AN ECONOMETRIC MODEL OF INDIA
1948–1961

AN ECONOMETRIC MODEL OF INDIA

1948-1961

RAMGOPAL AGARWALA

With a Foreword by Professor R. J. Ball

FRANK CASS & CO. LTD.
1970

First published in 1970 by
FRANK CASS AND COMPANY LIMITED
67 Great Russell Street, London, W.C.1

ISBN 0 7146 1200 6

Printed in Great Britain by
Billing & Sons Limited, Guildford and London

This book is dedicated
to my elder brother

M. P. Agarwala

whose devotion to knowledge
has always been a source of
inspiration to me

Contents

LIST OF TABLES

Foreword

Perhaps the most significant development in economics over the last fifteen years has been the increased application of quantitative methods to economic problems. This is so in the context of developments in techniques of analysis. In terms of subject-matter there is perhaps nothing so pressing as the problem of economic growth and development particularly in those countries whose standard of living for many of their people falls far below what we in the twentieth century can regard as tolerable. Thus the economics of underdeveloped and emerging nations lies at the heart of one of the principal problems of our time.

In the cause of improvement many underdeveloped countries have turned to a variety of forms of economic planning. From a technical point of view much use has been made of economic models of inter-industry relations in the form of input–output analysis. More aggregative statistical analysis based on national income concepts has largely been restricted to the more industrialised countries. In this book, however, Dr. Agarwala has brought together several of the problems facing the Indian Economy within the framework of an aggregate statistical approach along national income lines.

In adapting the national income approach to a model of the Indian economy, it has, of course, been necessary to integrate it with the problem of structure. In this treatment Dr. Agarwala picks out the relationship between the agricultural and non-agricultural sectors as crucial to an understanding of Indian development. In particular he focuses on the problem of the transference of the marketable food surplus from agriculture to the rest of the economy as a central issue. The data available for the study of this problem are sparse. None the less, within these constraints it has been found possible to provide a statistical macro-economic picture of the Indian economy.

Economic models change both as theory develops and new data become available. Dr. Agarwala's model provides an initial attempt to quantify the relevant relationships and to consider the implications of the structure for economic policy. Undoubtedly it lays a foundation of research on which other workers in the field can be expected to build.

London Graduate School of Business Studies
R. J. Ball

Preface

The idea of this study occurred to me when I was lecturing on macro-economics in Calcutta University. It seemed to me that the extent of emphasis we put on Keynesian economics was quite misplaced in the Indian context. It was, I thought, necessary to study macro-economics with the problems of Indian economy at the centre of our theory. This context accounts for the academic bias of the book and I very much hope that my modest effort will be of some use for teaching macro-economics in Indian universities and that it will stimulate further interest in this direction.

While grappling with economic data to test economic hypotheses one is inevitably impressed by the complexity of economic mechanism and the difficulty of arriving at policy prescriptions on the basis of simple models. I am therefore cautious about the validity of the policy conclusions emerging from my model. Even so I think there is some truth in my finding that it might have been better for India's economic growth to make greater use of her enormous labour power and to pay somewhat greater attention to agriculture. Although my research is based on Indian data, I believe that the general methodology and the broad conclusions may also be applicable to other thickly-populated, under-developed countries.

This book is an outcome of my Ph.D. thesis submitted to Manchester University in 1966. In this connection my greatest debt is to my supervisor Professor R. J. Ball. In spite of his extremely busy schedule, he always granted me a generous amount of his time and his comments and suggestions were most helpful to me; I am also grateful to him for writing a foreword to this book. I also received considerable help from many other members of the staff in Manchester University. On a wider field of academic debt, I must record my gratitude to Professor B. Datta from whom I had my first lessons in economics and Professor A. Datta who always encouraged me in problem-oriented thinking.

This study was made possible by the award of a Commonwealth Scholarship by the United Kingdom and I am very grateful to the Association of Commonwealth Universities for this generous award. I am also grateful to Calcutta University for sponsoring me for the award and for granting me the necessary study leave. While collecting the material for this study I had to use a number of libraries in the U.K. and I am grateful for their help and co-operation. In particular I must mention the name of Miss Thorne of India House Library without whose expert help life would have been very much more difficult for me. Lastly but not the least, I am thankful to my wife Bimala for her help in collecting and checking many statistical tables and for general forbearance.

R. AGARWALA

Economic Council of Canada

CHAPTER 1

Introduction

The post-war period has witnessed significant progress in the theory of economic development as well as in the theory of econometrics. Unfortunately, however, these twins seem to have been living largely separate lives and insufficient attempts seem to have been made to harness them together. The theory of economic development has been developed largely from intuitive reasoning and casual empiricism and not enough has been done to verify its premises with the help of econometric techniques. Empirical studies in this connection have been largely concerned with estimates of capital–output ratios, capital–labour ratios, saving–income ratios, etc. Econometric model-building, on the other hand, has been largely confined to the advanced industrialised countries. In the few cases where macro-models have been built for underdeveloped countries (e.g. the Narasimham model (112) for India) the underlying assumptions have been largely of the Keynesian type, and thus in our opinion unconnected with the theory of economic development. Ours is a modest attempt at econometric model-building on the basis of a model of development of an underdeveloped country.

1.1: THE MACRO-MODEL

The first problem that we face in this connection is the choice of an appropriate macro-model. Here, we must emphasise the importance of relativity in economics with respect to both time and space. In a sense, a universally valid theory is one of general equilibrium analysis where everything depends on everything else. But usually this is unmanageable. Such detailed data are not available and even if they were, we would face the insoluble statistical problem of identification; because, statistically, all the equations will look alike. The practising economist has to pick up a few strategic and crucial variables in the economy so that their inter-relationship can broadly account for the economic mechanism under study, and the question as to which of the variables are crucial and strategic is not a matter of logic, but of facts. Therefore, the design of the macro-model would depend on the institutional conditions in which it is to be applied and also on the problem for the solution of which it is being constructed.

The nature of the above points would become clearer if we consider the applicability of Keynes's *General Theory* (86) to the current Indian economic conditions.

In Keynesian economics, output and employment are determined by effective demand; the importance of the supply side is entirely ignored. According to some, the 45° line in the Keynesian diagram of income determination is Keynes's aggregate supply function. But it is a very strange type of supply function which remains invariant in the face of all changes in the supply of factors like labour, capital and land. In this framework the so-called supply function remains the same whatever be the size of the economy and whatever its factor-endowments. If we are to introduce a supply side at all in the Keynesian diagram of income determination, we should perhaps introduce a vertical aggregate supply function of the type suggested by D. Patinkin (117). Actually, however, the basic spirit of Keynes's analysis is to determine output solely by effective demand to the complete neglect of the supply constraints; and this is not unjustified as a simplification when one is concerned with the economics of depression. In our context on the other hand it is supply factors that act as the main constraints. With large doses of governmental spending being undertaken under planning, there is apparently no deficiency of aggregate demand. There might be certain sectors, e.g. trade, household industries, etc., where effective demand is the limiting factor, but in general it is the shortage of the factors of production that is limiting output. So in our context, for the explanation of real income, we should think not in terms of the propensity to consume or the marginal efficiency of investment, but in terms of the supply of land, labour and capital and their productivity.

In Keynes's theory of employment, money wages are assumed to be fixed till the level of full employment, and before that level is reached, increases in effective demand will bring about increases in employment even though it is associated with falling real wages. In the Indian context, however, increases in effective demand are associated with rising prices and not so much with rising employment. Increases in prices also are generally associated with demands for higher wages even if there is unemployment in the economy. It will be more plausible to assume that the supply curve of labour is infinitely elastic with respect to the subsistence level of real wages in the classical (Ricardian) sense than to regard it as infinitely elastic with respect to money wages in the Keynesian sense. In our context, unemployment is due not so much to the lack of effective demand as to the lack of fixed capital and the lack of means of subsistence of labourers. Again the existence of family-based labour in agriculture may necessitate the introduction of altogether new considerations. The family-based labour cannot be retrenched and employment may well be carried to the point where the marginal productivity of labour is zero.

The problem of unemployment in our context cannot thus be explained at all satisfactorily in Keynesian terms. In fact, in the Keynesian sense we are already in the full employment situation, since it is not in general possible to increase the level of employment and output by increasing effective demand. In this situation most of the Keynesian teachings become useless, if not misleading. For example, the simple multiplier analysis is valid only if the supply of goods could be increased, by increasing effective demand, a situation which, except for certain minor pockets, is not present in our economy. In this context it is wrong to assert that investment creates its own savings or that an increased propensity to save acts as an impediment to capital formation rather than as a stimulant to it.

Nor is Keynesian economics any more enlightening for the analysis of the impact of changes in the money supply. Here Keynes focuses primary attention on the influence of the money supply on the rate of interest and it is only through the effect of interest on investment and that of investment on effective demand that the level of prices is affected. If, as is thought plausible in Keynesian economics, there is a 'liquidity trap', changes in the money supply may not affect prices at all. This line of reasoning may be useful in a depressionary situation, but it is not in the current Indian economic context. With the relatively small bond market, the speculative demand for money is not likely to be very important. On the other hand, because of the predominantly trading character of financial capital, present prices and expected changes in prices may be the more important influence in the determination of demand for money. As we shall see below income-velocity is relatively stable in India and it is plausible to argue that spending decisions are influenced by the money supply to a greater extent than is supposed in Keynes's theory. Above all, because of the relatively underdeveloped financial institutions, a relatively stable interest rate, and the large degree of self-financing in the firms in India, it may be doubtful whether the rate of interest is an important endogenous economic variable.

The Keynesian economics is useful when the problem is to explain the short run fluctations of real income of the type considered in business cycle theories. In the Indian economy on the other hand, these endogenous cycles have not been important in the past, are not important at present, and with the government sector occupying an important place in our economy, are not likely to be important in future. The fluctuations present in our economy are of the random type mostly due to climatic variations in agriculture or to the random shocks in foreign trade or foreign aid. The main task of the economist in our context is:

(*a*) to explain the nature of the forces that have been holding the economy in the grip of stagnation for a long time;
(*b*) to determine the strategy for growth; and
(*c*) to consider how the various instruments in the hands of the Government can influence the time path of the economy.

For these purposes, Keynesian economics is not very helpful and we have to use a non-Keynesian model.

In spite of the considerable development in the theory of growth, it was not found possible to pick up any particular model from the existing literature on the subject. Instead we had to construct a model of our own. In doing so we have, of course, borrowed freely from the ideas thrown up in this connection and it would perhaps be tedious and rather useless to point out the similarities in this connection at each step. Briefly, the main building blocks of our model are the following:

(*a*) the Ricardian theory of diminishing returns in the wage-goods sector;
(*b*) the Nurkse–Lewis thesis of disguised unemployment and an unlimited supply of labour at subsistence wages;
(*c*) the hypothesis that employment function is connected with the marketed surplus of wage-goods;
(*d*) the quantity theory of money as determining the general price level;
(*e*) the hypothesis that capital formation in the non-wage-goods sector is dependent on the availability of foreign exchange.

Apart from these main building blocks we have, of course, made many other hypotheses. These will become clearer as we proceed.

1.2: THE DATA

The statistical estimates of the parameters of our model are mainly based upon the time-series data for the years 1948–49 to 1960–61. In some particular cases, where the data for the earlier years are available, we do use them. But in general we have not tried to extend our series beyond 1948–49; and this for two reasons. In the first place where data are not readily available it requires an enormous amount of labour to construct any series at all and even then these are likely to be rather shaky. Secondly, the Second World War and the attainment of Independence in 1947 are important watersheds in Indian history and there might have been some fundamental changes in attitudes and behaviour patterns. Therefore we confine our sample mainly to the years 1948–49 to 1960–61. The lack of sufficient data has also forced us to use only annual series and that too for a fairly aggregative scheme.

The model and the conclusions that emerge from it are therefore necessarily of a tentative character. But as Klein and Goldberger (91) emphasise, the econometric model building cannot be treated as a once-for-all affair; the model has to be continually revised and adapted to the developments in the economy. From the point of view of policy again, the conclusion of an aggregative economic system cannot be straight away applicable to real life. In real life there are too many details to consider and too many social and political pressures to accommodate. However, the results of the aggregative analysis can be a broad indicator of the optimum and if the actual plan departs too dramatically from it, one may think that there is an *a priori* case for having another hard look at the plan.

1.3: THE OUTLINE

The broad outline of the material will be as follows. In Chapter 2 we develop a simple model of an underdeveloped country. We show how there is a built-in tendency in the system towards stagnation. We also analyse the stages by which the economy could pass on to self-sustained growth. Then we briefly consider the role of money and the role of foreign sector in growth. In Chapter 3 we reformulate our theoretical model to make it suitable for statistical estimates. In three subsequent chapters we consider the statistical estimates of the equations concerned with output and employment (Chapter 4), money, wages and prices (Chapter 5), and investment and foreign trade (Chapter 6). In Chapter 7 we summarise the estimates and their statistical properties, and compare them with those of some other econometric models. In Chapter 8 we consider by the method of simulation, the performance of the model, the possible use of the model in determining the strategy of a developmental plan and the effects of various governmental measures over time. Lastly, in Chapter 9, we utilise our model to comment on some aggregative aspects of India's Third Five Year Plan.

CHAPTER 2

A Theory of Stagnation and Growth

In this chapter we try to develop a macro-model suitable for an economy of the Indian type. The main characteristic of the Indian economy is the fact of stagnation over a long period. During 1881–1921 both population and *per capita* incomes were roughly constant. Between the period 1921–41 population increased but *per capita* income was still roughly constant. During the plan periods there has been some growth in *per capita* as well as the total income, but still the production structure and employment pattern have changed only to a limited extent and there is as yet no sign of self-sustained growth.

The causes of economic stagnation in India over this period have been discussed by many economic historians, and, naturally enough, sentiments have played an important part in the emphasis and the explanations given by different authors. In this connection one comes across the whole spectrum of differing opinions. Some (mostly Western writers) attribute the stagnation solely to social institutions like the caste system, religious attitudes like 'cow-worship', etc., while some others (mostly Indian) attribute India's poverty solely to the British rule in India; and there are of course others who recognise the influence of both these factors. Thus, for example, L. C. A. Knowles (94) attributes India's poverty solely to her religious and social structure; Vera Austey (1) considers the excessive increase in population and uneconomic outlook of the people to be of much greater significance than the state economic policies; D. H. Buchanan (17) considers social organisation and state economic policies as factors of equal importance. On the other hand, R. Dutt (31) and M. G. Ranade (121) would attribute the poverty of India to the economic 'drain' from India in the form of various unrequited payments to Britain. Moreover, some emphasise the restrictive policies of British government in destroying the indigenous textile, metal and shipbuilding industry and not allowing the proper growth of new industries until a very late stage (see, e.g., V. V. Bhatt (13)).

In this connection, the principal blame is placed on the store-purchase policy, the tariff policy and the taxation policy followed by the Government.

It is, of course, difficult to prove any of these theses at all conclusively. Both types of influences might have worked in bringing about stagnation; but perhaps neither was necessary and sufficient. Without going into the details of these socio-political arguments we may note some broad points. The muslim-dominated areas of British India did not have any great influence of caste system or cow-worship, but economically these areas were on the whole no better than the Hindu-dominated areas. Again, social stratification did not prevent Japan from attaining economic progress. Similarly, some neighbouring states (e.g. Nepal or Tibet) or the Princely States in India which did not come under direct British rule did not exhibit any very different economic tendency than did British India. At the same time, the British rule in Malaya, Ceylon or Ghana did not prevent them from attaining a standard of living considerably higher than India's. Indian businessmen in spite of their social institutions did fairly well in East Africa and are doing much better now under planning in India. However, these are mostly sociological arguments into which we do not propose to enter. Our aim in this chapter is to see if we can develop an economic model which can lay bare the main economic forces that have been holding the country in stagnation for a long period.

For purposes of a theoretical model we have, of necessity, to ignore many aspects of reality, but it is hoped that in spite of these simplifications the system will be able to represent certain basic characteristics of the economy of the Indian type. We begin with the consideration of a closed system (Section 2.1). We consider how far there is an inherent tendency towards stagnation in such an economy. We also try to depict the stages through which such an economy passes towards 'self-sustained' growth. In Section 2.2 we introduce money in the system and consider its role in the determination of prices and its influence on growth. Lastly, in Section 2.3 we consider the role of the foreign sector in the economic growth of an underdeveloped country like India.

2.1: A MACRO-MODEL IN A CLOSED ECONOMY

2.1.1: A REFERENCE TO THE LITERATURE

The literature on economic development of underdeveloped countries is voluminous. However, we did not find any explicit model which we could use straight away for our theoretical and empirical work. The model that we have built naturally has many points of similarity with other models in this context. However, we consider only a few models that seem very close to our analysis. The pioneering paper in this direction is that of W. A. Lewis (100) and the discussion below draws heavily on his work. But Lewis did not present any explicit mathematical model and his verbal discussion is difficult to formulate exactly. An important contribution carrying Lewis's insight further is that by G. Ranis and J. C. H. Fei (123) and the model here is similar to theirs. However, their model was also insufficient for our purposes. Ranis and Fei do not discuss the forces of stagnation in the economy. In their discussion of the agricultural sector, it is not quite clear whether they are considering family-based agriculture or wage-based agriculture. From their reference to institutional wage rates and landlords it seems they were thinking of wage-based agriculture. In our context, the assumption of family-based agriculture will be more appropriate. Nor do they consider explicitly how the initial equilibrium is reached in the agricultural sector. Again, in the industrial sector they assume that employment is determined by the traditional point of intersection between the marginal physical productivity curve of labour and the horizontal supply curve of labour at a subsistence wage. However, this seems to ignore the point that marginal physical productivity refers to industrial output whereas the wage rate is fixed in terms of subsistence goods. Thus there is a crucial terms of trade variable involved in the equations and the traditional diagram cannot determine the level of employment and the terms of trade between agriculture and industry. Moreover, although they talk of stages in growth, they do not have any explicit investment function and they do not specify explicitly the forces that move the economy from one stage to another. They do not demonstrate as to how growth becomes self-sustained at the point where the disguised unemployment is exhausted and the economy is supposed to have reached a 'take-off' stage. Lastly, they do not consider explicitly money, absolute price and foreign trade in their model. It is for these reasons that while accepting the basic logic of the Ranis and Fei model we have to develop a model of our own.

Another attempt to develop a model of the dual economy has been made by D. W. Jorgenson (80). However, his model seems quite unsatisfactory for a number of reasons. For one thing Jorgenson assumes that 'output of the traditional or agricultural sector is a function of land and labour alone'. Actually, it seems to us, capital is a more important limitational factor in agriculture than labour. Secondly, Jorgenson assumes that an agricultural surplus is generated when agricultural output per man exceeds the level of income at which the rate of growth of population attains its physiological maximum (y^+). Actually, however, this physiological maximum is difficult to define and an agricultural surplus exists long before the income corresponding to this maximum is reached. Again, in his model, the industrial wage rate is determined by the usual marginal productivity considerations and he does not pay any attention to disguised unemployment in agriculture or the possibility of an unlimited supply of labour at the subsistence wage in the industrial sector. Moreover, as regards investment, there is no capital formation in agriculture. Even in the industrial sector 'workers do not save' and property owners do not consume. These assumptions seem unrealistic and rather unnecessary. Nor does Jorgenson consider the role of money, or the foreign sector in growth.

2.1.2: A SIMPLE MODEL WITHOUT PRICE VARIATIONS

The starting-point in our analysis (as in that of Lewis (100) and Ranis-Fei (123)) is the dualistic structure of an underdeveloped economy. There is a vast rural traditional sector side by side with a rather small but modern urban sector. In the traditional sector the production units are largely family based. Employment and consumption in this sector are undertaken on the basis of the family principle: 'From each according to his ability, to each according to his needs'. This sector may thus come to accommodate disguised unemployment in the sense that some people are consuming out of the income of the production unit even though their marginal contribution to production is zero. The urban sector is, however, organised on the basis of capitalistic principles and production and distribution are carried out in the light of the principle of profit-maximisation. Apart from this difference in the system of organisation, there is also a difference in the type of production undertaken by the two sectors. Ignoring some overlapping, we assume (as do Lewis and Ranis-Fei) that the traditional sector (Sector 1) produces wage-goods and the modern sector (Sector 2) produces services, luxury consumer goods and investment goods for both the sectors. We also assume (again at the cost of some realism), that the two sectors are vertically integrated so that intermediate goods do not come into the picture and the factors of production are land, labour and capital. The output of both the sectors is gross of depreciation and depreciation is assumed to be a fixed proportion of capital employed. To begin with we consider a closed economy and also ignore the question of money and prices; subsequently however, we relax these restrictive assumptions one by one.

In considering the determination of output and employment in Sector 1, we assume away the problem of aggregation. In other words, we assume that the form of functions and the rationale of economic behaviour at the micro-level is also applicable at the macro-level. The producer is faced with a production function of the type $Y_1 = f(K_1, L_1, LD)$ which shows the relationship between output (Y_1) and factors of production—labour (L_1), capital (K_1) and land (LD). However, since land is constant we ignore it in our aggregate production function. The production function in this sector is of the same type as it is in the capitalistic sector. But the cost curve of labour facing the family farm is of a different type from that facing the capitalistic entrepreneur. Up to the point where family labour is fully employed, the cost of labour for the farm is constant irrespective of the actual labour put in. Family members cannot be retrenched and the cost of maintenance of the family does not vary significantly with changes in the ultilisation of family labour. It could, of course, be argued that in our context we should take the cost of labour in terms of leisure sacrificed rather than the money cost and the cost of labour in the sense of dis-utility of work does rise with the amount of labour put in. Utility considerations, however, may not be very important for the head of the family at the level of work each member has to do in the presence of disguised unemployment. Moreover, we want to avoid the controversies connected with utility theory. However, we do refer to some of these aspects in Chapter 4.

After the point where family labour is fully employed, the cost curve will be upward sloping, say, at a constant rate. In symbols, the cost curve of labour is:

(2.1.1) $$c(L_1) = \bar{c} + \lambda_1(L_1 - \bar{L})$$

where $\bar{c}$ = the fixed cost of maintenance of the family which provides $\bar{L}$ labour units in the production period,

L_1 = labour employed,

$\lambda_1 = O$ when $L_1 \leqslant \bar{L}$

and $\lambda_1 > O$ where $L_1 > \bar{L}$

In the short run, capital is fixed and immobile between sectors so that the only decision to be taken is about labour input. Labour input will be carried to the point where the marginal productivity of labour is equal to its marginal cost. In the situation of surplus population, this point is reached before $L_1 = \bar{L}$ so that in equilibrium

$$\frac{\delta Y_1}{\delta L_1} = O.$$

In diagram we can show the situation as follows:
OD is the production function; ABC is the cost curve of labour. The marginal product of labour is zero at L_1, which is less than $\bar{L}$. In the context of disguised unemployment labour is no longer a limita-

tional factor in output and capital may be regarded as the only limitational factor of production. Let us assume that:

(2.1.2) $Y_1 = A K_1^{\alpha}$*

Next we have to consider the relationship between the wage-goods sector and the non-wage-goods sector. In the Indian economy the agricultural sector has been recognised as an important limiting factor on growth. It could also be argued that the demand generating aspect of agricultural production can hardly be very important because there seems to be an excess demand situation in the goods market. The supply of food has been more important than the supply of raw materials as a limitational factor. In our model the wage-

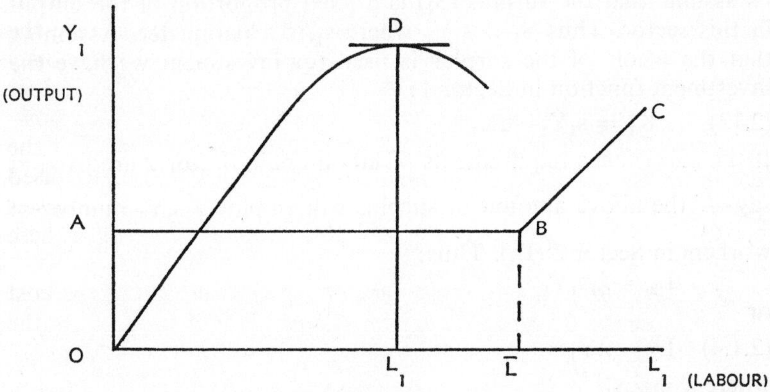

Figure 2.1

goods sector provides food. So to take this vital characteristic of the Indian economy into our model we make the assumption that the marketed surplus of wage-goods acts as a limitational factor on employment in the non-wage-goods sector. It is true that employment may be limited by capital before it is limited by a marketed surplus of wage goods. However, our theoretical production function allows continuous substitution between labour and capital so that the

* In this we have assumed the existence of disguised unemployment as it is commonly done in the literature on underdeveloped countries. Recently, some economists (see (36)) have questioned the validity of this assumption. We do not enter into this controversy at this point but we note our evidence on the issue in Chapter 4. As we would find below, our theory requires the assumption that $\alpha < 1$. This may seem rather strange. It could be argued that since labour is free, an increase in capital is also associated with an increase in labour and there should be constant returns to scale (i.e. $\alpha = 1$). However, this is unlikely to be the case because in agriculture (which produces wage-goods to a large extent) an important factor of production is land and land is kept constant. Thus, because of the fixity of land there are diminishing returns to capital in agriculture.

capital-labour ratio is variable; on the other hand, the amount of subsistence wage-goods required by labour is more or less constant. We adhere to the assumption made by Lewis (100) that at the early stage of development real wages are constant at the level of subsistence*. The dependence of employment in non-wage goods sector on the output in wage-goods sector may be analysed in a simple way, as follows.

The marketed surplus of wage-goods will depend on a number of factors such as the amount of contractual payments in the form of tax, rent or interest, the preference functions of the households in Sector 1, the size of the working force in Sector 1, the relative prices of the goods in the two sectors, etc. However, for simplification let us assume that the surplus (S_1) is a fixed proportion of the output in this sector. Thus $S_1 = s_1Y_1$ where s_1 is a parameter. Assuming that the whole of the surplus is used for investment we have the investment function in Sector 1:

(2.13) $\dot{K}_1 = s_1Y_1 - uK_1$

If the subsistence requirements of labourers in Sector 2 are fixed at say $\frac{1}{\lambda_1}$, the above amount of surplus will employ $\lambda_1 s_1 Y_1$ number of workers in Sector 2 (L_2). Thus:

$$L_2 = \lambda_1 s_1 Y_1$$

or

(2.1.4) $L_2 = \lambda Y_1$

where $\lambda = \lambda_1 s_1$

As regards the non-wage-goods sector, we make the assumption that production depends on the availability of factors of production —capital and labour; we also assume that the production function is of the Cobb–Douglas type with constant returns to scale.†

Thus we have:

(2.1.5) $Y_2 = BK_2^{\beta}L_2^{1-\beta}$

where Y_2 = gross output in Sector 2
K_2 = capital in Sector 2, and
L_2 = labour in Sector 2.

As regards capital formation in Sector 2 we again make the simplifying assumption that the savings are a constant proportion of income and depreciation is a constant fraction of the capital stock. Thus we have the net capital formation function:

(2.1.6) $\dot{K}_2 = s_2Y_2 - uK_2$

* See also N. Kaldor (82).

† The assumption of Cobb–Douglas type production function is further discussed in Chapter 3.

This completes the list of equations in our first model. Putting the equations together we have:

(2.1.2) $Y_1 = AK_1^{\alpha}$
(2.1.3) $\dot{K}_1 = s_1Y_1 - uK_1$
(2.1.4) $L_2 = \lambda Y_1$
(2.1.5) $Y_2 = BK_2^{\beta}L_2^{1-\beta}$
(2.1.6) $\dot{K}_2 = s_2Y_2 - uK_2$

A flow diagram of this system will look like the following:

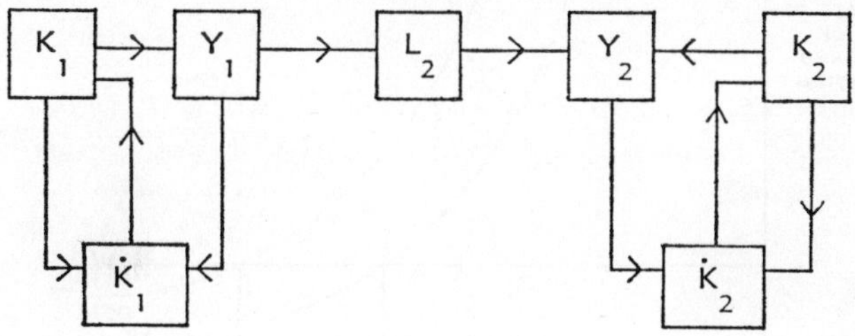

Figure 2.2

Next we consider the dynamic properties of this simple system. As is obvious, the main limiting factor in our production system is capital. True, output in the non-wage-goods sector depends on labour as well as capital. But labour in Sector 2 depends on output in Sector 1, which, in its turn, depends on capital in Sector 1. Thus ultimately capital is the only limitation factor of production. Therefore the dynamics of the system are concerned with the dynamics of capital accumulation.

Let us begin with the properties of the capital accumulation function in Sector 1. The relative rate of growth of capital in Sector 1 is given by:

$$\frac{\dot{K}_1}{K_1} = s_1\frac{Y_1}{K_1} - u$$

Substituting for Y_1,

(2.1.7) $$\frac{\dot{K}_1}{K_1} = s_1AK_1^{\alpha-1} - u$$

Now, in our model, labour is not a limitational factor so that an increase in capital may also be associated with the increased use of labour. However, land is fixed, so that there are diminishing marginal returns to capital. This would mean that $\alpha < 1$. In that case $\frac{\dot{K}_1}{K_1}$ diminishes as K_1 increases until it reaches a stable position with

$\frac{\dot{K}_1}{K_1} = 0$. In this situation gross investment is equal to depreciation, and the total amount of capital remains fixed.

Let us also consider the situation diagrammatically. In Figure 2.3 the horizontal axis shows the capital in Sector 1 and the vertical axis shows the gross rate of growth of capital and depreciation in Sector 1:

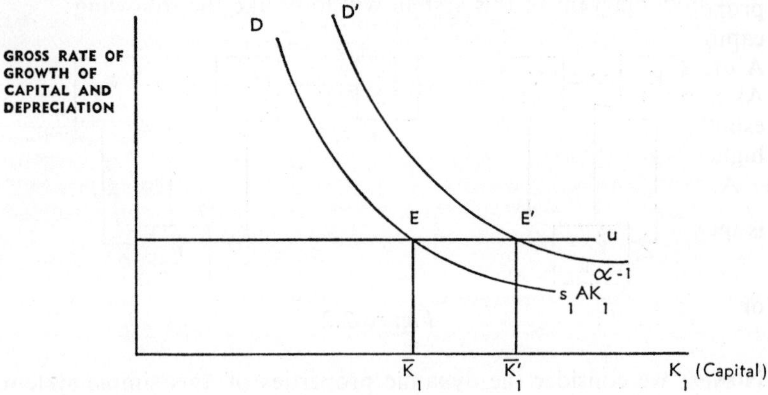

Figure 2.3

The gross capital accumulation function is given by curve D and depreciation by u. Whatever the level of capital is to begin with there is an inherent tendency in the system to move towards E, with capital $\bar{K}_1$. If $K_1 < \bar{K}_1$, $\frac{\dot{K}_1}{K_1}$ is positive and K_1 increases till it becomes equal to $\bar{K}_1$. Similarly, if $K_1 > \bar{K}_1$, $\frac{\dot{K}_1}{K_1}$ is negative and K_1 decreases till it becomes equal to $\bar{K}_1$. Thus the situation of stagnation has a built-in stability. The stagnation in K_1 will mean in our model stagnation in Y_1. Population may go on increasing till the per capita income reaches the subsistence level.

In the above scheme, the main force driving the economy towards stagnation is the law of diminishing returns and in this respect it resembles the scheme of the classical economists. However, whereas the classical economists were mainly thinking of the wage-economy we are considering a family-based production system with a considerable amount of disguised unemployment.

How may one escape from this stagnation? One possibility is that because of Government efforts and/or foreign capital, capital is increased to such an extent that the assumptions of the above system no longer apply. Thus labour may no longer be a non-limitational factor, the composition of wage-goods may change significantly in favour of industrial products where the law of diminishing returns may not operate. In this situation the assumptions of our present model are no longer valid and we may pass on to a different stage in economic growth, which we analyse later on.

Apart from exogenous increases in capital, an increase in the propensity to save will also bring about an increase in equilibrium capital and income; but the tendency towards stagnation will persist. A once-for-all increase in the propensity to save will shift the curve $As_1K_1^{\alpha-1}$ in Figure 2.3 to the right. The new equilibrium will be established at E′ with capital $\bar{K}_1'$. Here the level of income is higher but there is no tendency towards steady growth.

A steady growth may be brought about if the saving propensity is increasing continuously. Let us denote $\frac{\dot{K}_1}{K_1}$ by π_1, so that:

$$\pi_1 = s_1AK_1^{\alpha-1} - u$$

or

$$\pi_1 + u = s_1AK_1^{\alpha-1}$$

Now, taking log of both sides and differentiating with respect to time, we have:

$$\frac{\dot{\pi}_1}{\pi_1+u} = \frac{\dot{s}_1}{s_1} + (\alpha-1)\frac{\dot{K}_1}{K_1} \qquad (2.1.8)$$

In this situation there will be a stable rate of growth in K_1 given by:

$$\frac{\dot{K}_1}{K_1} = \frac{1}{1-\alpha}\cdot\frac{\dot{s}_1}{s_1} \qquad (2.1.9)$$

If $\frac{\dot{K}_1}{K_1} < \frac{1}{1-\alpha}\cdot\frac{\dot{s}_1}{s_1}$, the expression on the right hand side of (2.1.8) is positive and, therefore, $\dot{\pi}_1$ is positive (since neither π_1 nor u is expected to be negative). In that case the rate of growth of capital π_1 is increasing over time and this will continue until the equation (2.1.9) is satisfied. Similarly, if $\frac{\dot{K}_1}{K_1} > \frac{1}{1-\alpha}\cdot\frac{s_1}{s_1}$, $\dot{\pi}_1$ is negative so that $\frac{\dot{K}_1}{K_1}$ is decreasing. Thus there is a stable tendency towards the equation (2.1.9).

Similar results can be obtained from 'technical progress' in the sense of a shift in the production function. If there is a once-for-all 'technical progress' there will again be a shift in the curve $As_1K_1^{\alpha-1}$. This will bring about an increase in capital and income but the tendency towards stagnation will persist. If, however, there is continuous 'technical progress' there will be a tendency towards stable steady growth in capital and income. As before, we write:

$$\pi_1 = s_1 A K_1^{\alpha-1} - u$$

Manipulating as before, we have:

(2.1.10) $$\frac{\dot{\pi}_1}{\pi_1 + u} = \frac{\dot{A}}{A} + (\alpha - 1)\frac{\dot{K}_1}{K_1}$$

where 'A' is variable
and 's_1' is constant.

As above, it can be shown that $\frac{\dot{K}_1}{K_1}$ tends towards a stable value of $\frac{1}{1-\alpha}\cdot\frac{\dot{A}}{A}$.

The effects of increases in the propensity to save and of 'technical progress' are logically of the same type. However, whereas it is difficult to raise the propensity to save continuously over time it might be easier to have continuous technical improvement—for knowledge, in a way, feeds on itself. It should be noted that 'technical progress' will include the opening of better markets, the introduction of new products, etc. Historically also, technical revolution in agriculture (which is close to our Sector 1) is said to have been an important factor in economic growth in the West as well as in Japan.

Let us now consider capital accumulation in Sector 2. Here again we find that unless there is a parametric change the sector will tend towards stagnation. From equation (2.1.6) we have, after appropriate substitutions:

$$\frac{\dot{K}_2}{K_2} = s_2 B K_2^{\beta-1} L_2^{1-\beta} - u$$

or

$$\frac{\dot{K}_2}{K_2} = s_2 B \lambda^{1-\beta} A^{1-\beta} K_2^{\beta-1} K^{(1-\beta)} - u$$

(2.1.11) $$\frac{\dot{K}_2}{K_2} = D . K_2^{\beta-1} K_1^{\alpha(1-\beta)} - u$$

where $D = s_2 B \lambda^{1-\beta} A^{1-\beta}$

Now, we have shown that K_1 tends towards a stable level $\bar{K}_1$. Thus in the long run K_1 is a constant, $\bar{K}_1$. Therefore $\frac{\dot{K}_2}{K_2}$ tends towards:

(2.1.12) $$\frac{\dot{K}_2}{K_2} = D_1 K_2^{\beta-1} - u$$

where $D_1 = \bar{K}_1 . D$

Proceeding as before we can show that K_2 tends to a fixed level $\bar{K}_2$. With stagnation in both K_1 and K_2 there is stagnation in Y_2 as well. As before, we can show that stagnation can be escaped by continuous 'technical progress' and/or increasing the propensity to save. In this connection, it is important to note that a technical change or an increase in the propensity to save in Sector 1 will have effects in Sector 2, though not vice versa. This is, of course, a restrictive assumption. We relax it subsequently by introducing price considerations.

2.1.3: A MODIFIED MODEL WITH PRICE VARIATIONS

We have assumed so far that prices remain constant in both the sectors and that labour is employed in Sector 2 irrespective of marginal productivity considerations. We now relax this assumption. The employment in Sector 2 is still carried to the maximum extent permitted by the marketed surplus of Sector 1, but marginal value productivities are made equal to wages by changes in relative prices. The marginal productivity theory thus determines neither wages nor employment but only the terms of trade between the two sectors.

The modified model is as follows:

(2.1.13) $$Y_1 = AK_1^{\alpha}$$

(2.1.14) $$L_2 = \lambda Y_1$$

(2.1.15) $$Y_2 = BK_2^{\beta}L_2^{1-\beta}$$

(2.1.16) $$\bar{w} = \frac{p_2}{p_1}.BK_2^{\beta}(1-\beta)L_2^{-\beta}$$

where $\bar{w}$ = institutional real wage,

p_2 = price of the goods in Sector 2,

and p_1 = price of the goods in Sector 1.

(2.1.17) $$\dot{K}_1 = \frac{p_1 s_1 Y_1}{p_2} - uK_1$$

(2.1.18) $$\dot{K}_2 = s_2Y_2 - uK_2$$

A flow diagram of the model is given in Figure 2.4.

Next, we consider the dynamics of capital accumulation in this system.

We have, after appropriate substitutions:

$$\dot{K}_1 = \frac{s_1AK_1^{\alpha}}{\bar{w}}.BK_2^{\beta}(1-\beta)L_2^{-\beta} - uK_1$$

or

$$\dot{K}_1 = c_1K_1^{\alpha(1-\beta)}K_2^{\beta} - uK_1 \text{ (where } c_1 \text{ is a constant)}$$

Dividing both sides by K_1, we have:

(2.1.19) $$\frac{\dot{K}_1}{K_1} = c_1K_1^{\alpha(1-\beta)-1}K_2^{\beta} - u$$

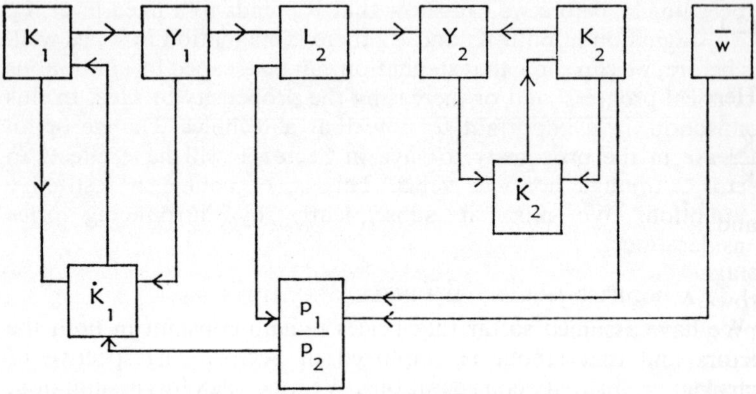

Figure 2.4

Similarly:

(2.1.20) $$\frac{\dot{K}_2}{K_2} = c_2 K_1^{\alpha(1-\beta)} K_2^{\beta-1} - u$$

From (2.1.19) and (2.1.20), we have:

$$\frac{1}{c_1}[\dot{K}_1 + uK_1] = K_1^{\alpha(1-\beta)} K_2^{\beta}$$

and $$\frac{1}{c_2}[\dot{K}_2 + uK_2] = K_1^{\alpha(1-\beta)} K_2^{\beta}$$

Since the right-hand side expressions of the above two equations are the same, we can have:

(2.1.21) $$\frac{1}{c_1}[\dot{K}_1 + uK_1] = \frac{1}{c_2}[\dot{K}_2 + uK_2]$$

Simplifying, and integrating, we have:

(2.1.22) $$CK_1 - K_2 = D_o e^{-ut}$$

where C and D_o are constants.

In the long run e^{-ut} tends towards zero (since $u<1$) so in the long run:

(2.1.23) $$CK_1 = K_2$$

Thus in the long run the capital formation function becomes:

$$\frac{\dot{K}_1}{K_1} = C_1 K_1^{\alpha(1-\beta)-1} K_1^{\beta} C^{\beta} - u$$

(2.1.24) $$\frac{\dot{K}_1}{K_1} = C^1 K_1^{(\alpha-1)(1-\beta)} - u$$

Putting $\frac{\dot{K}_1}{K_1} = \pi_1$ and taking log derivatives as before we have:

$$(2.1.25) \qquad \frac{\dot{\pi}_1}{\pi_1+u} = (\alpha-1)(1-\beta)\frac{\dot{K}_1}{K_1}$$

Here $(\alpha-1)(1-\beta)$ is negative, so $\frac{\dot{K}_1}{K_1}$ will tend towards zero. If $\frac{\dot{K}_1}{K_1}>0$, $\dot{\pi}_1$ is negative and $\frac{\dot{K}_1}{K_1}$ decreases. Similarly if $\frac{\dot{K}_1}{K_1}<0$, $\dot{\pi}_1>0$ and $\frac{\dot{K}_1}{K_1}$ increases. There is thus an inherent tendency for K_1 to be stagnant at a level say $\bar{K}_1$. Similarly, it can be shown that K_2 tends towards a stagnant level. As before, it can be shown that 'technical progress' and/or increases in the propensity to save provide escape from stagnation. An important difference now is that technical change or increased thrift in either of the sectors will affect both the sectors.

2.1.4: AN EXERCISE IN 'STAGES IN GROWTH'

So far we have been concerned with the nature of an under-developed country with surplus population. It is interesting to know in what precise ways the economy changes as it proceeds towards growth.

The analysis given above may be said to represent Stage I of economic development. In this phase there is a considerable amount of disguised unemployment in the subsistence sector. Labour is free in this sector and employment is carried to the point where the marginal product of labour is zero. Total output could be increased if the disguised unemployed could be transferred to the organised sector, but this transfer is limited by the availability of the marketed surplus of wage goods produced in the subsistence sector. In this situation, as we have shown, there is an inherent tendency towards stagnation, checked only by 'technical progress', foreign capital and increases in the propensity to save. If these forces are strong enough they may bring about an exhaustion of the excess supply of labour in the subsistence sector and thus mark the beginning of the second phase of economic development.

In Stage II the excess family labour is exhausted. The family-based system of production breaks up and there is a commercialisation of the economy and of the outlook of the people. Capital and labour are freely mobile between the sectors. Both the sectors have to pay an institutional wage for labour. However, the economy is not yet rich enough to provide full employment to all persons because of the rapidly increasing population and possibly also because of increasing participation of women in outside work. The real wages in both the sectors are at an institutionally fixed level.

Employment is carried to the point justified by the capitalistic principle of profit maximisation. There may thus be some open unemployment—and these people may have to be maintained by public or private charity. In this situation, as we note below, the inherent tendency towards stagnation may persist if the law of diminishing returns operates in the consumer goods sector. If constant returns to scale obtain, there is no tendency towards stagnation nor any towards self-sustained growth.

In Stage III, capital accumulation has gone far enough so that the marginal product of labour is higher than the subsistence level even in the full employment situation. Both labour and capital are mobile and the allocations are made in the light of the profit maximisation principle. In this situation, we find, there is a tendency towards a stable steady rate of growth of capital.

Having described the broad characteristics of the three stages, let us note their properties in more precise terms. In Stage II, when the economy is commercialised, the distinction between the subsistence sector and the modern organised sector is no longer valid. The whole economy is organised on capitalistic principles. In this context we replace the earlier distinction between sectors by the distinction between a consumer goods sector (Sector 1) and a capital goods sector (Sector 2). However, since we have assumed that even in this stage wages are at a subsistence level, the consumer goods sector is likely to be dominated by the agricultural sector and therefore we retain the assumption of the law of diminishing returns to capital and labour in Sector 1.

Production in Sector 1 (Y_1) depends on labour (L_1) and capital (K_1). Labour is a limitational factor in Sector 1 in Stage II, whereas in Stage I, it was not. The production function is:

(2.1.26) $$Y_1 = AK_1^{\alpha}L_1^{\alpha_1}$$

where $\alpha+\alpha_1<1$

There is no basic change in the form of production function for Sector 2 in Stage II. As before, we write:

(2.1.27) $$Y_2 = BK_2^{\beta}L_2^{1-\beta}$$

In Stage I capital was specific to the sectors. In Stage II, however, capital is mobile and we have a capital allocation equation:

(2.1.28) $$K_1+K_2 = K$$

where K = total capital.

The allocation of capital is carried out in such a way as to ensure equality between the marginal product of capital and the rental rate (r) in both the sectors:

(2.1.29) $$r = A\alpha K_1^{\alpha-1}L_1^{\alpha_1}$$

(2.1.30) $$r = pB\beta K_2^{\beta-1}L_2^{1-\beta}$$

where p = price of capital goods in terms of consumption goods.

The real wage in terms of consumption goods ($\bar{w}$) is institutionally determined and employment in each sector is determined by the marginal productivity condition. Thus we have:

(2.1.31) $$\bar{w} = AK_1^{\alpha}\alpha_1 L_1^{\alpha_1-1}$$

(2.1.32) $$\bar{w} = pBK_2^{\beta}(1-\beta)L_2^{-\beta}$$

In Stage I the output of Sector 1 was a constraint on employment in Sector 2. But in Stage II capital is freely mobile between the two sectors and allocations are made between the two sectors on marginal productivity considerations. Thus, if the output of Sector 1 was insufficient to meet the demands on labour in Sector 2, the relative price of its output with respect to that of Sector 2 will rise and capital will flow into this sector (which it could not do in Stage I).

The value of the output of the capital goods sector is equal to the savings which we assume to be a fixed proportion of total income in terms of consumption goods.

(2.1.33) $$pY_2 = s.Y$$

Total income (Y) is given by:

(2.1.34) $$Y = Y_1 + pY_2$$

Putting together these equations, we have:

(2.1.26) $$Y_1 = AK_1^{\alpha}L_1^{\alpha_1}$$

(2.1.27) $$Y_2 = BK_2^{\beta}L_2^{1-\beta}$$

(2.1.28) $$K = K_1 + K_2$$

(2.1.29) $$r = A\alpha K_1^{\alpha-1}L_1^{\alpha_1}$$

(2.1.30) $$r = pB\beta K_2^{\beta-1}L_2^{1-\beta}$$

(2.1.31) $$\bar{w} = AK_1^{\alpha}.\alpha_1 L_1^{\alpha_1-1}$$

(2.1.32) $$\bar{w} = pBK_2^{\beta}(1-\beta)L_2^{-\beta}$$

(2.1.33) $$pY_2 = s.Y$$

(2.1.34) $$Y = Y_1 + pY_2$$

The above system of equations contains 9 equations in 9 variables: Y, K, Y_2, K_1, L_1, K_2, L_2, p, r. Assuming that the usual conditions of consistency and independence are satisfied, the system is determinate.

Let us now analyse the dynamics of the model. From (2.1.33) and (2.1.34) we have:

$$pY_2 = sY_1 + spY_2$$

or

(2.1.35) $$pY_2 = \frac{s}{1-s}.Y_1$$

From (2.1.29) and (2.1.30) we have:

$$p = \frac{A\alpha K_1^{\alpha-1}L_1^{\alpha_1}}{B\beta K_2^{\beta-1}L_2^{1-\beta}}$$

Substituting this value of p in (2.1.35) and using (2.1.26) and (2.1.27) we have:

$$\frac{A\alpha K_1^{\alpha-1}L_1^{\alpha_1}}{B\beta K_2^{\beta-1}L_2^{1-\beta}}.BK_2^{\beta}L_2^{1-\beta} = \frac{s}{1-s}.AK_1^{\alpha}L_1^{\alpha_1}$$

Simplifying, we have:

(2.1.36) $$\frac{\alpha}{\beta}.K_2 = \frac{s}{1-s}.K_1$$

Using (2.1.28):

$$\frac{\alpha}{\beta}.K_2 = \frac{s}{1-s}(K-K_2)$$

or

(2.1.37) $$K_2 = \frac{\beta s}{\alpha(1-s)+\beta s}.K$$

Therefore, taking the log of both sides and differentiating with respect to time, we have:

(2.1.38) $$\frac{\dot{K}_2}{K_2} = \frac{\dot{K}}{K}$$

Similary, we can obtain:

(2.1.39) $$\frac{\dot{K}_1}{K_1} = \frac{\dot{K}}{K}$$

By similar manipulations it is easy to show that:

(2.1.40) $$\frac{\dot{L}_1}{L_1} = \frac{\dot{L}_2}{L_2}$$

From equation (2.1.31) we have:

$$\bar{w} = AK_1^{\alpha}\alpha_1 L_1^{\alpha_1-1}$$

or

$$L_1^{1-\alpha_1} = \frac{\alpha_1 A}{\bar{w}} K_1^{\alpha}$$

or

(2.1.41) $$(1-\alpha_1)\frac{\dot{L}_1}{L_1} = \alpha\frac{\dot{K}_1}{K_1}$$

Now the rate of growth of capital is given by the amount of production in the capital goods sector minus depreciation. So we have:

$$\dot{K} = Y_2 - uK$$

where u = rate of depreciation.

Therefore, the relative rate of growth of capital (π) is given by:

$$\pi = \frac{Y_2}{K} - u$$
$$= \frac{1}{K}.BK_2^{\beta}L_2^{1-\beta} - u$$

Taking u on the left-hand side and differentiating with respect to time, we have:

$$\frac{\dot{\pi}}{\pi+u} = -\frac{\dot{K}}{K} + \beta\frac{\dot{K}_2}{K_2} + (1-\beta)\frac{\dot{L}_2}{L_2}$$
$$= (\beta-1)\frac{\dot{K}}{K} + (1-\beta)\frac{\alpha}{1-\alpha_1}\frac{\dot{K}}{K} \quad \text{—using (2.1.38) (2.1.40) and (2.1.41)}$$
$$= \frac{\dot{K}}{K}.(\beta-1)\left[1-\frac{\alpha}{1-\alpha_1}\right]$$

Therefore:

(2.1.42) $$\frac{\dot{\pi}}{\pi+u} = \frac{\dot{K}}{K}(\beta-1)\left[\frac{1-(\alpha_1+\alpha)}{1-\alpha_1}\right]$$

Now $\beta<1$ and $\alpha+\alpha_1<1$. Therefore, the coefficient of $\frac{\dot{K}}{K}$ is negative. In other words, whenever $\frac{\dot{K}}{K}$ is greater than zero, $\dot{\pi}$ is negative, i.e. $\frac{\dot{K}}{K}$ falls over time. Again, when $\frac{\dot{K}}{K}$ is negative, $\dot{\pi}$ is positive and $\frac{\dot{K}}{K}$ increases. Thus there is always a tendency towards $\frac{\dot{K}}{K}=0$. Moreover, when $\frac{\dot{K}}{K} = 0, \frac{\dot{K}_1}{K_1} = \frac{\dot{K}_2}{K_2} = 0$ because of (2.1.38) and (2.1.39). Further because of (2.1.40) and (2.1.41) $\frac{\dot{L}_1}{L_1} = \frac{\dot{L}_2}{L_2} = 0$. Thus even when the economy is commercialised there is a tendency towards stagnation. The main cause of stagnation is the law of diminishing returns in the consumption goods sector and not the family-based structure. If the law of constant returns to scale prevails in the consumption goods sector (which may be the case when consumption goods are no longer dominated by agricultural products), $\alpha+\alpha_1 = 1$. In that situation our equation (2.1.42) becomes:

(2.1.43) $$\frac{\dot{\pi}}{\pi+u} = \frac{\dot{K}}{K}(\beta-1)\frac{1-1}{1-\alpha_1} = 0$$

In this situation, the growth path of K is neutral. There is no inherent tendency towards stagnation or towards any stable self-sustained growth. The rate of growth of capital can be at any level depending on the saving propensity, the rate of depreciation and the production function in capital goods. This stage is an advance on the earlier stage to the extent that commercialisation (which is ultimately the characteristic of an economy with self-sustained growth) has been introduced and the consumer goods sector has moved away from diminishing returns. Here again the main ways of increasing the rate of increase of capital are increases in the propensity to save, foreign capital and 'technical progress'. If this process continues for a time so as to exhaust the reserve army of labour we may be able to pass on to Stage III.

In Stage III capital accumulation has proceeded far enough to provide employment for the whole of the labour force. Analytically this means the introduction of another equation:

(2.1.47) $$L_1+L_2 = L$$

where L_1 = labour in Sector 1
L_2 = labour in Sector 2, and
L = total labour force.

Moreover, because of the increased productivity of labour and the absence of a reserve army of labourers, real wages are no longer tied to an institutionally determined level. Real wages are equal to the marginal productivity of labour which is now higher than the subsistence level. Lastly, because of the increased standard of living, consumer goods are no longer dominated by agricultural products and we can assume that constant return to scale prevails in the consumer goods sector as it does in the capital goods sector. With these modifications the new model is as follows:

(2.1.44) $$Y_1 = AK_1^{\alpha}L_1^{1-\alpha}$$
(2.1.45) $$Y_2 = BK_2^{\beta}L_2^{1-\beta}$$
(2.1.46) $$K_1 + K_2 = K$$
(2.1.47) $$L_1+L_2 = L$$
(2.1.48) $$r = A\alpha K_1^{\alpha-1}L_1^{1-\alpha}$$
(2.1.49) $$r = pB\beta K_2^{\beta-1}L_2^{1-\beta}$$
(2.1.50) $$w = AK_1^{\alpha}(1-\alpha)L_1^{-\alpha}$$
(2.1.51) $$w = pBK_2^{\beta}(1-\beta)L_2^{-\beta}$$
(2.1.52) $$pY_2 = s.Y$$
(2.1.53) $$Y = Y_1+pY_2$$

The symbols are the same as those in the model for Stage II. Here we have one new equation, equation (2.1.47), and one more unknown,

w. The level of capital (K) and the labour force (L) are exogenous as before.*

Manipulating as before, we find that both capital and labour in each sector are a fixed proportion of total capital and total labour. Thus we have:

$$\frac{\dot{K}_1}{K_1} = \frac{\dot{K}_2}{K_2} = \frac{\dot{K}}{K} \tag{2.1.54}$$

and

$$\frac{\dot{L}_1}{L_1} = \frac{\dot{L}_2}{L_2} = \frac{\dot{L}}{L} \tag{2.1.55}$$

The relative rate of growth of capital is given by:

$$\frac{\dot{K}}{K} = \frac{Y_2}{K} - u$$

Putting $\frac{\dot{K}}{K} = \pi$ and using (2.1.45) we have:

$$\pi + u = \frac{BK_2{}^{\beta}L_2{}^{1-\beta}}{K} \tag{2.1.56}$$

Taking logs of both sides and differentiating with respect to time, we have:

$$\frac{\dot{\pi}}{\pi + u} = \beta\frac{\dot{K}_2}{K_2} + (1-\beta)\frac{\dot{L}_2}{L_2} - \frac{\dot{K}}{K}$$

$$\frac{\dot{\pi}}{\pi + u} = (\beta - 1)\left(\frac{\dot{K}}{K} - \frac{\dot{L}}{L}\right) \tag{2.1.57}$$

using (2.1.54) and (2.1.55).

In this case we find that there is an inherent tendency for capital to grow at the same rate as labour is growing. Thus, if $\frac{\dot{K}}{K} < \frac{\dot{L}}{L}$, $\dot{\pi}$ is positive; so $\frac{\dot{K}}{K}$ increases towards $\frac{\dot{L}}{L}$. Similarly, if $\frac{\dot{K}}{K} > \frac{\dot{L}}{L}$, $\dot{\pi}$ is negative and again $\frac{\dot{K}}{K}$ tends towards $\frac{\dot{L}}{L}$. In this situation, even if there is no 'technical progress', or foreign capital, the economy tends to grow on its own.

2.2: MONEY IN GROWTH

In our analysis so far we have ignored (as has been done in most other growth models) the influence of money on the determination of income, investment, employment, etc. Actually, however, casual

* At this stage, our model becomes very similar to the two-sector model of H. Uzawa (165).

observation as well as historical studies suggest that economic development has always been associated with an increasing money supply and increasing prices, and it is possible that there is some causal link behind this observed association. We should, therefore, try to indicate the place of money in our model.

2.2.1: A REFERENCE TO THE LITERATURE

The debate on the role of money has old roots. The mercantalists emphasised the importance of the accumulation of precious metals in increasing the wealth of nations. 'For them money was—to use the terminology of today—a factor of production on the same footing as land' (Heckscher (75), Vol. II, p. 200). Whether this was because the mercantalists confused precious metals for wealth of nations (as Adam Smith asserts) or because they understood the relation between money, interest and capital accumulation (as Keynes (86) would have it) we need not discuss. Whatever the precise reasoning in their minds the fact remains that mercantalists thought that increases in the stock of money increased the wealth and welfare of nations. This conception of the role of money was sharply criticised and completely abandoned by the classical economists. It was argued that the wealth of nations depends on the production of real goods and services. Money is only a medium of exchange that facilitates transactions but does not affect them. If, for example, money is doubled, all the prices will be doubled and nobody will be any richer. Thus money is a pure 'veil' over the real economic forces; and not only is it possible to take off this veil, but it is also necessary to do so in order to see the underlying reality. Thus in classical economics money has no place in equilibrium analysis of value and distribution; but money might influence the dis-equilibrium situation of business-cycles type as analysed by Wicksell, Hayek and Hawtrey and monetary policy might be useful in controlling short run deviations in the economy from the long run equilibrium. Keynesian economics effected a *volte face* in this respect. In Keynes' system money does influence the equilibrium values of output and employment, but monetary policy is not considered important for controlling economic fluctuations. In subsequent discussions, D. Patinkin (117) has tried to integrate value theory and monetary theory by introducing the real balance effect as the connecting link. He has further demonstrated in this modified and sophisticated system the validity of the essential classical conclusion that increases in money raise prices proportionately and do not change the equilibrium rate of interest or the level of employment.

The Indian economy is of a pre-industrial type—perhaps closer to the mercantalist world than to the Keynesian world. In this situation, as we note below, money may have certain important effects on the production possibility curve of the system. However, these effects are mostly of a qualitative nature and it was not found possible to introduce them explicitly in a simple macro-model. Broadly speaking, we find that the classical quantity theory may well be valid in the Indian context. In our scheme the direct influence of money is on prices, though it may also influence investment, production, etc., via prices. We do not deny the theoretical plausibility of integrating the real and monetary sector by the real-balance effect or the like; but we do consider this type of effect rather minor and not worth the sacrifice of the simplicity of our macro-system.

2.2.2: SOME QUALITATIVE EFFECTS OF THE INTRODUCTION OF MONEY

Money, it is well known, has three important roles: it is a unit of account, it is a medium of exchange, and it is a store of value. In all these respects money plays a vital role in stimulating growth. As a unit of account money helps to develop a sense of accounting and commercial calculations in economic activities. In a primitive society, where money does not exist, it is difficult to think rationally of the problems of allocation and exchange because of the absence of a common unit for calculation. In such a situation there is a continual danger of confusion between the use value and the exchange value of goods and factors of production. Here the introduction of money facilitates the measurement, and, therefore, the achievement of economic efficiency. It is true that such considerations are relevant only when we are considering the question of the existence or non-existence of money and not when we are considering changes in the quantity of money. But the discussion remains relevant because in many underdeveloped countries, including India, a considerable part of the economy is non-monetised, and for this part, the introduction of money will have the effect of developing the commercial outlook which is essential for economic growth.

As a medium of exchange money increases the scope of exchange and thus increases the division of labour and economic efficiency of the factors of production. In the absence of money barter is the only form of exchange, and in this situation the scope for exchange is restricted because barter requires reciprocal coincidence of demand and supply. Introduction of money widens the market and people can concentrate on producing the goods in which they are most efficient instead of trying to produce by themselves as much of their requirements as they can. In both these ways the introduction of money helps the process of rational allocation and thus brings about a shift in the production function.

Thirdly, as a store of value money stimulates savings and helps in the better allocation of savings. In the absence of money the main form of accumulation available to the household is the accumulation of goods of direct use—grain, cattle, etc. In these cases the cost of storage and risk of damage tend to be high after a certain point and thus the rate of return is rather low. Money provides an asset which is relatively costless and riskless (except for the fall in the purchasing power of money). Thus the presence of money increases the effective rate of return on savings and consequently stimulates savings.

2.2.3: EFFECTS OF CHANGES IN THE QUANTITY OF MONEY

The above analysis refers to the effects of the introduction of money into the non-monetary sector. This is not irrelevant to our purpose because the non-monetary sector in the Indian economy is about 30 per cent (see, for example, H. V. R. Iengar (76)). However, the more important question is: what are the effects of an increase in the money supply in the monetary sector? In this connection the main conflict is between the classical quantity theory of money and the Keynesian theory of money. According to the quantity theorists, increases in the money supply will lead ultimately to proportionate increases in prices (with real income constant) though in the short run, the interest rate may also fall temporarily. On the other hand, according to the Keynesian theorists, the main effect of changes in money supply is on the interest rate; price may or may not change as a secondary effect.

The main source of conflict between these two theories is the assumption about how the discrepancy between demand and supply of money is sought to be corrected. According to the quantity theorists, when the money supply is increased, the community will have unwanted cash holdings and it will seek to spend the excess cash balance on goods until prices of goods have gone up to such an extent that the increased balances are necessary to transact the ordinary business of the community at higher prices. Since it is assumed that the community wants to hold a fixed proportion of its money income as cash balances, an equilibrium is restored only when prices have increased proportionately to the change in the money supply. According to the Keynesian mechanism, however, when actual cash balances exceed desired cash balances people go out and buy additional securities. This pushes down the rate of interest and the latter may affect the rate of investment, the level of income and prices. There may be thus some secondary effects on prices; however, if the demand for idle balances is elastic with respect to the rate of interest, and the rate of interest has fallen, some part of the addition to the money supply will end up as idle balances;

and the increase in money income cannot be proportional to the increases in the money supply. More sophisticated versions of the quantity theory do not preclude the Keynesian mechanism to begin with. They argue that even if the initial effect of changes in the money supply is on the interest rate, prices might rise proportionately to the money supply if the demand for money is interest inelastic. Thus the increase in the money supply lowers the rate of interest to begin with; but the lower rate of interest stimulates investment and discourages savings and these in turn bid up the prices of goods and services. Since the decline in the rate of interest cannot induce people to hold more money the expansion of money income and prices will proceed until all the cash balances are required for transaction purposes. Still another rationalisation of the quantity theory has been provided by D. Patinkin (117) who demonstrates that if there is no money illusion in the holdings of idle cash balances, their volume should increase as prices are increasing, and therefore equilibrium is restored only when prices have risen proportionately to the increase in the money supply.

From the above brief review of the controversy it is clear that it is not a logical issue but an empirical one. It all depends on how developed are the financial markets and what is the behaviour pattern in different markets. In an underdeveloped country financial markets are underdeveloped. So the main alternative to holding money is to spend it on goods and services. Thus, on the whole, the unsophisticated classical quantity theory may well be applicable to an underdeveloped country. It is true that financial markets are also developing rapidly in these countries; but their importance in the economy as a whole is insignificant. Most people do not have an adequate knowledge of or confidence in other financial assets. However, one alternative to spending excess cash balances on current goods and services may be spending them on durable goods like land or gold. Thus it is possible that increases in the money supply will be used to bid up the price not of currently produced goods and services but of land and gold. Actually, however, this line of reaction does not invalidate the quantity theory. In the first place, the amount of gold and land actually traded in a particular year is likely to be a small proportion of the total income. Secondly, we should not stop at the first step of the analysis where the prices of gold and land are bid up. The question then arises, what do the sellers of land and gold do with their new cash balances? Most probably they would spend them on goods and services. Thus the impact of the money supply is felt in the commodity market at one remove.

The results of the above process can be demonstrated in a simple model of the Patinkin type. Suppose there are three markets in the economy: commodity market, land market, and money market. Equilibrium in the commodity market is established when:

$$Y_o = D(Y_o, \frac{p_L . L_o}{p}, \frac{M_o}{p}) \tag{2.2.1}$$

where Y_o = supply of goods and services in the current period
L_o = the fixed supply of land and such other assets
p_L = price of land
p = general price level of goods and services
M_o = money supply.

We assume that the wealth value of holding land or gold is determined in terms of their value in purchasing current goods and services. Therefore, the relevant land variable becomes $\frac{P_L L_o}{p}$.

$$L_o = L(Y_o, \frac{p_L L_o}{p}, \frac{M_o}{p}) \tag{2.2.2.}$$

$$\frac{M_o}{p} = M(Y_o, \frac{p_L L_o}{p}, \frac{M_o}{p}) \tag{2.2.3}$$

Because of Walras's law, only two of the above equations are independent and they determine the two unknowns in the system: p and p_L. Suppose at a particular set of values of the exogenous variables the equilibrium values of p and p_L are p_o and $(p_L)_o$. We assume that this is a unique solution system so that with one set of values of the exogenous variable only one set of endogenous values are possible. Now, if M_o is increased to $2M_o$, and p_o and $(p_L)_o$ are also increased to $2p_o$ and $2(p_L)_o$ we find by substitution that all these equations are satisfied. Now with Y_o, L_o and $2M_o$ there can be only one set of solution values for p and p_L and $2p_o$ and $2(p_L)_o$ is one such set; therefore, $2p_o$ and $2(p_L)_o$ is the only solution with the new values of the exogenous variables. Thus without going into the details of the dynamic adjustment process and mathematical solution we can assert that the presence of land and gold as alternative ways of spending excess cash balances does not invalidate the quantity theory hypothesis.

Having demonstrated the validity of the quantity theory hypothesis in the presence of gold and land, we can return to the situation where currently produced goods are the only type to be exchanged against money and consider the exact formulation of our hypothesis. The effects of introducing money in a non-monetary economy are of a qualitative type and we do not propose to include them in our model. As regards the quantity theory hypothesis, it would have been more in keeping with our assumption of a dualistic economy if we could refer to separate money equations for the two sectors.

Actually, however, the separate monetary data in the two sectors are unlikely to be available; and we have to consider one money equation for the whole economy. Making the money supply an independent variable we can write:

(2.2.4) $$pY = \alpha + \beta M$$

where p = general price
Y = total income level in real terms
M = total money supply.

Now the value of β in this equation depends on institutional conditions of the economy and these are likely to change over time. So we include a time variable to indicate this change in institutional conditions. We have:

(2.2.5) $$pY = \beta_0 + \beta_1 M + \beta_2 t$$

where t = time variable.

Thus, in our simple system the main influence of the money supply is on prices. However, since prices affect wages, investment, etc., the money supply may also indirectly affect these real variables.

2.3: GROWTH AND THE FOREIGN SECTOR

In the preceding sections we have considered the process of growth in the context of a closed economy. In this section we relax the assumption of a closed economy and consider the impact of the foreign sector on economic growth in an underdeveloped country. We begin with the consideration of the importance of trade and pass on to consider the importance of capital movements and food aid of the P.L. 480 variety.*

2.3.1: TRADE AND GROWTH

The traditional discussions of the gains of trade centre on the comparative cost principle. In terms of the typical two-commodity, two-country model, it is argued that even when both the countries can produce both the goods, it is better for each to specialise in the

* This refers to the Surplus Agricultural Commodities Disposal Programme (Public Law 480) of the U.S.A., under which the U.S.A. has been giving agricultural commodities to foreign countries on favourable terms. Since October, 1956 India has received large quantities of wheat, rice, coarse grains, cotton, tobacco and milk products under this programme. According to the agreement, the Indian Government is to pay the Government of the U.S.A. the rupee equivalent of the dollar costs of these commodities and 50 per cent of the ocean freight costs and these are to be deposited in the U.S. Title Account in India. The remaining 50 per cent of the freight is to be borne by the Government of India. Further under the agreement, the counterpart funds representing the rupee deposits to the U.S. Title Account are to be used as assistance to the Government of India in the shape of grants or loans, and a small portion is retained by the U.S. Government partly for its own use and partly for giving loans to U.S. firms or their affiliates for investment in India.

production of the commodity in which it enjoys a comparative cost advantage. This basic Ricardian theorem has been presented in various forms—e.g. in terms of opportunity costs by Haberler (72) and in terms of factor endowments by Heckscher and Ohlin. But essentially it is always based upon the static general equilibrium theory of welfare economics and it does not consider structural disequilibrium of the type present in underdeveloped countries. As is often argued (see below), this line of argument does not provide an adequate rationalisation of trade in the context of economic growth in underdeveloped countries. Our position is that to appreciate the significance of trade in our context we have to give up the assumption that both the commodities can be produced in both the countries. The main benefit to underdeveloped countries of trade with the developed countries springs from the fact that trade provides new commodities and new knowledge which could not be produced at home unless the underdeveloped country decides to re-enact the whole drama of the industrial revolution, the outcome of which is not certain in any case. It is in this sense that foreign exchange availability can become a constraint on economic growth, quite apart from the availability of domestic capital, labour and other factors of production. To put it differently, the main justification for foreign trade lies in its being a carrier of 'technical progress' rather than its static efficiency.

It is easy to see why the traditional rationalisation of trade does not hold water in underdeveloped countries. As is generally agreed, the market costs of labour and capital in underdeveloped countries do not reflect their true social cost, and specialisation on the basis of market prices can lead to the wrong choice. W. A. Lewis (100) has put the argument very neatly: 'We assume that two countries can produce the same things and trade with each other. A is the country where labour is scarce; B is the country where unlimited supply of labour is available in the subsistence (food) sector. Using the classical framework for comparative costs, we write that one day's labour

in A produces 3 food or 3 cotton manufactures
in B produces 2 food or 1 cotton manufactures

This, of course, gives the wrong answer to the question "who should specialise in which?" since we have written the average instead of the marginal products. We can assume that these coincide in A and also in cotton manufacture in B. Then we should write in marginal terms that one day's labour

in A produces 3 food or 3 cotton manufactures
in B produces 0 food or 1 cotton manufacture

B should specialise in cotton manufacture and import food. In practice, however, wages will be 2 food in B and between 3 food and 6 food in A, at which level it will be "cheaper" for B to export food and import cotton' (W. A. Lewis (100)). There is thus a conflict between market cost and social cost and for optimisation from a social point of view, B should protect its textile industry. Another variant of this argument has been presented by E. E. Hagen (73). He argues that because of the wage disparity between the manufacturing industry and agriculture, 'manufacturing industry having a real comparative advantage will be under-sold by imports when foreign exchanges are in equilibrium. Protection which permits such industry to exist will increase real income in the economy' (op. cit.).

Our model throws out essentially similar reasons for protection in underdeveloped countries. In the typical pattern of trade the underdeveloped countries export primary products in exchange for manufactures for the developed countries. The primary goods will mean the products of the wage-goods sector in our model. This holds even when the exports are commercial crops like indigo, tea or jute, which are not wage-goods themselves, but which are opportunity costs of food-grains production. In our model, the export of wage-goods will bring about a reduction in employment in Sector 2. Since the marginal productivity of labour in Sector 2 is positive, the output of Sector 2 will decline and the unemployed labour will be thrown back to Sector 1 to live with other family members on the family farms. This addition of labour to Sector 1 will not, however, increase output in Sector 1 because the marginal product of a labourer in this sector is zero. There is thus a loss in total output which could have been prevented by protecting the indigenous manufactures.

The above line of argument, which is generally accepted in the context of the theory and policy of economic development, implies that the underdeveloped countries should try to restrict imports and consequently exports. Actually, however, the imports of the underdeveloped countries are rising fast and these countries are very anxious to expand their exports. The key to this paradox perhaps lies in the fact that the comparative cost doctrine does not underline the real advantages of trade between developed and underdeveloped countries of today. This doctrine was developed in the context of trade amongst countries with a roughly similar level of technical knowledge (note, for example, the assumption of the same production functions for the two trading countries); and it misses the main advantage of trade between the developed and underdeveloped countries. Imports are necessary to the underdeveloped countries not because they are cheaper than the cost of production (relative or absolute) at home, but because they embody new knowledge which is not available at home. It is not sufficient to characterise them as 'capital goods' because theoretically any type of non-consumed goods is a 'capital good' and in that sense, capital goods are also produced at home. Their main importance springs from the fact that these are new types of capital goods which are not producible at home. This seems to us to be an important neglected dimension of trade theory in the modern context. A proper consideration of this aspect would require a heterogeneous capital model of the Solow (151) type and our model as it stands is incapable of dealing with it satisfactorily. To a certain extent, however, we can accommodate it in our model by making the rate of 'technical progress' in the underdeveloped country a function of imports. For an empirical verification of this hypothesis, we have to relate the 'technical progress' factor for every year with the imports. If the production function is $Y_2 = BK_2^{\beta}L_2^{1-\beta}$ the 'technical progress' factor can be put as $(\frac{\Delta B}{B})_t$ for the year t. Our hypothesis will imply that $(\frac{\Delta B}{B})_t = f(M_t)$, where M_t = imports in year t.

Another way of introducing the foreign sector may be by emphasising the import-content of investment in underdeveloped countries —especially in their modern sector. Analytically, we can write $GI_2 = f(M)$, where GI_2 is gross investment in the modern sector and M is imports in real terms. It is possible that in the absence of foreign imported machines investment plans may not be realised. In this case imports play a vital role in the process of growth. However, imports have to be paid for. In a situation of equilibrium in the balance of payments, $p_x.X = p_mM$ where p_m = price of imports, p_x = price of exports and X = exports. Using this balance of payments equation we have $GI_2 = f(\frac{p_x}{p_m}.X)$. Thus capital formation and growth of the economy may be closely connected with its terms of trade and export possibilities.

Unfortunately for underdeveloped countries there seem to be low price and income elasticities of demand for primary products and fluctuating and secularly declining terms of trade of primary producers. The fluctuating prices of primary commodities are, of course, well known, but these could be taken care of by some buffer stock operations. The secular trend of terms of trade of primary producers is a more serious matter and it has been a subject of dispute from both statistical and theoretical points of view*, though broadly speak-

* For a review of this discussion see T. Morgan (104).

ing a tendency towards the worsening of terms of trade of the primary goods-producing countries is accepted. This tendency may be apparently puzzling, for from a theoretical point of view it may seem, as Keynes (84) and Robertson (132) argued, that since the law of diminishing returns works more powerfully in primary production, the terms of trade of primary producers should improve as production expands. The explanation of the observed tendency towards declining terms of trade has proceeded along two lines: demand-based argument and cost-based argument. Explanations of the latter type have been advanced by Raul Prebisch (120) and W. A. Lewis (100). Prebisch argues that the characteristic lack of organisation among workers employed in primary production prevents them from obtaining wage increases (in the boom) comparable to those of the industrial countries, and from maintaining the increases to the same extent in depression as is done in industrial countries. According to Lewis, the poor terms of trade experience of the underdeveloped countries is due to the fact that wages in export industries are fixed by peasant earnings, which have been stagnant over time, whereas the wages of the industrial countries have shown an upward tendency. Of the demand-based explanations we may note the ones advanced by C. Kindleberger (90) and E. M. Bernstein (10). According to Kindleberger the worsening of the terms of trade is due to the operation of Engel's law and the incapacity of underdeveloped countries to withdraw resources from the losing industries and to enter into the more productive ones. Similarly, Bernstein argues that the falling terms of trade are due to the chronic surplus in raw materials content of industrial output.

In our opinion, the demand-based explanations of Kindleberger and Bernstein are closer to truth than the cost-based explanations of Prebisch and Lewis. For one thing, wage-cost is only a part of the total cost and low wages may not always lead to low prices because of diminishing returns (as Keynes and Robertson emphasised) and because of the cost of capital, land, etc. Secondly, the constancy of wages refers to real wages, i.e. to the relative prices of wage-goods *vis-à-vis* money wages, whereas the terms of trade depend on the absolute prices of exports, *vis-à-vis* imports. Thus even if real wages are constant, money wages may be rising very fast and thus the prices of exports in terms of imports may go up. For the determination of terms of trade, it is, therefore, more important to know the demand situation. We present below a simple model of terms of trade which shows the rate of change of terms of trade as a function of various demand elasticities and the rates of growth of income.

Exports (X) can be assumed to depend positively on the rest of the world income (Y_w) and negatively on the terms of the trade ($\frac{p_x}{p_m} = P$). Assuming a constant elasticity function we have:

$$(2.3.1) \qquad X = AP^{-\alpha}Y_w^{\beta}$$

The imports of the country (MT) may be assumed to depend positively both on the income of the country (Y) and the terms of trade (P). Again, assuming a constant elasticity function, we have:

$$(2.3.2) \qquad MT = BP^{\gamma}Y^{\sigma}$$

In equilibrium the earnings from exports ($p_x.X$) must be equal to those from imports ($p_m(MT)$). Thus:

$$(2.3.3) \qquad p_x.X = p_m(MT)$$

or

$$PX = (MT)$$

Any discrepancy between demand and supply is likely to be corrected through movements in the terms of trade. If the exchange rate is free to vary, the required change in the terms of trade may be obtained by variation in exchange rate. When, however, the exchange rates are fixed, the process may operate through the internal price level. When there is a surplus in the balance of payments, the central bank of the country accumulates foreign assets, but it has to pay the exporters in terms of local currency and thus expand the money supply and vice versa for deficits. This expansion or contraction of the money supply will in our model affect absolute prices, until equilibrium is restored.

Assuming that the values of Y_w and Y in equations (2.3.1) and (2.3.2) respectively are determined independently of trade we have in the above system three equations and three unknowns: X, MT, P. Subject to the usual qualifications, the system is thus determinate. From this system it is also possible to state the determinants of the trends in the terms of trade in a precise manner. From (2.3.3) we have:

$$P = \frac{(MT)}{X}$$

Using (2.3.1) and (2.3.2) and simplifying, we have:

$$P^{1-\alpha-\gamma} = \frac{B}{A}Y^{\sigma}Y_w^{-\beta}$$

Taking the derivatives of the log of both sides and dividing by $(1-\alpha-\gamma)$ we have:

$$(2.3.4) \qquad \frac{\dot{P}}{P} = \frac{1}{1-\alpha-\gamma}.\frac{\dot{B}}{B} - \frac{1}{1-\alpha-\gamma}.\frac{\dot{A}}{A} + \frac{\sigma}{1-\alpha-\gamma}.\frac{\dot{Y}}{Y} - \frac{\beta}{1-\alpha-\gamma}.\frac{\dot{Y}_w}{Y_w}$$

From the above formula it is obvious that it is difficult to make any *a priori* statement about the trend in terms of trade; it would depend upon the empirical values of the parameters involved. Historically, perhaps the rising preference for foreign goods ($\frac{\dot{B}}{B} > O$), the substitution of synthetic products for natural raw materials by the industrial countries ($\frac{\dot{A}}{A} < O$) combined with the low income elasticity of demand for primary products (Engel's law) have been responsible for the fall in the terms of trade of the primary goods producing countries. For a precise quantitative statement in this respect we have to obtain the statistical estimates of the parameters. But broadly speaking neither the terms of trade nor the volume of exports seem to hold much hope for the future of primary producing countries.

2.3.2: CAPITAL MOVEMENTS AND GROWTH

It is in this context that foreign capital assumes great significance for the growth of underdeveloped countries. The difference between trade and capital movement is, of course, not a difference in the nature of the goods traded but a difference in the method of payments. Capital goods are imported even in trade, but they have to be paid for by exports. In the case of a capital inflow, however, the imports do not have to be paid for in the current period. In this sense, the capital inflow augments the investible resources in the economy. To the extent that the capital inflows are regarded as only adding to the savings in the economy, their effects would be formally similar to the increase in domestic savings in the economy. We have already noted that in the context of our model the increase in savings will bring about an increase in the level of capital and income, but it does not provide the basis for continuous growth—the tendency towards stagnation remains. Similarly, unless the amount of capital is so large as to enable the economy to skip over the first stage of economic growth as analysed above, the capital inflow will not provide an escape from stagnation, though it will increase the level of income. The main significance of foreign capital lies in its qualitative aspect. Thus proceeding with the assumption that gross investment in the modern sector depends on imports, we have:

(2.3.5) $$GI_2 = f(MT)$$

and

(2.3.6) $$p_m.(MT) - p_x.X = FC$$

where FC = net inflow of foreign capital.

Thus:

(2.3.7) $$GI_2 = f(\frac{FC + p_x.X}{p_m})$$

In this way, foreign capital may play an important part in capital formation and the growth of underdeveloped countries. Its precise significance can be understood only by estimating the parameters of the function (2.3.7) above.

Historically, the foreign capital has not formed a quantitatively significant part in the growth of the present-day developed countries. As K. Berrill (11) concludes from his survey of the conditions of take-off in Britain, France, Germany, Japan, Finalnd, U.S.A., Australia, New Zealand, Scandinavian countries and Canada: 'The first characteristic which strikes the observer is that in terms of quantity foreign capital is very much the minor part of capital supply during the two or three decades of take-off. On average over this period the foreigner usually supplied less than 20 per cent of the necessary savings and sometimes very much less. Possibly the only exception to this rule was Canada' (op. cit.).

Thus so far as foreign capital only supplements domestic investible funds, it is unlikely to be of any great significance in growth. But actually, the real importance of foreign capital lies not in its quantitative aspect but in its qualitative one; not in adding to the amount of capital but in transforming the nature of capital. The inflow of foreign capital is generally associated with an inflow of foreign entrepreneurs and management as well as foreign techniques of production. This may have the important effects of spreading the training among local workers and management. Similarly, a considerable part of foreign capital has gone into public utilities and transport and this has played an important part in building up the infra-structure of the economy. The exact extent of the stimulation provided by these types of investment would, of course, depend on the technological nature of the industry into which capital has flowed (see, e.g., R. E. Baldwin (5)). For example, a network of railways for transport of jute or tea may have considerable effects on the degree of mobility in the economy, whereas the transport of oil by pipeline may not affect mobility at all. Apart from these tangible effects, the foreign sector may have important socio-economic effects. Foreign capitalists are less likely to be bothered about traditional social prejudices and they may help to increase the mobility of labour in the economy. They may also help in the development of commercial attitudes in the society which are essential for transition from Stage I to Stage II of our model of growth. All these are very important aspects of the impact of the foreign sector. But unfortunately, as noted above, our simplified model is incapable of taking into account all these socio-economic effects in any precise manner. All we can do is to put these effects under the catch-all category of 'technical progress' and make the latter a function of foreign capital as well. The figures of imports of goods include the figures of capital inflow as well. So the effect of capital inflow on technical progress is taken into account when we make the rate of technical progress a function of imports.

2.3.3: FOOD AID AND GROWTH

In recent years the possibility of food aid for economic growth has attracted considerable attention and since in our model the marketed surplus of wage-goods (of which food is an important part) plays a crucial role in the determination of employment and output in the non-wage-goods sector, we should consider the impact of food aid in the context of our model. At present the U.S. programme of surplus food disposal under P.L. 480 is mainly concerned with the disposal of food-grains, but it is possible (and it has been suggested) that P.L. 480 be combined with some foreign exchange aid which would purchase other items of wage-goods. Therefore, we consider the P.L. 480 aid as the free import of wage-goods.

The possible effects of P.L. 480 in underdeveloped countries have been a subject of keen controversy. A sample of these contrasting opinions is provided by the symposium on this issue reported in the *Journal of Farm Economics*, December 1960. It has been argued by T. W. Schultz (141) that P.L. 480 imports of food-grains will depress the agricultural prices and thus adversely affect the production and investment of agriculture in the recipient country. These imports are, therefore, not in the long run in the interest of agriculture even though it may serve the interest of consumption and productivity in the non-agricultural sector in the short run. S. R. Sen (146), on the other hand, argues that there has been no such tendency in India where large-scale schemes of development have been creating considerable demand for food. On the other hand, 'P.L. 480 supplies have helped considerably to mitigate the shortage in the economy and give protection to a large vulnerable section of the population'. The same conclusion seems to have been supported by the experience of P.L. 480 funds in Japan and Pakistan as noted by M. Ezekiel (38). In a similar vein, it has been argued by D. R. Khatkhate (87) that even if these imports depressed agricultural prices, they may not affect agricultural production, since 'in an economy where the subsistence sector looms large, agricultural production does not respond to price changes, while the marketed surplus has a negative response, which is totally opposed to what happens in an economy with a predominance of big landholders'. The above discussion relates to the effects of agricultural prices relative to other prices. But there is also some controversy about the effects on the absolute level of prices. According to some the P.L. 480 funds are helpful in checking the inflationary pressures in the economy whereas others argue that the use of local currency holdings arising from surplus disposal is inflationary.

Let us now consider this problem in the context of our model. We begin with the real effects of P.L. 480 type aid. In the context of our model employment in the non-wage-goods sector is determined by the availability of wage-goods. Now since the food aid increases the availability of wage-goods, it is likely to increase the employment potentiality in Sector 2. Thus we have to modify our earlier employment function to write:

$$L_2 = \alpha + \beta Y_1 + \gamma M_1 \qquad (2.3.8)$$

where M_1 = import of wage-goods.

The coefficient of M_1 is likely to be different from that of Y_1, since the imported wage-goods are likely to be largely available for Sector 2, whereas only a fraction of Y_1 is available for Sector 2.

Thus, according to our model, the food aid will facilitate an increase in employment and therefore output of Sector 2. It is true that employment of labour is not possible without some additional capital. But it is always possible to change the techniques and product-mix in such a way that more labour could be employed with the same amount of capital. However, this increase in the level of employment at the constant level of capital will bring about a fall in the marginal productivity of labour and since in our model the terms of trade between the two sectors depend on the marginal productivity of labour (see equation 2.1.16), the fall in marginal productivity of labour will bring about a fall in the ratio of price of Sector 1 to the price of Sector 2. However, in our analysis the production of the Sector 1 is determined by the availability of factors of production and it is not sensitive to relative prices. In this sector, labour is utilised to the point where the marginal product of labour is zero and this is independent of prices. However, if the P.L. 480 aid relates only to food-grains there will be a fall in the price of food-grains relative to other wage-goods and this may bring about a shift from food-grains to other types of wage-goods. But this need not reduce the value of the total output of Sector 1 and in fact this type of compositional change may be desirable for the economy. As regards the investment in subsistence sector, we note that private investment may be somewhat reduced because though the income level is constant the terms of trade have turned against this sector. However, as we note in our statistical analysis later, the terms of trade effect is quantitatively small. Moreover, the availability of P.L. 480 funds is likely to facilitate public investment, a part of which at least will go to the subsistence sector. Thus on the whole investment will be higher as a result of P.L. 480 food aid. To sum up therefore, in the context of our model, food aid is likely to have considerable good effects on employment, output and investment in the underdeveloped countries. This type of aid is, moreover, doubly desirable, because it also enables the food surplus countries to get rid of their embarrassing surpluses.

Next, let us consider the monetary implications of the P.L. 480 funds disposal. The imports of food-grains under P.L. 480 are paid for in local currency and according to some this has an inflationary effect on the economy. In our model, the effect on the general price level will depend on the effects on the money supply and the level of output, and we have to consider how the P.L. 480 affects these variables. The effects of P.L. 480 in this respect will depend on the method of payments and the use of the counterpart funds. Let us consider two cases:

Case I. When the food-grains arrive in the recipient country the Government pays the American Embassy by borrowing the necessary amount from the Central Bank (i.e. by creating new money). The whole of the food-grains are then disposed of in the market and the Government pays back the Central Bank from its sales receipts. The counterpart funds with the American Embassy are then spent either through loans to the Government or directly in the market.

In this case there is no net creation of money. The initial monetary expansion is neutralised as soon as sales receipts of the Government are utilised to pay back the Central Bank. Assuming that the time lag between the Government's purchase and sale is not significant, we can say that what has happened essentially is that food-grains have been sold by the American Embassy to the public. There is no increase in the money supply. So according to our analysis, there should be no expansion in the total money expenditure in the economy. On the other hand, there has been an increase in the supply of goods in the current period. To that extent there should be a disinflationary effect of P.L. 480 aid. This effect will not be present in subsequent years if the whole of the P.L. 480 funds are utilised for consumption purposes. However, to the extent that the rate of capital formation is increased, the flow of goods and services may be permanently raised. This will bring about a disinflationary effect even in subsequent years.

Case II. Next we consider the situation in which a part of the food-grains is kept aside for buffer stocks and the rest is sold to the public in the open market. The American Embassy is, however, paid in full and it spends the whole amount. In this case, there is a net expansion in the money supply; for the Government does not pay back the whole of its borrowings from the Central Bank for this purpose. This expansion in the money supply will have a multiplier effect on total expenditure—the multiplier being given by the income velocity. On the other hand, the real goods are increased by the amount of P.L. 480 imports in the current period and by their effect on production in subsequent periods through capital formation. Thus the net effect might be inflationary or deflationary depending on the statistical values of the parameters involved. So we would consider it again when we have obtained the statistical estimates of the parameters in our model (see Chapter 8.4 and Table 8.6).

2.4: THE SUMMARY

In the preceding sections we have tried to present a thcorctical analysis of an underdeveloped economy. Collecting the equations from different sections, our model for the Indian economy can be presented as follows:

(2.4.1) $$Y_1 = AK_1^{\alpha_{1\cdot 0}}$$

(2.4.2) $$L_2 = \alpha_{2\cdot 0}+\alpha_{2\cdot 1}Y_1+\alpha_{2\cdot 2}M_1$$

(2.4.3) $$Y_2 = BK_2^{\alpha_{3\cdot 0}}L_2^{1-\alpha_{3\cdot 0}}$$

(2.4.4) $$\bar{w} = \frac{p_2}{p_1}BK_2^{\alpha_{3\cdot 0}}(1-\alpha_{3\cdot 0})L_2^{-\alpha_{3\cdot 0}}$$

(2.4.5) $$I_1 = \frac{p_1 s_1 Y_1}{p_2} - uK_1$$

(2.4.6) $$Y = Y_1+Y_2$$

(2.4.7) $$pY = \alpha_{7\cdot 0}+\alpha_{7\cdot 1}M+\alpha_{7\cdot 2}t$$

(2.4.8) $$p = p_1\frac{Y_1}{Y}+p_2\frac{Y_2}{Y}$$

(2.4.9) $$X = CY_w^{\alpha_{9\cdot 0}}\left(\frac{p_x}{p_m}\right)^{\alpha_{9\cdot 1}}$$

(2.4.10) $$p_m(MT) = FC+p_x.X$$

(2.4.11) $$I_2 = \alpha_{11\cdot 0}+\alpha_{11\cdot 1}(MT)-uK_2$$

where Y_1 = output in wage-goods sector
K_1 = capital in wage-goods sector
L_2 = employment in non-wage-goods sector
M_1 = import of wage-goods
K_2 = capital in non-wage-goods sector
Y_2 = output in non-wage-goods sector
$\bar{w}$ = subsistence real wage
p_2 = price of non-wage-goods
p_1 = price of wage-goods

p = general price
p_x = price of exports
M = money supply
p_m = price of imports
Y = aggregate output
I_1 = net investment in wage-goods sector
I_2 = net investment in non-wage-goods sector
X = exports
Y_w = world income
FC = foreign capital inflow
MT = imports

The above system has 11 equations and subject to the usual conditions of consistency and independence, it determines the 11 unknowns: Y_1, Y_2, L_2, Y, p_1, p_2, p, I_1, I_2, X, MT. The rest of the variables are exogenous.

A flow diagram of the system can be presented as follows:

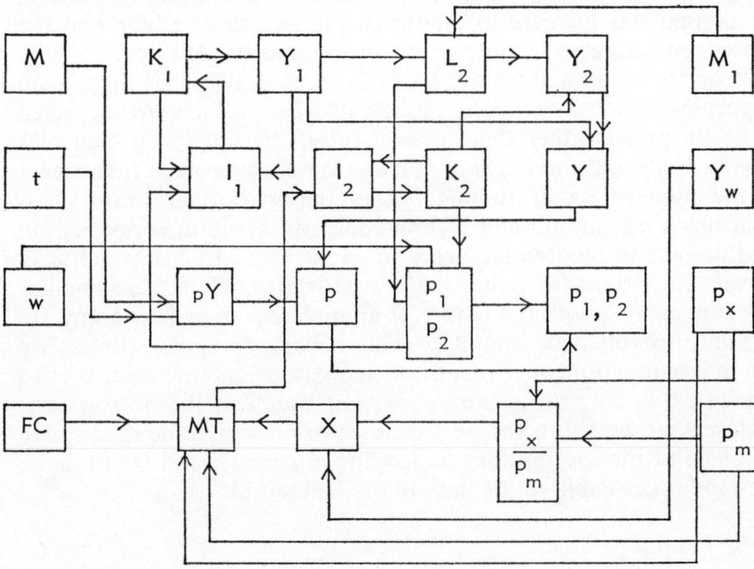

Figure 2.5

In constructing our model we have made many simplifying assumptions without making much effort to justify them. However, every theory involves some simplifications. Its justification lies in bringing to focus some important aspect of the problem not immediately obvious. We feel that our model possesses this type of justification. We have found that in the absence of 'technical progress' there may be an inherent tendency towards stagnation in an economy where consumer goods sector is dominated by agricultural products because of the law of diminishing returns in agriculture. Thus steady growth can be ensured only when the consumer goods sector is dominated by industrial products where constant returns to scale may operate. Thus industrialisation may well hold the key to self-sustained growth in underdeveloped countries. However, this does not mean that the whole of the available capital should go to the industrial sector. For industrialisation requires labour as well as capital. The transfer of labour from the agricultural to the industrial sector is possible only if there is some capital investment in agriculture. The optimum allocation of capital for the sake of industrialisation itself will require considerable investment in agriculture. More precisely, in the optimum situation the direct marginal productivity of capital in the industrial sector should be equal to the indirect marginal productivity obtained by increase in capital in agriculture, the consequent increase in labour in the industrial sector and the consequent increase in production in the industrial sector.

In our discussion above we have also seen that money may be an important factor in growth; though its *direct* effects are expected to be on prices rather than interest rates. We have also seen that foreign trade and foreign capital may play a vital role in investment in the modern sector though not in the traditional sector. This indicates a certain amount of non-competitiveness in investment in traditional and modern sectors, a proper appreciation of which may be very important for policy makers. However, while these qualitative statements about the nature of an underdeveloped economy are certainly useful, they cannot provide a basis for policy unless we can make quantitative estimates of the parameters involved. It is to this task that we turn in our subsequent chapters. It is in this connection that we try in the next chapter to present some descriptive rationale of the assumptions underlying our model and try to make the model amenable to the data in the real world.

CHAPTER 3

The Statistical Form of the Model

In the preceding chapter we have presented a theoretical model suitable for an underdeveloped economy of the Indian type. Our next task is to estimate the parameters of the various structural equations in the model. However, for statistical estimation we have to recast our model so as to make it amenable to the data available. For one thing, the system as it stands does not take into account dynamic considerations in the form of lags or expectations; but in statistical analysis concerned with the data of the real world, we have to take these into account. Similarly, it is difficult to define a wage-goods sector in practice. So for statistical purposes we have to divide the economy between agricultural and non-agricultural sectors—the agricultural sector being a close approximation to the wage-goods sector. Again, for the employment function in the non-agricultural sector, we have to take the output of food-grains rather than total agricultural output as the determining influence. Thus, while keeping the basic logic of the model intact, we have to modify our system of equations in a number of ways. It is these statistical problems that are considered in this chapter. In the first four sections (Sections 3.1 to 3.4) we consider in turn the statistical forms of production functions, employment functions, investment functions, and the functions for money, wages and prices. In Section 3.5 we introduce some equations which are required for closing the system. Then in Section 3.6 we put together these equations and consider the limitations of the model and compare it with other similar models. Lastly, in Section 3.7, we consider the statistical problems of the estimation of the parameters of the model.

3.1: PRODUCTION FUNCTIONS

In our statistical analysis we continue to adhere to the Cobb–Douglas type of production function. We have chosen the Cobb–Douglas type of production function rather than the fixed-coefficient type used by Harrod–Domar or the variable elasticity of substitution type used by K. J. Arrow, H. B. Chenery, B. S. Minhas and R. M. Solow (SMAC) (3). The fixed coefficient type of production function has been used quite extensively in actual planning experiments (e.g. Mahalanobis (102)). However, we feel that while it is quite appropriate in the industry-level analysis, it is not so at the aggregative level. At the aggregative level there is scope for a substitution between capital and labour not only by variation in techniques of production of individual products but also by changing the product-mix. Similarly, in the agricultural sector especially, there is a possibility of diminishing returns to capital and labour and this is difficult to bring out with the fixed-coefficient production function (unless we decide to fit it separately at different levels of capital and labour). By comparison the Cobb–Douglas production function allows for considerable flexibility in factor proportions. It also provides easy measures of the elasticity of production with respect to labour and capital.

The SMAC production function is:

$$P = \gamma[\delta K^{-\rho} + (1-\delta)L^{-\rho}]^{-\frac{1}{\rho}}$$

where P = output
K = capital
L = labour

This function is homogeneous of degree one in inputs, though increasing returns or diminishing returns can be allowed for by making the exponent equal to $-\frac{v}{\rho}$, with v greater than or less than unity. Here γ is the efficiency parameter which changes output for given quantities of inputs; δ is the distribution parameter which determines the division of factor income; ρ is the substitution parameter and is a simple function of the elasticity of substitution $(\sigma)[\sigma = \frac{1}{1+\rho}]$. This function is obviously more general than the Cobb–Douglas or the fixed-coefficient function. It has been shown that SMAC tends towards Cobb–Douglas or fixed-coefficient production function as ρ tends to zero or infinity.

However, the empirical evidence is not yet conclusively in favour of the SMAC. Zvi Griliches (71) has shown that the Cobb–Douglas is better than SMAC in certain cases. From our point of view the most serious objection against SMAC is that it is not possible to compute its parameters in any simple way. The elasticity of substitution in SMAC is estimated from functions of the type:

$$\log \frac{V}{L} = \log a + b \log w + u$$

where V = total value added
L = labour force
w = wage rate
u = error term.

This procedure requires the assumption of a competitive economy and the applicability of the marginal productivity theory of wages; it does not enable us to establish a direct technical relation between input and output. This problem is especially serious in the context of Indian agriculture where, as we have seen, the traditional wage theory is not applicable. Thus it seems that the Cobb–Douglas production function is the best suited to our context, though we might consider the linear production function also in certain cases.

The next task is to define the various variables entering into our equation. The first is production. Ideally it should refer to the material units of standard type. Actually, however, the units are heterogeneous and the only alternative is some monetary measure of output deflated by a price index. This, of course, brings us face to face with all the index number problems for which so far there is no known solution. Then again because of the data deficiency attention is generally confined to value added figures. We also do the same in our time-series study. However, in a cross-section study of agricultural production function, we have the data of gross output also and we try to use both the gross production figures and value added figures. For the major part however, we are concerned with value added.

The variable 'labour' is also measured in an approximate fashion. Ideally we should measure the standard labour unit with no variation in skill or intensity. Actually, however, we do not even have the figures of man-hours. For the most part, we have to use the figures of total number of persons in employment. Only in a cross-section study of the industrial production function do we have the figures of man-days worked. In a family-based agricultural sector the working force may be the relevant variable. However, if disguised unemployment prevails, as is supposed to be the case in Indian agriculture, even this variable need not appear in the production function.

The most difficult thing to measure is, of course, capital and a considerable amount of theoretical controversy has raged around it. Joan Robinson (133), for example, does not accept the idea of a composite capital total at all. The capital stock at any time, she would argue, consists of a collection of heterogeneous capital equipments at various stages of their life cycles and at various degrees of obsolescence. Nor is it easy to provide a price measure because, as Mrs. Robinson points out, the unit of measurement varies with the rate of profit and the relative prices of equipment are determined by the future profit expectations. These difficulties are formidable no doubt, and it would be more desirable to obtain some 'vintage model' of capital as Solow (151) has done. However, in our case such detailed data on capital are not available and we have to be satisfied with some crude measures.

Even if we accept the idea of homogeneous capital, it is important to note that what is relevant is not the stock of capital at any point of time but the capital services over a period of time. This introduces the problem of variation in the stock over time and of the variation in the rate of utilisation. The first point is that capital is a stock concept and relates to a point of time, whereas production is a flow concept relating to a period of time. By introducing arbitrary change in the time period under study, we can introduce changes in the coefficients of capital in a linear production function (capital–output ratio). To be consistent we should define capital as

$$K = \frac{1}{T}\int_{t_1}^{t_1+T} K(t)\, dt$$

where K(t) is the time path of capital stock and T is the unit period under study. Actually, however, it is not possible to compute a complete time path of capital series. As an approximation we assume the time path to be linear and take the mid-year capital figures. As regards the problem of the varying intensity of utilisation of capital no easy method is available. Sometimes the degree of unemployment is used as a deflator for the capital series. There is, of course, a considerable amount of unemployment in India; however, this unemployment is not cyclical but mostly secular. Therefore figures can hardly be applied to account for the degree of utilisation of capital nor does it seem possible to estimate how much of this unemployment is 'cyclical'. We do not, therefore, make any adjustment in this respect. We derive some comfort from the theoretical point that so long as we are using a Cobb–Douglas type of production function (which allows infinite substitution between labour and capital), we should not assume under-utilisation of capital because of inadequate labour. Moreover in the present inflationary economy of India the excess capacities may be only marginal and may, therefore, be neglected in a broad aggregative analysis of our type.

Lastly a word about the statistical technique of measurement of capital. The usual technique of measuring fixed capital is the 'perpetual inventory method'. An inventory is maintained of the capital stock at the base year prices by adding gross investment and by deducting capital consumption annually. Other methods of estimating gross fixed capital include, first, collecting valuations for fire insurance (T. Barna (9)) and second, multiplying the property income stream by the reciprocal of the estimated rate of return (in

Giffen method). We have used a variation of perpetual inventory method with this difference: that instead of subtracting from gross investment the figures of capital replacement obtained on the basis of assumption of life time of assets, we have subtracted the depreciation figures which are perhaps only accounting figures. This, of course, makes no allowance for gestation lags or the age structure of the equipment. But at the present state of data in India it seems difficult to obtain a very sophisticated measurement of capital.

In addition to labour and capital, we consider another important influence determining agricultural production, namely, climate. The importance of this factor is recognised by every model builder but hardly anyone tries to incorporate it in the model. It is, of course, difficult to represent various aspects of climate in any single variable. We have to take into account, for example, the amount of rain and its timing in the year, as also the sunshine and its timing. All natural disasters like flood, earthquake, pestilence, will affect agricultural production. Over and above these is the problem of aggregation over different regions which have very different climatic conditions. In spite of these formidable difficulties, however, it seems that we should try to introduce some indicator of weather; for weather is an important factor in Indian agriculture and some attempt at measuring it, however crude, is worth making. Klein and Shinkai (93) in their model of Japan use the series on damaged crop area as an indicator of weather, pestilence and other natural phenomena. In the Indian context we do not have the figures for damaged crop area, and in any case it seems to us theoretically better to try to obtain some direct measure of climate. In our analysis we try to incorporate the effect of rainfall only. And in this respect again we shall be concerned only with the annual rainfall and not its distribution over the year. For aggregation over different meteorological divisions we might take the weighted average of annual rainfall figures. However, this seems to be inappropriate; for the regions are so heterogeneous that the impact of variation in the amount of rainfall in different regions will be quite different. For example, a variation of annual rainfall by 20 inches in Rajasthan will make a substantial difference to crop prospects in Rajasthan whereas a similar movement in the reverse direction in Assam will not make much difference to the crops in Assam. Thus, if we take the average of the absolute value of these two rainfalls the deviation will come out to be zero (if the areas are equal), though in fact, from the point of view of effect on agriculture, they should not. This problem may to a certain extent be avoided if we take the percentage deviation of actual rainfall from the normal rainfall in different regions and take a weighted average of these. We try this measure and we denote it by R_1. However, it could be argued that even this is not a good measure of the effect of variation in rainfall. For both the positive and the negative variations from the normal rainfall are harmful for agricultural production and they should not be averaged out. In order to take this point into account also, we compute the weighted average, not of the algebraic values but of the absolute values of the deviations from the normal rainfall. Thus, both negative and positive deviations will magnify the deviation coefficient. This coefficient we call R_2.

In addition to the factors considered above we add a time trend indicating the shift of production function and a stochastic term indicating the specification and other errors. The function for agriculture is:

(3.1.1) $$Y_a = A(t).K_a^{\alpha_{1\cdot 0}} R_2^{\alpha_{1\cdot 1}} e^{u_1}$$

where Y_a = agricultural production (value added) at 48–49 prices (in Rs. crores)
K_a = capital in agriculture at 48–49 prices (in Rs. crores)
R_2 = the weighted average of the absolute values of the percentage deviation of actual rainfall from the normal rainfall
u_1 = stochastic variable
t = time trend.

The labour variable does not appear in the final equation because, as we have argued, there appears to be a huge amount of disguised unemployment in agriculture and thus labour is not a limitational factor in production.

The production function for the non-agricultural sector is, similarly, given by:

(3.1.2) $$Y_i = B(t)K_i^{\alpha_{4\cdot 0}} L_i^{\alpha_{4\cdot 1}} e^{u_4}$$

where Y_i = non-agricultural production (value added) at 48–49 prices (in Rs. crores)
K_i = capital in non-agricultural sector at 48–49 prices (in Rs. crores)
L_i = employment (number of workers in 10,000) in the non-agricultural sector.

This production function includes such diverse sectors as small-scale industries, large-scale manufactures, services, etc.; but this seems the essential price of aggregative analysis. However, this aggregation is not unmixed evil. It allows substitution between labour and capital by variation in output mix which will be difficult at a very disaggregate level. For measuring the influence of technical progress we have introduced a simple time-trend. More sophisticated methods for measuring the technical progress such as those employed by R. Solow (151) were not found practicable for lack of sufficient data. As a measure of capital we are taking the value of capital at the middle of the year. We are ignoring the variation in capital utilisation as being relatively non-significant in the context of planning. Indirectly, this equation should also provide some test of our hypothesis that the Keynesian theory of output determination by effective demand is not applicable in our context. For if output varied significantly because of variation in demand without variation in capital or labour, this function should not give us a good fit to the data on output, capital and labour.

3.2: EMPLOYMENT FUNCTION

In our analysis in Chapter 2 we have assumed that employment is limited by the marketed surplus of wage-goods and/or capital and that the marginal product of labour equation determines the relative prices of the wage-goods and the non-wage-goods sector. However, since it is statistically difficult to accommodate two alternative restraints in a regression analysis, we use only the supply of wage-goods as the more important constraint. The argument is that the capital/labour ratio can be changed by variation in techniques but not the wage-goods requirement at subsistence level.

In the statistical data available we have not been able to identify a wage-goods sector. Instead we have used the agricultural sector as the nearest approximation. However, in the agricultural sector a considerable part of the output consists of commercial crops which are not relevant to the supply of wage-goods. So we take the food-grains output as equivalent to wage-goods output. Food-grains do constitute a large and vital part of wage-goods in India and the marketed surplus of wage-goods can constitute a bottleneck to employment. Thus we can use the marketed surplus of food-grains as the determining influence on employment. Unfortunately, we do not have the figures for the marketed surplus of food-grains over the period under consideration. Some rough figures for a few years (1951–58) were presented in the Ford Foundation Report on India's food crisis (63) but these relate to only a few years and no explanation is given as to how these are obtained. Therefore, it was not considered desirable to utilise these figures. Instead we make the assumption that the marketed surplus is a linear function of total output. Thus employment becomes a function of the total output of food-grains:

(3.2.1) $$L_i = \alpha + \beta F_a$$

Apart from domestic production we have also to consider the

import and export of food-grains. In the years under consideration India has been a net importer of food-grains. However, the net import figures cannot be aggregated with domestic production figures. This is so because imports of food-grains are primarily used for urban population and industrial labour whereas only a part of the domestic production of food-grains comes to urban areas. Therefore, the coefficients of these two factors in employment function are likely to be different and they have to be treated as two separate variables. Lastly, we introduce a stochastic variable to take into account the effect of omitted variables. The function is:

(3.2.2) $$L_i = \alpha_{3 \cdot 0} + \alpha_{3 \cdot 1} F_a + \alpha_{3 \cdot 2}(M - X)_a + u_3$$

In the above we have food-grains production as an independent variable. On the other hand, our production function is concerned with agricultural production as a whole. Thus to make our system determinate we have to introduce an equation determining the allocation of total agricultural production between food-grains and other crops. This distribution is likely to depend on the relative prices of food-grains and other cash crops in areas where substitution is possible. In fact it is reasonable to presume that a Cobweb cycle might be operating in some cases such as jute and rice in North Bengal and Assam. However, as we find in Chapter 4, these considerations are not important at an aggregative level and therefore we take a simple relation between output of food-grains and total agricultural production with a stochastic variable:

(3.2.3) $$F_a = \alpha_{2 \cdot 0} + \alpha_{2 \cdot 1} Y_a + u_2$$

3.3: INVESTMENT FUNCTIONS

Investment behaviour at both the micro and macro level has been a subject of intense theoretical and empirical controversy* and it is desirable to see where our simple investment functions of Chapter 2 stand in the light of these theories. The investment theories can be conveniently grouped into three categories: (i) the profit maximisation or marginal theories; (ii) the more technically oriented accleration approach; and (iii) inductive generalisations based upon institutional and empirical studies. In marginal theories the entrepreneur tries to maximise his profits by equating the marginal efficiency of capital with the rate of interest. Thus, the expected rate of profit and the rate of interest become important determinants of the rate of investment. On the acceleration hypothesis, however, the rate of investment is a linear function of the rate of increase of output. This simple presentation has been, of course, qualified in a number of

* Survey of the discussion is available in several places. See J. R. Meyer and E. Kuh (103), E. Kuh (97).

ways so as to take account of excess capacity, expectations, financial restraints, gestation lags and so on. An important modification of the acceleration hypothesis which we will consider in our statistical analysis is that presented by H. B. Chenery (20). Chenery shows that if firms seek to minimise the cost of production over time, they will on the average build ahead of demand, where there are economies of scale and they will have a normal degree of over-capacity. To allow for the usual rate of excess capacity because of as yet unexploited scale economies, Chenery modifies the basic acceleration hypothesis by inserting the factor which he terms the 'capacity factor' before capital stock at the beginning of period:

$$\Delta K_{t+\theta} = b(\beta X_t - \lambda K_t)$$

After a bit of transformation he contrasts his capacity principle with the acceleration principle in the following way:

$$\text{Capacity Principle: } \frac{\Delta K_{t+\theta}}{K_{t+\theta-2}} = b\left(\frac{X_t}{K_t}\right) - b\lambda$$

$$\text{Accleration Principle: } \frac{\Delta K_{t+\theta}}{K_{t+\theta-2}} = b\left(\frac{\Delta X_t}{X_t}\right) + C$$

where X = output
K = capital.

In some other modifications of accelerator hypothesis, profits have been considered as determinant of investment in addition to changes in output (e.g. Tsiang (160)). While these modifications have brought the acceleration hypothesis closer to reality, they have also robbed it of its distinctive character.

The third group of theories emphasises the importance of retained profits in determining the rate of investment. In recent years big companies have shown a strong preference for financing from internal funds. This is said to be partly because of the increasing risk in the case of borrowed funds and partly because of the possibility of the weakening of the power of the 'control group'. This group of theories has also emphasised the businessman's strong desire to maintain or improve their share of the market.

The above theories have mostly been developed in the context of advanced countries like the U.S.A., and it is not possible to apply them in a straightforward manner to an underdeveloped economy of the Indian type. In fact, it may be argued that it is doubtful whether anything called investment function (expressing entrepreneurs' propensity to invest) has been allowed to operate in India during the period under review, because of the various restrictions put on private investment by the Government. However, our feeling is that while the influence of Government should be taken as an important variable influencing investment, we should not reject the idea of an investment function altogether. For one thing, government controls can only put an upper limit to investment and cannot compel the private sector to invest. Thus, a better understanding of the forces behind investment will enable the Government to choose better and more effective means of controlling private investment. Secondly, in sectors such as agriculture, government control on private investment is negligible and it might be possible to construct an investment function in this context.

In the context of Indian agriculture the expected demand for agricultural products is unlikely to be an important factor in the determination of investment. There is more or less a competitive situation in agricultural products and any individual farmer can hope to sell any increased amount of his produce at market prices. This would suggest that the acceleration theories of investment which put emphasis on the demand induced character of investment are unlikely to be important in Indian agriculture. As we find in Chapter 6, our statistical experiments confirm this intuitive judgment.

The more important factor determining investment in agriculture is likely to come from the supply side, namely, the availability of investible funds. Thus the analysis of factors behind the availability of funds may throw some light on the factors determining investment. From the *All-India Rural Credit Survey Report* (127) we know that in the year 1951 current income and past savings formed the main source of investible funds for investment in capital other than land and livestock. The Table 3.1 gives the percentage distribution of sources of credit for investment in capital other than land and livestock:

TABLE 3.1

SOURCES OF FUNDS FOR RURAL INVESTMENT

Sources	*Percentage Distribution*
1. Current income	54·4
2. Past savings	12·1
3. Sale of assets	1·3
4. Borrowings	31·0
5. Others	1·2
	100·0

Source: *All-India Rural Credit Survey Report*, Vol. I, Reserve Bank of India, Bombay 1956.

From the above table it is obvious that a significant proportion of investible funds comes from income. Moreover, a further analysis of borrowings shows that a major portion of borrowing comes from relatives, landlords, agricultural money lenders, trade and commission agents. The resources of these agencies are likely to depend on agricultural income so that in an aggregative model, where we are considering agricultural income of farms and the related agencies together, we may treat this part of investible funds also as coming from agricultural income, present as well as past.

TABLE 3.2

SOURCES OF CREDIT IN RURAL AREAS

Credit Agencies	*Percentage Distribution*	
1. Government	2·7	
2. Co-operatives	3·2	
3. Relatives	11·8	55·7
4. Landlords	2·2	
5. Agricultural moneylenders	33·2	
6. Traders and commission agents	8·5	
7. Professional moneylenders	32·4	
8. Commercial banks	0·5	
9. Others	5·5	
	100·0	

Source: *All-India Rural Credit Survey Report*, Vol. I, Reserve Bank of India, Bombay 1956.

From the above discussion it seems reasonable to presume that incomes (past and present) may be the main determinants of private investment in Indian agriculture. One way to take this into account will be to make investment a function of current and past income levels with the weights of past incomes declining in a definite pattern. Using the assumption of geometrically declining weights and applying the Koyck transformation, we get the investment function in a simple form:

$$I_a = \alpha + \beta(Y_a - T_a) + \lambda I_{a-1} \tag{3.3.2}$$

where I_a = private investment in agriculture

$Y_a - T_a$ = disposable income calculated by subtracting the land revenue from the agricultural income.*

* Agricultural income tax may also be subtracted. However, this tax applies only in a few states in India and is quantitatively rather small. So we have not considered it.

The above formulation will be more appropriate than an unlagged equation because of its ability to consider the effect of past as well as present savings. However, we find from our statistical analysis that the long-run investment function obtained from the above equation does not differ significantly from the function obtained from the equation which does not consider the lag. So we accept the simpler form of investment function and write:

$$\text{(3.3.3)} \qquad I_a = \alpha + \beta(Y_a - T_a)$$

There remains, however, a problem of relative prices. The disposable income of agriculture is deflated by the price index of agricultural goods whereas investment at constant prices is obtained by deflating monetary investment by investment cost index. Thus investment at constant (capital goods) prices depends on the relative prices of agricultural goods and investment goods apart from the savings in the agricultural sector in real terms. Suppose the savings function in agriculture in real terms is:

$$S_a = -\alpha + \beta(Y_a - T_a)$$

then in money terms,

$$p_a S_a = -\alpha p_a + \beta p_a (Y_a - T_a)$$

In terms of investment goods prices this is:

$$\frac{p_a S_a}{p_{inv.}} = -\frac{p_a}{p_{inv.}}\alpha + \beta \frac{p_a (Y_a - T_a)}{p_{inv.}}$$

The left-hand side expression is saving-investment at constant prices. However since the taxation data are generally given in current prices, it is more convenient to write the second term on the right-hand side as $\frac{p_a Y_a - T_a}{p_{inv.}}$. Further, adding a constant term and a stochastic variable, we have:

$$\text{(3.3.4)} \qquad I_a = \alpha_{14\cdot 0} + \alpha_{14\cdot 1}\frac{p_a Y_a - T_a}{p_{inv.}} + \alpha_{14\cdot 2}\cdot\frac{p_a}{p_{inv.}} + u_{14}$$

where T_a = agricultural tax at current prices (in Rs. crores).

It can be further argued that investment in the private sector in Indian agriculture is very much dependent on public outlays providing necessary overhead facilities. The *All-India Rural Credit Survey Report* (127) remarks 'Situations favourable for capital formation in the country appear to be either in the regions or districts in which a generally high level of economic activity was attained, or in districts or locations where owing to state initiative or otherwise developmental activity in particular directions had been stimulated' (op. cit.). The latter feature indicates that it might be desirable to introduce Government expenditure on public works in agriculture as an additional determinant of investment in agriculture. Thus our equation for investment in agriculture becomes:

$$(3.3.5) \quad I_a = \alpha_{14\cdot 0} + \alpha_{14\cdot 1}\frac{p_aY_a - T_a}{p_{inv.}} + \alpha_{14\cdot 2}\frac{p_a}{p_{inv.}} + \alpha_{14\cdot 3}G_a + u_{14}$$

where G_a = government investment in agriculture at constant prices.

However, our statistical analysis does not yield good results with G_a as an additional variable. So we accept the simpler form of agricultural investment function given by (3.3.4).

Next, we consider the determinants of investment in the non-agricultural sector. In our theoretical discussion we made investment a simple function of income. Even in the non-agricultural sector in India there is a considerable part that is organised along family lines and the savers may be the investors in this as they are in the agricultural sector. However, the more important and dynamic part of the non-agricultural sector is the one organised on company lines and here the net income (profits) of the companies rather than the total value added is likely to be the more important determinant of investment. Profits are important both as a source of finance (the third group of investment theories considered above) and as an indicator of the profitability of investment (the marginal theory of investment). Internal financing is especially important in India because the stock markets are not so developed as to reach the mass of the public and the banks are generally reluctant to give long-term loans. So it seems that profit theory of investment should be applicable to the Indian context. However, we also consider acceleration theories as well as the interest rate hypothesis. They do not fare as badly there as they did in the agricultural sector and it seems that at a disaggregative level both the acceleration hypothesis (e.g. in certain industries) and the interest rate hypothesis (e.g. in the analysis of changes in paid-up capital of public limited companies) may be useful. But on the whole we find that the profit hypothesis fares better. Moreover, we find that for the purpose of solution of the system a disposable income variable is more suitable than a profit index.

In addition to the above we must consider the influence of government control on private investment which is known to be quite significant during the period under discussion. It is difficult to devise a simple indicator of government control in the licensing of capital projects and in issuing permits for the foreign exchange. We tried two indicators—one was the position of foreign exchange reserves of India as an indicator of the foreign exchange shortage and thus, an indicator of the Government's strictness in issuing licences for projects involving foreign exchange. The other was the consent for capital issues granted as a percentage of applications for capital issues. On empirical grounds it was found that the latter is a better variable in explaining investment. So we include it in our investment function. Adding a stochastic variable we get:

$$\text{(3.3.6)} \qquad I_i = \alpha_{15\cdot 0} + \alpha_{15\cdot 1}\frac{p_i Y_i - T_i}{p_{inv.}} + \alpha_{15\cdot 2} GC + u_{15}$$

where I_i = private net investment in non-agricultural sector at 48–49 prices (in Rs. crores)

GC = the indicator of government control as explained above.

In our statistical analysis, we found that in the form (3.3.6) the regression coefficient of GC comes out to be small and this limits the scope of government control over private investment to an unrealistic extent. So we tried another form of introducing GC. The realised investment I_i is a proportion of the investment demand and this proportion is given by GC. Moreover, we found that the rate of change of price has significant influence on investment demand. This may be partly because rising prices stimulate profit expectations and partly because they stimulate inventory investment. The final form of the investment function for the non-agricultural sector is:

$$\text{(3.3.7)} \qquad I_i = GC\left(\alpha_{15\cdot 0} + \alpha_{15\cdot 1}\frac{p_i Y_i - T_i}{p_{inv.}} + \alpha_{15\cdot 2}\cdot\frac{\dot{p}}{p} + u_{15}\right)$$

In the above scheme of investment determination we have ignored the influence of the foreign sector on investment. This will be valid theoretically when the non-agricultural sector is assumed to produce goods which could be either consumed or invested. Actually, however, in the Indian context at present a significant part of investment goods—especially in the non-agricultural sector—has to be imported and therefore, the import capacity may be a severe limitation on investment, apart from the domestic demand for investment and the availability of domestic resources. We try to bring in the foreign exchange situation in the following way. Imports in real terms depend on investment in the non-agricultural sector and income in the non-agricultural sector. The import content of investment in agriculture is small and can perhaps be neglected. The non-agricultural income creates a demand for imported raw materials as well as consumer goods. The merchandise import equation therefore, is:

$$\text{(3.3.8)} \qquad MT = \alpha_{19\cdot 0} + \alpha_{19\cdot 1} Y_i + \alpha_{19\cdot 2}(I_i + G_i) + u_{19}$$

In our statistical analysis, we found that Y_i and $(I_i + G_i)$ are significantly correlated and the estimates of the parameters in the form (3.3.8) are unreliable. So we considered a disaggregated form of import demand. The import of capital goods (M_k) is dependent on the total domestic investment in the non-agricultural sector (I_i+G_i). Thus we have:

(3.3.9) $$M_k = \alpha_{19\cdot 0}+\alpha_{19\cdot 1}(I_i+G_i)+u_{19}$$

The demand for consumer goods and raw materials (M_c) may be assumed to be dependent on income in the non-agricultural sector (Y_i) and a time trend (t) which will indicate the importance of import-substitution. However, because of the collinearity between Y_i and t, it was found convenient to make $\frac{M_c}{Y_i}$ the dependent variable in the equation. Thus we have:

(3.3.10) $$\frac{M_c}{Y_i} = \alpha_{20\cdot 0}+\alpha_{20\cdot 1}t+u_{20}$$

Total imports (MT) would, of course, be equal to the sum of M_k, M_c and import of miscellaneous goods (M_o). Thus we have:

(3.3.11) $$MT = M_k+M_c+M_o$$

Exports depend on world income (Y_w) and the ratio of domestic price of exports and the price of exports of competitors, namely, the underdeveloped countries $\frac{p_x}{p_{xu}}$. The influence of domestic demand in exportables is assumed to be reflected in the price of exports (p_x). Thus we have:

(3.3.12) $$X = \alpha_{17\cdot 0}+\alpha_{17\cdot 1}Y_w+\alpha_{17\cdot 2}\frac{p_x}{p_{xu}}+u_{17}$$

Lastly, there is the balance of payments constraint, according to which the imports bill must be equal to the exports bill plus foreign capital inflow (FC), where the latter term includes all net inflow of invisibles, private capital and government loans and grants. Thus we have:

(3.3.13) $$p_m.MT = p_x.X+FC$$

The inflow of foreign capital can be assumed to be exogenous and so are the prices of imports. Export prices can be assumed to depend partly on the domestic price situation (p) and partly on the foreign demand situation for the primary products. Assuming that the world demand situation for primary products is indicated by the prices of exports of the underdeveloped countries as a whole, we have:

(3.3.14) $$p_x = \alpha_{16\cdot 0}+\alpha_{16\cdot 1}p+\alpha_{16\cdot 2}p_{xu}+u_{16}$$

where p = the general domestic price level

p_{xu} = the export price index of the underdeveloped countries as a whole.

These six equations above ((3.3.9) to (3.3.14)) will determine the six unknowns p_x, X, M, (I_i+G_i), M_k, M_c with Y_i already determined by equation (3.1.2). Now if private investment in non-agriculture is already determined, government investment (G_i) remains a residual. However G_i can be varied by adjusting the percentage of capital issue sanctioned (GC) in our equation of private investment in the non-agricultural sector.

3.4: MONEY, WAGES AND PRICES

We have argued in Chapter 2 that in the Indian context the quantity theory of money may not be altogether unsuitable. When the market in financial assets is not very developed and the speculative demand for money is not very strong, the main alternative to holding money is spending on goods. And thus the money supply does tend to determine the spending on goods and, therefore, their prices. Thus, the income velocity may be a stable ratio in Indian economy though we have to allow for the changing degree of monetisation in the economy. We try the statistical analysis of velocity hypothesis in various forms but ultimately concentrate on the form presented recently in the work of M. Friedman and D. Meiselman (43). Our aggregate money income equation is:

(3.4.1) $$pY = \alpha_{7.0}+\alpha_{7.1}M+\alpha_{7.2}t+u_7$$

where p = general price index
M = money supply
t = time trend which might reflect the changing degree of monetisation
u_7 = error term.

However, it is reasonable to presume (and it is supported by empirical evidence) that an increase in money supply might take more than a year to exert its full influence on money income. Thus it might be desirable to include lagged effects of money supply as well. We assume a geometrically distributed lag and applying the Koyck transformation, we have:

(3.4.2) $$pY = \alpha_{7.0}+\alpha_{7.1}M+\alpha_{7.2}(pY)_{-1}+u_7$$

Now with real income already determined by the supply of factors of production this equation determines the absolute price level.

In the above equation we have assumed the money supply to be exogenously determined. As an attempt to analyse the determinants of money supply, we try to explain the variation in the money supply with reference to variations in high-powered money—namely, currency and coins, and a time trend reflecting the changing banking habits of the public and other determinants of 'money-multiplier'.* Thus we can write:

(3.4.3) $$M = \alpha_{6\cdot 0} + \alpha_{6\cdot 1}C + \alpha_{6\cdot 2}t + u_6$$

where C = notes and currency.

With absolute prices determined we have to consider the determination of relative prices. In our model, relative prices are determined by the marginal productivity of labour equation:

$$\bar{w}p_a = p_i \frac{\delta Y_i}{\delta L_i}$$

However, for statistical purposes it will be desirable to consider the two parts of the equation separately. Thus, according to the first part, the real wage is constant at the subsistence level in the initial stage of growth. Thus, money wages move in accordance with the consumer price index. However, at the beginning of the period under discussion, real wages were (as an aftermath of war and partition) at a very low level—lower than the pre-war period. Therefore, we have to include a time trend in real wages. Thus the equation for money wages becomes:

(3.4.4) $$W_i = \alpha_{13\cdot 0} + \alpha_{13\cdot 1}p_c + \alpha_{13\cdot 2}t + u_{13}$$

In our statistical analysis, we found that increases in money wages as a result of increases in consumer price index, are spread over a number of years. So assuming a geometrically declining lag and applying Koyck transformation, we have:

(3.4.5) $$W_i = \alpha_{13\cdot 0} + \alpha_{13\cdot 1}p_c + \alpha_{13\cdot 2}W_{i_{-1}} + u_{13}$$

In the context of developed economies, money wages are supposed to depend not only on the consumer price index but also the degree of unemployment and the productivity of labour. In the Indian context these latter forces are not likely to be important. As regards unemployment, the problem is a secular one rather than cyclical. There is a huge unemployed labour population available at prevailing wages and since wages are at a subsistence level already and they cannot be competed down because of institutional reasons, variation in the size of the unemployment pool does not affect wages. It was

* 'Money multiplier' is determined as follows. Suppose C is the amount of currency created by the Government, M is the total money supply (cash plus deposits), R is the reserve with the banks, r the reserve ratio of the banks, b the fraction of its money holdings that non-bank public holds in currency and D is the deposit. Then we have the following equations for a fully loaned up banking system:

$$M = bM + D$$
$$C = bM + R$$
$$R = rD$$

from which we have:

$$M = \frac{1}{1-(1-b)(1-r)} \cdot C$$

found difficult to test this hypothesis for the year-by-year figures of unemployment are not available. But broadly speaking we know that the volume of unemployment continued to grow during the period without any obvious adverse effect on real wages. As regards the influence of productivity we made some tests and we find that there is no significant relation between the two. Thus it seems that we can ignore unemployment and productivity in our wage determination equation.

With money wages determined the prices in the non-agricultural sector will be determined by the equation:

$$p_i = W_i . \frac{1}{\frac{\delta Y_i}{\delta L_i}}$$

Since we are taking the implicit price deflator of manufactures only in income statistics, the price of raw materials does not come into the equation. We try a fit to this equation in two forms. First, we linearise it as:

$$(3.4.6) \qquad p_{im} = \alpha_{11\cdot 0} + \alpha_{11\cdot 1} W_i + \alpha_{11\cdot 2}\left(\frac{\delta Y_i}{\delta L_i}\right) + u_{11}$$

Here the coefficient of $\left(\frac{\delta Y_i}{\delta L_i}\right)$ is expected to be negative. In another form we assume a distributed lag and apply Koyck transformation. We have then:

$$(3.4.7) \qquad p_{im} = \alpha_{11\cdot 0} + \alpha_{11\cdot 1}\frac{W_i}{\frac{\delta Y_i}{\delta L_i}} + \alpha_{11\cdot 2}(p_{im})_{-1}$$

From our statistical results, it seems that the equation (3.4.7) is better.

3.5: MISCELLANEOUS EQUATIONS

With the above, our system is substantially complete. However, we have to add a few more equations and definitions to tie up some loose ends. For one thing, in the preceding discussion we have introduced a number of prices in order to suit particular equations. Thus in our theoretical discussion the price index of the non-agricultural sector was the same as that of investment goods and the price of agricultural goods the same as the price of consumer goods. But in the statistical system we have introduced different prices. For example, wages are dependent not on prices of agricultural goods but on the consumer price index. Similarly, an investment cost index is introduced which is different from the manufacturing price index. Now, in order to complete our system we have to tie them up together by a number of price equations. These are, of course, only statistical approximations and we do not go into the details of the theory of determination of these relative prices. The equations are:

(3.5.1) $p_c = \alpha_{9\cdot 0} + \alpha_{9\cdot 1} p_a + u_9$

(3.5.2) $p_{inv.} = \alpha_{12\cdot 0} + \alpha_{12\cdot 1} p_{im} + \alpha_{12\cdot 2} W_i + u_{12}$

(3.5.3) $p_i = \alpha_{10\cdot 0} + \alpha_{10\cdot 1} p_{im} + u_{10}$

Next, we have to note a few definitions and identities:

(3.5.4) $K_a = [K_a^o + (K_a^o)_{+1}]/2 = (K_a^o + K_a^o + I_a + G_a)/2$

(3.5.5) $K_i = [K_i^o + (K_i^o)_{+1}]/2 = (K_i^o + K_i^o + I_i + G_i)/2$

where K_a^o, K_i^o are capital in agriculture and non-agriculture respectively at the beginning of the year, $(K_a^o)_{+1}$ and $(K_i^o)_{+1}$ are capital figures at the end of the year. These are obtained by adding private as well as government investment in each sector to the initial capital. Foreign investment is not treated separately as it is spread over private and government investment depending upon whether it comes through private or government channels. The mid-year capital is obtained as the average of the capital at the beginning and end of the year.

The general price index is a weighted average of the individual prices indices:

(3.5.6) $p = p_a . \frac{Y_a}{Y} + p_i . \frac{Y_i}{Y}$

The weights are the proportions of total output formed by output in the agricultural and non-agricultural sectors.

Aggregate output at constant prices is the sum of agricultural output at constant prices and non-agricultural output at constant prices:

(3.5.7) $Y = Y_a + Y_i$

3.6: THE MODEL AS A WHOLE

3.6.1: THE EQUATIONS

Putting the above equations together and arranging them in an order convenient for the solution of the system, we have our model as follows:

(3.6.1) $Y_a = A(t) K_a^{\alpha_{1\cdot 0}} R_2^{\alpha_{1\cdot 1}} e^{u_1}$

(3.6.2) $F_a = \alpha_{2\cdot 0} + \alpha_{2\cdot 1} Y_a + u_2$

(3.6.3) $L_i = \alpha_{3\cdot 0} + \alpha_{3\cdot 1} F_a + \alpha_{3\cdot 2} (M - X)_a + u_3$

(3.6.4) $Y_i = B(t) K_i^{\alpha_{4\cdot 0}} L_i^{\alpha_{4\cdot 1}} e^{u_4}$

(3.6.5) $Y = Y_a + Y_i$

(3.6.6) $M = \alpha_{6\cdot0} + \alpha_{6\cdot1}C + \alpha_{6\cdot2}t + u_6$

(3.6.7) $pY = \alpha_{7\cdot0} + \alpha_{7\cdot1}M + \alpha_{7\cdot2}(pY)_{-1} + u_7$

(3.6.8) $p = p_a\dfrac{Y_a}{Y} + p_i\dfrac{Y_i}{Y}$

(3.6.9) $p_c = \alpha_{9\cdot0} + \alpha_{9\cdot1}p_a + \alpha_{9\cdot2}(p_c)_{-1} + u_9$

(3.6.10) $p_i = \alpha_{10\cdot0} + \alpha_{10\cdot1}p_{im} + u_{10}$

(3.6.11) $p_{im} = \alpha_{11\cdot0} + \alpha_{11\cdot1}\dfrac{W_i}{\dfrac{\delta Y_i}{\delta L_i}} + \alpha_{11\cdot2}(p_{im})_{-1} + u_{11}$

(3.6.12) $p_{inv.} = \alpha_{12\cdot0} + \alpha_{12\cdot1}p_{im} + \alpha_{12\cdot2}W_i + u_{12}$

(3.6.13) $W_i = \alpha_{13\cdot0} + \alpha_{13\cdot1}p_c + \alpha_{13\cdot2}(W_i)_{-1} + u_{13}$

(3.6.14) $I_a = \alpha_{14\cdot0} + \alpha_{14\cdot1}\dfrac{p_aY_a - T_a}{p_{inv.}} + \alpha_{14\cdot2}\dfrac{p_a}{p_{inv.}} + u_{14}$

(3.6.15) $I_i = GC\left[\alpha_{15\cdot0} + \alpha_{15\cdot1}\dfrac{p_iY_i - T_i}{p_{inv.}} + \alpha_{15\cdot2}\dfrac{\dot{p}}{p} + u_{15}\right]$

(3.6.16) $p_x = \alpha_{16\cdot0} + \alpha_{16\cdot1}p + \alpha_{16\cdot2}p_{xu} + u_{16}$

(3.6.17) $X = \alpha_{17\cdot0} + \alpha_{17\cdot1}Y_w + \alpha_{17\cdot2}\dfrac{p_x}{p_{xu}} + u_{17}$

(3.6.18) $p_m(MT) = p_x . X + FC$

(3.6.19) $M_k = \alpha_{19\cdot0} + \alpha_{19\cdot1}(I_i + G_i) + u_{19}$

(3.6.20) $\dfrac{M_c}{Y_i} = \alpha_{20\cdot0} + \alpha_{20\cdot1}t + u_{20}$

(3.6.21) $MT = M_k + M_c + M_o$

(3.6.22) $G_i = (I_i + G_i) - I_i$

(3.6.23) $K_a = \dfrac{K_a^o + K_a^o + G_a + I_a}{2}$

(3.6.24) $K_i = \dfrac{K_i^o + K_i^o + G_i + I_i}{2}$

where Y = net national output (value added) at 48–49 prices (in Rs. crores)

Y_a = net agricultural output (value added) at 48–49 prices (in Rs. crores)

K_a = mid-year capital in agriculture at 48–49 prices (in Rs. crores)

F_a = output of food-grains (in 10,000 metric tons)

L_i = employment in non-agricultural sector (number of workers in 10,000)

Y_i = net output (value added) in non-agricultural sector at 48–49 prices (in Rs. crores)

K_i = mid-year capital in non-agricultural sector at 48–49 prices (in Rs. crores)

I_a = private net investment in agricultural sector at 48–49 prices (in Rs. crores)

I_i = private net investment in non-agricultural sector at 48–49 prices (in Rs. crores)

(I_i+G_i) = total net investment in non-agricultural sector at 48–49 prices (in Rs. crores)

p = general price index of aggregate national product (base 1948–49 = 100)

p_a = price index of output of agricultural sector (base 1948–49 = 100)

p_i = price index of output of non-agricultural sector (base 1948–49 = 100)

p_c = consumer price index (base 1948–49 = 100)

$p_{inv.}$ = investment cost index (base 1948–49 = 100)

p_{im} = price index of manufactured goods (base 1948–49 = 100)

W_i = money wage (earnings) index in industrial sector (base 1948–49 = 100)

M = money supply (in Rs. crores)

MT = imports of merchandise at 48–49 prices (in Rs. crores)

M_k = import of capital goods at 48–49 prices (in Rs. crores)

M_c = import of consumer goods (excluding food-grains) and raw materials at 48–49 prices (in Rs. crores)

X = exports of merchandise at 48–49 prices (in Rs. crores)

G_i = net investment in non-agricultural sector by the government at 1948–49 prices (in Rs. crores)

px = price index of exports (base 1948–49 = 100)

R_2 = climate indicated by the absolute value of percentage deviation of actual annual rainfall from the normal annual rainfall

$(M-X)_a$ = net imports of food-grains (in 10,000 metric tons)

T_a = tax in agriculture (in Rs. crores)

T_i = tax in non-agricultural sector (in Rs. crores)

GC = government control on private investment indicated by the capital issues sanctioned as a percentage of applications for capital issues.

K_a^o = capital in agriculture at the beginning of the year at 48–49 prices (in Rs. crores)

K_i^o = capital in non-agricultural sector at the beginning of the year at 48–49 prices (in Rs. crores)

C = notes and currency (in Rs. crores)

G_a = government investment in agriculture at 48–49 prices (in Rs. crores)

Y_w = index of world G.N.P. at constant factor cost (base 1958 = 100)

p_m = price index of imports of India (base 1948–49 = 100)

FC = net inflow of foreign capital at current prices (in Rs. crores)

p_{xu} = export price index of underdeveloped countries (base 1958 = 100)

M_o = import of food-grains and miscellaneous goods at 48–49 prices (in Rs. crores)

t = time trend, 1948–49 = 0

$(pY)_{-1}$ = aggregate net value added of the previous year in current prices (in Rs. crores)

$(p_c)_{-1}$ = consumer price index of the previous year (base 1948–49 = 100)

$(p_{im})_{-1}$ = price index of manufactured goods of the previous year (base 1948–49 = 100)

$(W_i)_{-1}$ = money wage index of the previous year (base 1948–49 = 100)

$(p)_{-1}$ = general price index of the previous year (base 1948–49 = 100).

The system has 24 equations and 44 variables. Of these variables the last 20 are either predetermined variables or exogenous variables. Thus, subject to the usual conditions of independence and consistency of the equations, our system is determinate; it has 24 equations and 24 endogenous variables. Of these equations 7 are constraints or identities and only 17 are true equations. A flow diagram of the system is presented in Figure 3.1.

3.6.2: LIMITATIONS OF THE MODEL

The model presented above is a highly simplified one and it is difficult to presume that any simple model will represent at all faithfully an economy of the diversity and enormity of the Indian type. Thus our attempt is primarily exploratory and we hope to expand the model in subsequent attempts. A few of the directions in which development is needed are noted below:

1. The model is highly aggregative both over sectors and over time. We have considered only two sectors: the agricultural and non-agricultural. It might be desirable to subdivide the agricultural sector into at least two groups: commercial crops and food crops. It seems plausible that the cobweb theorem might be applicable in the matter of the distribution of the crop between the two groups.

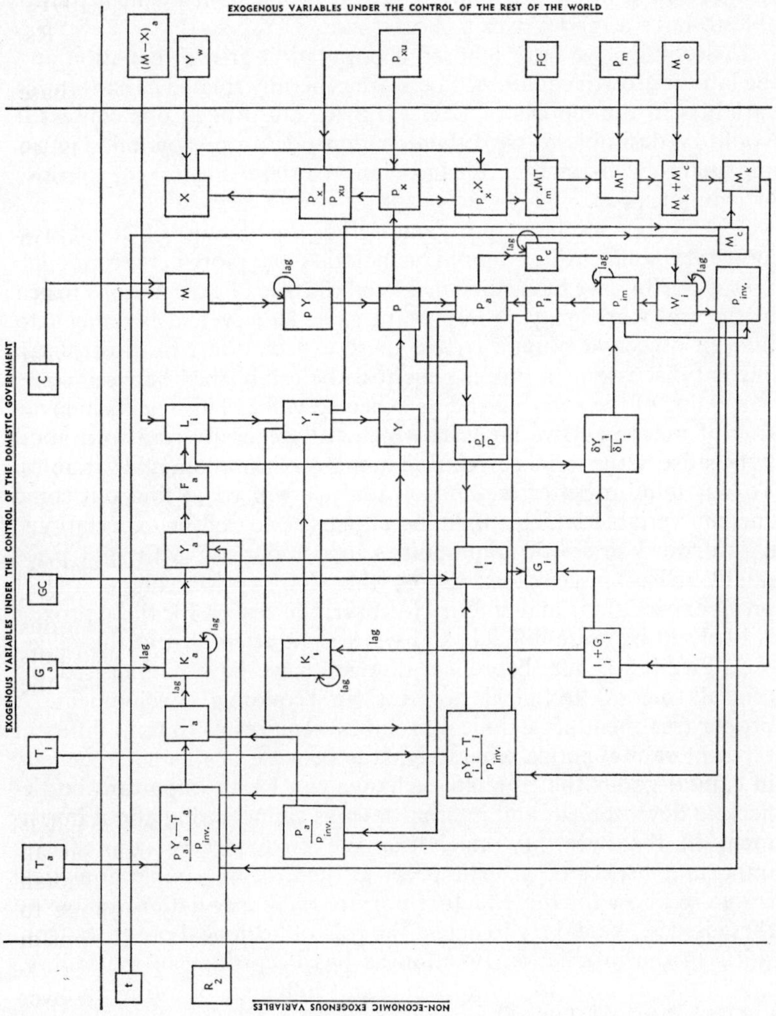
EXOGENOUS VARIABLES UNDER THE CONTROL OF THE REST OF THE WORLD
EXOGENOUS VARIABLES UNDER THE CONTROL OF THE DOMESTIC GOVERNMENT
NON-ECONOMIC EXOGENOUS VARIABLES
lag

Figure 3.1

In the non-agricultural sector again it might be desirable to consider the household sector, government sector and organised manufacturing sector separately. Similarly, we have been concerned only with annual figures while for many practical problems it might be desirable to have a model over a shorter run.

2. Secondly, we have ignored a population growth equation and the labour growth equation. These are generally treated as exogenous variables in the models of U.K., U.S.A., etc. But in our context it would be desirable to treat them as dependent on economic factors and analyse these factors. We have ignored these only for the purpose of simplification.

3. Thirdly, we have not considered the details of fiscal and monetary policy, which should be included in a more detailed model.

4. Fourthly, we have not considered the role of expectations which in the real world play an important part. However, it is difficult to find an objective counterpart of these expectations. In most of the current discussions a link is sought to be established between some past value of the variable and its expected value. This results in some sort of autoregressive analysis which will generally lead to a good fit because of the serial correlation in many of the economic variables. To our mind a better method of analysis will be to find out some current variable which might be supposed to reflect expectations, e.g. forward prices of commodities in comparison with spot price might reflect price expectations, the share prices might reflect profit expectations and so on. However, the search for these proxies is likely to be quite difficult and we do not attempt it at this stage.

5. Fifthly, in our theoretical discussion we have emphasised the crucial role of 'technical progress' in economic development. A proper treatment of 'technical progress' requires us to treat different types of capital goods separately. It is because of this heterogeneity in capital goods that foreign exchange can be an important bottleneck in development and internal savings cannot bring about investment in the necessary machines. We have largely ignored this important aspect of growth because there is no simple analytical frame to allow for these factors nor are there any data available on these issues. We did try to detect the role of 'technical progress' from shifts in the production function as has been done in the U.S.A., but in our case we found no significant influence of a time trend.

6. Sixthly, we do not have an explicit consumption function. We have assumed that the output is determined by the supply of factors of production and that investment decisions are realised. In that situation, consumption is a residual and it should not have any determinant other than those entering into the production and investment functions. In fact, the time series of consumption given

in *Estimates of Gross Capital Formation in India* (51) calculates consumption as a residual. In a more sophisticated system, we should have considered the joint influence of demand and supply on output determination.

3.6.3: COMPARISON WITH SOME SIMILAR MODELS

Before we go on to consider the statistical estimation of our model it is worth making some brief comments on similar attempts at model building in India and abroad. An early attempt at the construction of an econometric model in the Indian context was made by C. M. Palvia (115).

His model is similar to ours in so far as the economy is disaggregated into two sectors only and output is determined by the supply of factors of production rather than by effective demand as in the Keynesian models. However, on the whole, the model is constructed on the lines of a classical system in a competitive wage economy and the dualistic character of underdeveloped economies is not considered at all. For example, the problem of disguised unemployment is not even mentioned. Nor is it discussed as to how we can assume full employment in the economy as a whole and the marginal productivity theory of wages in both the sectors when the farm sector is known to be operating largely on a family basis and substantial unemployment and underemployment are known to prevail. The model, again, does not consider absolute price formation or the role of monetary factors at all. Nor are the investment functions considered. Lastly, from a statistical point of view an important deficiency of the model is that the parameters are adopted from the studies in developed countries and no attempt is made to obtain these from the analysis of the Indian data.

A more extensive and a more well-known model was constructed by Narasimham (112). However, Narasimham follows the Keynesian approach towards income determination where the expenditure propensities are the determining influence on income. According to our analysis, on the other hand, it is the supply of factors of production that is crucial to income determination. Nor does Narasimham give any consideration to the dualistic aspect of the economy, disguised unemployment, etc. Investment again is considered only at an aggregative level. In price formation monetary aspects are completely ignored—without any attempt at justification, either theoretical or statistical. Lastly, the data relate only up to 1952 and these have to be built up from scanty sources in a rather rough and ready manner. Somewhat better data have since been available and they may be expected to improve the results.

A very large number of models have been constructed in the

context of developed countries such as the U.S.A., U.K., Canada, Japan, etc. These models are not of much relevance to us since they relate to very different types of economies and they are mostly based on the Keynesian theory of income determination. However, they are important in connection with general methodology and some individual equations and we refer to them in the relevant places.

3.7: METHOD OF ESTIMATION OF THE PARAMETERS OF THE MODEL

ORDINARY LEAST SQUARES V. SIMULTANEOUS EQUATION METHODS

The main choice we have to face in this connection is the choice between applying ordinary least squares (OLS) to each equation of the model and simultaneous equation methods like two-stage least squares (TSLS), limited information maximum likelihood (LIML), full information maximum likelihood (FIML) or any of Theil's k-class estimators. The debate on the relative merits of the different methods has been long and rather inconclusive. An excellent summary of the debate has been provided by J. Johnston (79) and we need not go into the details. In our case FIML is ruled out because of computational difficulties. The main choice is between OLS and TSLS and LIML. It is well known that OLS estimates in a simultaneous equation system are biased and this bias cannot be eliminated by increasing the sample size. The other estimators developed for simultaneous equation systems are also, in general, biased but this bias tends to vanish as the sample size increases. On the other hand, it has been shown by H. Theil (154) that the generalised variance of ordinary least squares estimates of the parameters in a single equation is at least as small as that LIML estimates. Thus it is plausible and has been found to be the case in Monte Carlo Studies that the bias of OLS may be more than offset by its better efficiency so that the root mean square of OLS may be lower than that of TSLS or LIML. It is, of course, difficult to be sure what weightage one should apply in general to the properties of consistency and efficiency. However, in a sample as small as ours (for the most part only 13 observations) the large sample property of the consistency of TSLS or LIML may not free it from bias, whereas the efficiency property of OLS remains. Another important problem with the simultaneous equation methods is that they are very sensitive to specification error and in a preliminary system of our type it seems risky to allow specification error in one equation influence the estimates of all the others. The problem of specification is especially important in this case, because the simultaneous equation methods generally require the assumption of linearity so as to make them computationally manageable. However, it is well known that the actual economy may contain many non-linearities. Even the simple model that we have presented above involves certain non-linearities. These non-linearities can be easily tackled with OLS but are difficult in a simultaneous equation estimate. It is also easier to experiment with alternative variables and alternative forms of equations in the case of OLS. For these reasons, it seems to us that in spite of the theoretical appeal of TSLS or LIML methods it will not be proper for us to reject the OLS and rely exclusively on the simultaneous equation methods. In fact, for the major part of our analysis we are concerned with OLS though for the sake of comparison we also obtain the TSLS and LIML estimates for certain sub-systems in our model.

CHAPTER 4

Production and Employment

In this chapter we consider the results of statistical analysis of the first four equations in our model. We begin in Section 4.1 with the consideration of statistical evidence on the assumptions implicit in our agricultural production function. In Section 4.2, we consider the relationship between the output of food-grains and total agricultural output. Next, in Section 4.3, we consider the relation between employment in the non-agricultural sector and the output and net import of food-grains. Lastly, in Section 4.4, we consider the statistical estimates of the non-agricultural production function.

4.1: AGRICULTURAL PRODUCTION FUNCTION

In our statistical analysis of agricultural production function our objectives are threefold: (1) to test the hypothesis that the marginal product of labour in agriculture is zero as is implied in our assumption that labour is not a limitational factor in agricultural production; (2) to test the hypothesis that the law of diminishing returns to scale works in agriculture; and (3) to obtain the output elasticity with respect to capital and to assess the role of weather and 'technical progress'.

4.1.1: MARGINAL PRODUCTIVITY OF LABOUR

To begin with, we regress the figures of agricultural output on labour, capital, land and rainfall, for the period 1948–49 to 1960–61.* The coefficient of labour is not statistically significant in any of the regressions. This is what we would expect if labour was not a limitational factor in production, though of course this cannot be treated as a definite proof of the validity of our hypothesis. For one thing, this might have been due to the collinearity of the explanatory variables. Actually we find that over the period 1948–49 to 1960–61

* For details of experimental results, see author's Ph.D. thesis submitted to Manchester University in 1966.

labour and capital are highly correlated; the simple correlation coefficient between them is 0·99. The inevitable result of this multicollinearity is that the regression coefficients are unstable and frequent switches of signs of coefficients occur when we vary the independent variables. This is so both in the linear and in the log-linear form of the production function. Thus to measure the marginal productivity of labour we have to try to get other data.

We extend our search for new data in two directions: in the first place, we try to extend the time-series data backwards beyond 1948–49, and secondly, we use the cross-section data made available by the *Studies in Economics of Farm Management* (67). The data on labour and capital before 1948–49 are very meagre and the series that we have built up for the period, 1920–21 to 1947–48 is based on a number of assumptions.

We computed separate regressions for the periods, 1920–21 to 1960–61 and 1920–21 to 1947–48. Unfortunately, the results are not very much different from those for the period 1948–49 to 1960–61. The coefficient of simple correlation between labour and capital is still 0·99 for the period 1920–21 to 1960–61. When labour and capital are both included as independent variables the regression coefficient of labour is negative, though not very highly significant. The addition or omission of labour as an explanatory variable does not make much difference to the goodness of fit as indicated by R. Thus, subject to the qualification of the multi-collinearity problem, we can again assert that the labour does not appear to be a limitational factor in agricultural production function. Over the period 1920–21 to 1947–48 labour and capital are less closely correlated. The simple correlation coefficient is 0·88. Here again, the regression coefficient of labour is negative, though not statistically significant. However, in this case, the overall fit of the equation is not so good. Thus, from all the three sets of regressions we find that the hypothesis of labour not being a limitational factor is not rejected; though it is difficult to be very sure of the result in view of the problem of multicollinearity. Further investigation is obviously necessary for this purpose.

We turn next to the cross-section data. The original data are in the form of gross output per farm (and per acre) in farms of different size groups. In order to make the results comparable with the time-series results, we calculate the value-added figures by making some rough adjustments. Another problem is that the data were collected for two districts in each state and by two different techniques of survey. The number of size-groups is small and unless we pool the results of different districts and different techniques we do not have sufficient degrees of freedom for our regression equations. So we pool together the data on different districts and different techniques and in order to test the validity of this procedure we use dummy variables for place as well as for technique of survey. Whenever we find that the dummy variable is not significantly different from zero we ignore the dummy variable and run the regression for the pooled data. When, however, we find that the dummy variable is significant we treat the data in separate regressions. Another problem that we face in this connection is the problem of heteroscedasticity. The data are given in the form of group averages and as the groups are of different sizes this introduces the problem of heteroscedasticity. We use weighted regression equations to take this difficulty into account.

The coefficient of intermediate inputs is always very highly significant and generally much greater than unity (nearly 2 in most cases). If this result is correct, it will imply that the availability of intermediate inputs like fertiliser, manure, better seed, irrigation facilities, etc., bring into play a part of the idle labour and capital and thus output increases by much more than the value of intermediate inputs. This result will also indicate that the supply of intermediate products is much more important than that of labour or capital for increasing the output of Indian agriculture.

In sharp contrast with our time-series results, the regression coefficient of labour is highly significant in most of the regressions, while that of capital is not. The only exception is the case of Madras where the regression coefficient of labour is not significant.

Some amount of discrepancy between the time-series and cross-section studies is not altogether unexpected. As has been found by many others (e.g. E. Kuh (97)) the regression coefficients of cross-

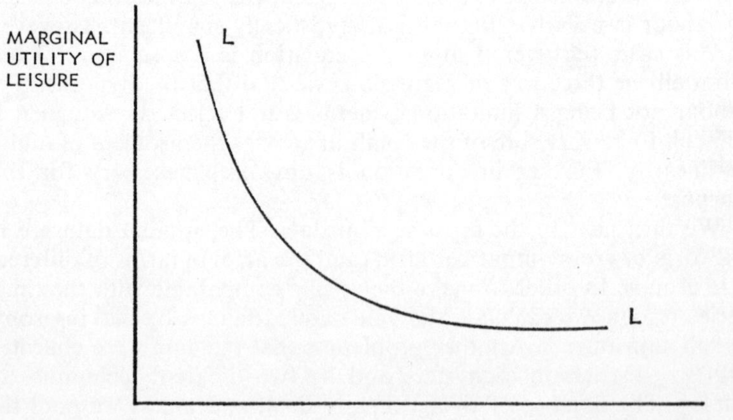

Figure 4.1

section and time-series may give quite different types of results In our case, the discrepancy is large and demands an explanation.

It should be noted that in time-series 'labour' refers to the number of labourers in the agricultural sector, whereas in cross-section analysis 'labour' refers to the number of man-days actually put in agricultural production. We suggest a situation of what we call 'leisure trap' in agricultural families in order to reconcile the two types of findings:

Let LL represent the marginal utility curve of leisure for an individual. After a certain number of hours of leisure the utility curve flattens out. This indicates the situation where any amount of leisure can be spent without a decline in its marginal utility. The corresponding curve indicating the disutility from work is like WW, in Figure 4.2:

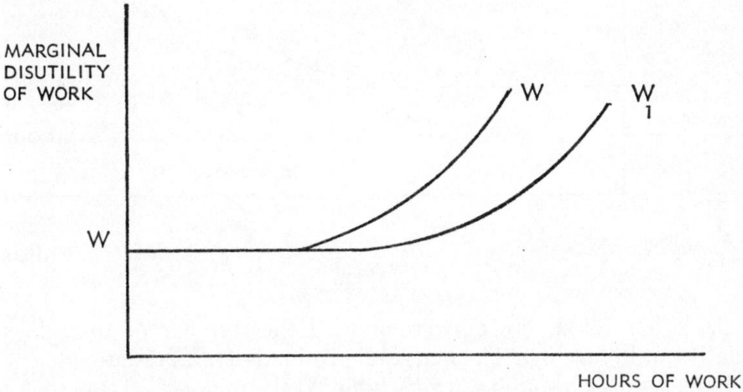

Figure 4.2

This would suggest that up to a certain number of hours of work the alternative to work is the monotony of leisure and the marginal disutility of work does not increase. From this type of curve for the individual we can easily get the family curve indicating the marginal disutility of work by horizontal summation of these curves. Thus for a family of n working members we would have a curve like WW_n in Figure 4.3:

In Figure 4.3 PP indicates the curve for marginal productivity of work. The point of intersection of WW_n and PP indicates the amount of work supplied and the marginal productivity of man-hours. Now suppose that the number of family workers increases from n to n+1 and consequently the WW_n curve shifts to WW_{n+1}. Since there is no change in capital, land and other factor endowments of the family, the PP curve remains where it was. Thus in the new situation, even though the number of workers is increased, the number of man-hours put in agriculture is not and, therefore, output does not increase.

If the above analysis is correct, the contrasting evidence of time-series and cross-section can be reconciled. The time-series data show the increases in number of workers over time. But because of the 'leisure trap' the increased hours were largely utilised in increased leisure rather than increased work. The cross-section data

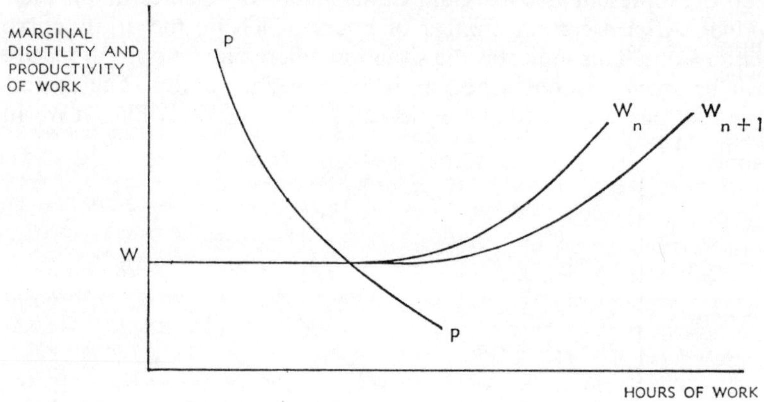

Figure 4.3

on the other hand, are concerned with the number of man-days actually put in farming. The marginal productivity of labour, actually put in, is positive, though not very high. At the micro-level those who work harder get better results; but on the macro-level, when a family expands, increased man-hours are largely dissipated in increased idleness.

What implication does our analysis have for the hypothesis that a large amount of labour could be withdrawn from the agricultural sector without any adverse effects on its production? Our analysis seems to suggest that it should be valid. If some members of a family are taken away, the rest would take a bit less leisure and the total number of man-hours would remain constant. However, there is an important possibility of asymmetry in this respect which may be noted. When family size is increasing the increase is spread more or less evenly over the entire agricultural sector. But when labour is withdrawn for employment in the non-agricultural sector, the main group to respond first might be those who are working as land-less labourers in big farms. These big farms are operated on the wage economy principle and in their cases the marginal productivity of labourers may not be zero. However, it is difficult to assess the exact extent of this asymmetry from our data and we do not go into any further details of this problem.

4.1.2: DIMINISHING RETURNS TO SCALE

Our next task is to see if our hypothesis that there are diminishing returns to scale is invalidated by the data. For this purpose, we have to see whether the elasticities in the log-linear form sum up to unity or more or less than unity. We find that the elasticities do sum up to less than unity. The elasticity of output with respect to capital when capital is the only explanatory variable is also less than unity as is required by our theoretical discussion in Chapter 2. In this case the cross-section data from Farm Management Studies also support the time-series finding. The sum of the output elasticities with respect to labour (L) and capital (K) obtained from cross-section studies is given below:

TABLE 4.1

RETURNS TO SCALE IN AGRICULTURE (CROSS-SECTION RESULTS)

The Regression Equation $Y = AL^{\alpha}K^{\beta}(LD)$
where Y = value added
L = labour
K = capital
LD = land.

	(α)	(β)	($\alpha+\beta$)
1. West Bengal (55–56) OLS	0·641	−0·035	0·506
2. ,, ,, ,, WLS	0·269	0·212	0·481
3. West Bengal (56–57) OLS	0·679	−0·088	0·591
4. ,, ,, ,, WLS	0·459	0·015	0·474
5. Ahmednagar (55–56) OLS	0·936	−0·171	0·765
6. ,, ,, WLS	1·110	−0·160	0·950
7. Ahmednagar (56–57) OLS	0·767	0·170	0·937
8. ,, ,, WLS	0·424	0·263	0·687
9. Madras (55–56) OLS	0·144	0·109	0·253
10. ,, ,, WLS	0·568	−0·056	0·512
11. U.P. and Punjab (55–56) WLS	0·236	0·191	0·427

Note: OLS = Ordinary Least Squares.
WLS = Weighted Least Squares.

From the above results it would seem that the hypothesis of diminishing returns in agriculture is not refuted by the data we have.

4.1.3: ROLE OF CAPITAL, WEATHER AND 'TECHNICAL PROGRESS'

Let us begin with the consideration of 'technical progress'. In the context of advanced countries (especially U.S.A.) 'technical progress' has been found to be a very important influence in increasing agricultural production. In our context also we expect from our theoretical discussion of Chapter 2 that 'technical progress' would be the main hope of escape from stagnation of the economy of the Indian type. However, our statistical analysis does not give us any definite evidence on this issue. We find that for the period 1948–49 to 1960–61 the coefficient of the time trend t as an indicator of disembodied 'technical progress' is positive but it is not statistically significant at a 95 per cent level of significance. For the period 1920–21 to 1960–61 however, the coefficient of t is negative and statistically significant, thus indicating that there was negative 'technical progress' in agriculture. Perhaps these two findings could be rationalised in the following way. In the period before 1948–49 land was being subjected to intensive use without adequate return to the land in the form of manure or fertiliser, so that the fertility of the soil was going down. In other words, the production function which includes only labour and capital was shifting downwards. In the period 1948–49 to 1960–61, however, the negative trend is no longer there though the positive trend has not yet asserted itself sufficiently strongly. Thus compared with the previous period there was relative 'technical progress' in agriculture, although its magnitude is rather small. However, because of the correlation between capital (K_a) and the time-trend (t), the regression coefficients of these two variables, when both are included amongst the explanatory variables, become statistically insignificant. Thus it seems to us that it will be desirable on statistical grounds (and not too objectionable on economic grounds) if we omit the time trend (t) in our final equation.

Next, we consider the weather effects. *A priori*, we expect that a deviation from normal rainfall will have adverse effects on agricultural production. For the period 1920–21 to 1960–61 we find that the coefficient of (log R_2) has the desired negative sign, but it is not statistically significant. This is probably due to the fact that our weather index is not a very satisfactory indicator of the effects of weather on agricultural production. But in view of the importance of weather in agricultural production and the non-availability of any better weather index, we decided to keep our weather variable in our analysis.

Lastly, we consider the output elasticity with respect to capital. For the period 1920–21 to 1960–61 the regression coefficient of log K_a is highly significant statistically and quite plausible on *a priori* grounds. The regression coefficient for the period 1948–49 to 1960–61 is slightly higher, perhaps because of the increased proportion of 'non-traditional capital' (see T. W. Schultz (142)) in this period. However, the regression coefficient of weather (log R_2) for the latter period is not plausible and we therefore take the regression equation for the period 1920–21 to 1960–61. This is:

$$(4.1.1) \quad \log Y_a = \underset{(0{\cdot}575)}{2{\cdot}9142} + \underset{(0{\cdot}0785)}{0{\cdot}6543} \log K_a - \underset{(0{\cdot}0228)}{0{\cdot}0347} \log R_2$$

$$\bar{R}^2 = 0{\cdot}7204; \ \delta^2/S^2 = 1{\cdot}8622$$

It would have been desirable if we could check our estimate of capital elasticity with reference to the cross-section data. Unfortunately, the cross-section data yield quite different results altogether. The regression coefficient of capital comes out to be statistically insignificant in most of the cases. The result may be due to the inaccuracy of the data but assuming that both the findings are correct, we may suggest a reconciliation. The capital in cross-section data mainly includes the traditional type of capital of farmers—bullocks, ploughs, etc. It may be that the marginal productivities of these traditional types of capital are low. The capital in time-series data on the other hand, includes government capital as well as private capital. Government capital is mostly in non-traditional forms of capital like irrigation, land improvement, etc. It is possible that this non-traditional type of capital is the main influence behind increased production in agriculture in the time-series. However, it was not possible to test the hypothesis of low (or zero) marginal productivity of private capital in the time-series. We could build up the series of private capital; but the correlation between the private capital series and the total capital series is high and the regression coefficients of both of these come out to be statistically non-significant. Thus the discrepancy between the time-series and cross-section results in this connection remains an interesting problem and our explanation is only a tentative one.

Before we pass on to the next equation, it may be interesting to note a few points about the role of land in agriculture. We have not included land as a separate variable. It can be argued quite plausibly that the extension of land in the Indian context is largely through capital expenditure in reclamation, land improvement, etc., and these are taken into account in the capital estimates. Statistically also we find that the addition of land does not improve the results very significantly and when both capital and land are included as independent variables, the regression coefficient of land is not statistically significant. Thus, in the time-series we find that the neglect of land as a separate variable does not seem to affect the results.

At the micro-level, of course, land is likely to be important because an individual can increase his land by buying from others. Thus it was not surprising to find that cross-section data give significant coefficients on land. The comparative estimates of the marginal products of land and capital are given below.

TABLE 4.2

MARGINAL PRODUCT OF LAND AND CAPITAL (CROSS-SECTION RESULTS)

The Equation: $Y = \alpha + \beta L_a + \gamma K_a + \delta LD$

	Marginal Product of Land (δ)		*Marginal Product of Capital* (γ)	
1. W. Bengal (55–56) OLS	0·105	(0·048)	−0·244	(0·103)
2. ,, ,, WLS	0·068	(0·045)	−0·028	(0·106)
3. ,, (55–57) OLS	0·006	(0·051)	0·065	(0·179)
4. ,, ,, WLS	0·040	(0·042)	−0·037	(0·158)
5. Bombay (55–56) OLS	−0·030	(0·031)	0·049	(0·063)
6. ,, (56–57) OLS	0·069	(0·037)	0·220	(0·077)
7. Ahmednagar (55–56) OLS	0·002	(0·041)	−0·136	(0·075)
8. ,, ,, WLS	0·006	(0·040)	−0·109	(0·074)
9. ,, (56–57) OLS	0·257	(0·110)	0·147	(0·180)
10. ,, ,, WLS	0·223	(0·099)	0·086	(0·161)
11. Madras (55–56) OLS	0·052	(0·022)	0·198	(0·060)
12. ,, ,, WLS	−0·033	(0·035)	0·177	(0·089)
13. U.P. and Punjab (55–56) OLS	0·218	(0·036)	−0·490	(0·158)
14. ,, ,, ,, WLS	0·155	(0·022)	−0·190	(0·187)

In the above table we find that there are 4 cases (numbers 3, 5, 7, 8) where neither land nor capital has a significant coefficient. Of the remaining 10 cases we find that land scores over capital in 7 cases (numbers 1, 2, 4, 9, 10, 13, 14) whereas capital scores over land in only 3 cases (numbers 6, 11, 12). This would suggest that from an individual farmer's point of view an increase in land is on the whole even more profitable than investment in capital assets.

If the above finding is valid, it would indicate one of the reasons why farmers in India are so very land conscious. The high propensity to invest in land rather than in other capital goods may not be a reflection of irrational social or personal psychology but the result of valid economic calculus. Under present circumstances the most important forms of capital investment open to the farmers are bullocks, ploughs, etc. The marginal productivity of these forms of capital is found to be less than that of land. So, from the personal point of view, the preference for investment in land may be quite rational. Perhaps the best way to attract investment away from land is to introduce new forms of capital with higher marginal productivities or to increase the marginal productivity of the present forms of capital by providing external economies.

4.2: FOOD-GRAINS PRODUCTION FUNCTION

Given total agricultural output we have to determine how much is devoted to food-grains. This is necessary for a number of reasons. In the first place, the agricultural production function that we have analysed so far gives value added figures, whereas for employment purposes some figure of gross output in physical terms may be more relevant. Secondly, part of agricultural production is devoted to commercial crops and we should eliminate this part to estimate agricultural output close to wage-goods. For this purpose we have a simple relation given by the regression of food-grains output on total agricultural value added (equation 4.2.1). The value of $\bar{R}^2$ is quite satisfactory in this case and the coefficient of Y_a has the right sign and it is highly significant statistically.

The main defect of the regression seems to be the low von Neumann ratio. The null hypothesis of zero auto-correlation is accepted at 1 per cent significance level (where the limits are 0·9033 and 3·4603) but it is rejected at 5 per cent significance level (where the limits are 1·2301 and 3·1335). It seems, therefore, that we might have omitted some other significant variable.

One important omitted variable that easily suggests itself is the relative price of food-grains and other commercial crops. Actually, it has been reported that in some cases there is a cobweb cycle operating in particular regions with respect to rice and jute (see e.g. R. Clark (22)). We test this hypothesis in an indirect manner. If a cobweb cycle has been operating, the supply of this year will depend on last year's prices [i.e. $F_a = f(Y_a, p_{a_{-1}})$] and the prices of last year on the supply of last year [i.e. $p_{a_{-1}} = g(F_{a_{-1}})$]. Making the substitution we find that in the case of a cobweb we should have $F_a = \alpha + \beta Y_a + \gamma F_{a_{-1}}$ where β is positive and γ is negative. Actually, however, the coefficient of $F_{a_{-1}}$ comes out to be positive and statistically insignificant; nor is the value of the von Neumann ratio appreciably better. Another form of this equation that we try is

$$\frac{F_a}{Y_a} = \alpha + \beta\left(\frac{F_a}{Y_a}\right)_{-1}.$$

Here the value of the coefficient is statistically significant and the von Neumann ratio is quite high but the sign of the coefficient is positive and not negative as expected. Nor does the situation improve with the introduction of a time trend t and the introduction of a two-period lag. Thus, in spite of the *a priori* plausibility, there is no empirical evidence of a cobweb cycle. One possible explanation is that even though in some areas there is a possibility of substitution between food-grains and commercial crops, their impact on the aggregate is not significant. Therefore, in spite of the low value of the von Neumann ratio, we have to accept the first simple approximation of food-grains production equation. We have:

$$(4.2.1) \qquad F_a = -3823{\cdot}301 + 2.0675\, Y_a$$
$$(780{\cdot}4809) \quad (0{\cdot}1554)$$
$$\bar{R}^2 = 0{\cdot}9412;\ \delta^2/S^2 = 0{\cdot}9766$$

4.3: EMPLOYMENT FUNCTION

Next, we consider the dependence of employment in the non-agricultural sector on the output of food-grains. One employment index for the period 1950–61 has been provided by the Planning Commission in the *Third Five Year Plan* (69). But this index relates to the organised sector only and it does not agree with the figures of employment given by Kalra (83) in *Census of India*, 1961, for the non-agricultural sector as a whole. Therefore, we had to build up a series of employment, which is given in Appendix I.

We have considered four sets of food-grains figures. In the first place we have the form where home production of food-grains (F_a) and the net imports of food-grains ($(M-X)_a$) are considered as separate variables. Apart from this we also consider the total available food-grains (net output plus net imports) for the current year (TF_a), total available food-grains with a one-year lag ($TF_{a_{-1}}$), and the two-year moving average of total available food-grains ($TF_{a_{M.A.}}$).

All these regressions give good results. But the equation (4.3.2) seems the best on statistical as well as economic grounds. Statistically the correlation coefficient and the von Neumann ratio are the highest in this case. The regression coefficients are all highly significant and considerably stable. The regression coefficient of net imports is higher than that of food-grains production at home and this is what we expect on *a priori* grounds because most of the imports are used for the non-agricultural sector.

We also considered the impact of taxation in the agricultural sector on this function. *A priori* one would expect that the higher the level of taxation of agriculture the greater would be the marketed surplus of food-grains and the level of L_i. Statistically we found that the regression coefficient of the tax variable is of the expected sign and is statistically significant. However, its contribution to $\bar{R}^2$ is not very great and its introduction considerably complicates the process of solution of our system. So while recognising the importance of taxation for the present equation, we ignore it for the purposes of simplification. We also tried to see the importance of total population (N) in this equation. However, because of the collinearity between N and F_a the coefficient of F_a changes sign and becomes statistically insignificant. For this reason we have to give up this line of refinement as well. Lastly, we tried to see if we could obtain a demand function for food-grains dependent on L_i, total population (N) and total income. Here again, the multi-collinearity made the results nonsensical. Thus, after considerable experimentation we find that the equation with domestic food-grains production and net imports of food-grains as explanatory variables seems to be the best. Therefore we have:

$$(4.3.1) \quad L_i = \underset{(279{\cdot}1535)}{1803{\cdot}044} + \underset{(0{\cdot}0393)}{0{\cdot}3347} F_a + \underset{(0{\cdot}3044)}{1{\cdot}1844} (M-X)_a$$

$$\bar{R}^2 = 0{\cdot}8697; \ \delta^2/S^2 = 2{\cdot}3674$$

4.4.: NON-AGRICULTURAL PRODUCTION FUNCTION

A number of studies of production functions of manufacturing industries have been made in India. Some of the results of these studies are presented below in Table 4.3.

TABLE 4.3

PRODUCTION FUNCTIONS OF MANUFACTURING INDUSTRIES

Production Function: $Y_i = AL_i^{\alpha}K_i^{\beta}$

	Exponent of Labour (α)	*Exponent of Capital* (β)
1. Tewari (153)		
Year: 1946	0·66	0·31
,, 1947	0·68	0·47
2. Dutt (30)		
Year: 1946	0·77	0·23
,, 1947	0·57	0·50
3. Divatia and Trivedi (29)	0·402	0·598
4. Bhatia (12)		
Year: 1948	0·67	0·26
,, 1949	0·59	0·44
5. Murti and Sastry (110)		
Year: 1951	0·59	0·40
,, 1952	0·53	0·50

We did not, however, think it proper to take the estimates from any of these studies. For one thing, they all relate to manufacturing industries only whereas we are concerned with the non-agricultural sector as a whole. Secondly, these estimates are rather unstable; the exponent of labour, for example, varies between 0·402 and 0·77. Thirdly, better data have become available since these studies were made and we should utilise them. In our estimation we have utilised three sets of data:

(1) the time-series data referring to the non-agricultural sector as a whole;

(2) the Annual Survey of Industries (A.S.I.) cross-section data (48);

(3) the Census of Manufacturing Industries (C.M.I.) data (62), both cross-section and time-series.

We study industries as well as the non-agricultural sector as a whole, because it is the industrial sector that forms the most dynamic and the most important part of the non-agricultural sector.

As in the agricultural production function, so in the non-agricultural one, multi-collinearity presents a major statistical problem. The simple correlation coefficient between labour and capital is 0·99. The natural result is the instability of the coefficients. In the linear form the coefficient of labour comes out to be negative although it is not statistically significant. In the log-linear form the coefficient of $\log L_i$ changes sign as the time trend t is included or excluded. Again, the sum of the elasticities of output with respect to labour and capital turns out to be unrealistically low. Therefore, in order to avoid the problem of multi-collinearity we introduce the assumption of constant returns to scale. Under this assumption the Cobb–Douglas production function takes a simple form and if the trend (t) is ignored there is only one independent variable. We find that when t is an independent variable along with $\log \frac{K_i}{L_i}$, the regression coefficients of both these terms turn out to be statistically insignificant. Thus for the sake of statistical efficiency we also ignore the trend variable and choose the equation with $\log \frac{K_i}{L_i}$ as the only explanatory variable. With this restriction the multiple correlation coefficient is slightly lower than the unrestricted case. But it seems that this disadvantage is more than balanced by the advantage of avoiding the problem of multi-collinearity. Thus we have:

$$(4.4.1) \qquad \log \frac{Y_i}{L_i} = \underset{(0{\cdot}0734)}{-0{\cdot}4407} + \underset{(0{\cdot}0628)}{0{\cdot}5599} \log \frac{K_i}{L_i}$$

$$\bar{R}^2 = 0{\cdot}8675; \ \delta^2/S^2 = 0{\cdot}7095$$

In the analysis of the ASI data we find that the unrestricted regression gives the sum of the exponents of labour and capital in the log-linear case as less than unity. However, in the industrial sector, diminishing returns to scale does not seem very plausible. So we obtain the estimates with the restriction: $\alpha + \beta = 1$. The results are very similar to the time-series estimates. The exponents of capital and labour are 0·566 and 0·434 respectively. It is interesting to note that the wage-share in value added for large-scale manufacturing sector (calculated from the input–output table (1951–52) for India presented in *National Income and Allied Topics*, Vol. I (125)) comes out to be 0·427.

The results of the analysis of C.M.I. data are not so encouraging. In time-series regression the exponent of labour turns out to be greater than unity. In the cross-section study, however, the exponents nearly sum to unity. The time-series regression with the restriction $\alpha+\beta=1$ gives meaningful results, but the exponent of capital turns out to be lower than that found in the A.S.I. study and we preferred the A.S.I. estimate because the A.S.I. data are more recent and have a greater coverage. However, while these cross-section studies give us some additional information about the production structure of our economy, it is preferable for the purposes of our model to stick to the time-series equation obtained from the data for the non-agricultural sector as a whole.

CHAPTER 5

Money, Wages and Prices

In this chapter we consider the statistical results of the equations dealing with the absolute price, the wage rate and relative prices. We begin with the equations connected with the determination of the absolute price level (Section 5.1). Then, in Section 5.2, we consider our wage-rate hypothesis. Lastly, in Section 5.3, we consider the determination of other prices like consumer goods prices, price of manufactured goods, price of investment goods, etc.

5.1: THE MONEY SUPPLY AND THE ABSOLUTE PRICE LEVEL

We have argued in Chapter 2 that on *a priori* grounds it seems that the quantity theory of money may well be valid in the Indian context. Our task now is to see if the Indian data reject this hypothesis and if they do not, what the relevant parameters are. The quantity theory hypothesis has been presented in a number of different forms. Of course, all these forms assert basically the same thing; but it is desirable to distinguish between them for the sake of the clarity of exposition. We divide the different approaches into three groups:

(1) Velocity of Money Approach: In this approach the ratio of income (or transactions) over a period of time to the stock of money is considered to be a stable ratio and a knowledge of this ratio enables us to predict total money expenditure and thus the absolute prices, once we know the volume of money supply and the level of real income (or transactions).

(2) Demand for Money Approach: In this approach, which is associated with the Cambridge school, the demand for money is considered to be a stable function of income and such other tangible factors. The demand function for money along with the supply function of money enables us to determine the value of money which is the inverse of the absolute price level.

(3) Money Income Generation Approach: In this variant of the quantity theory, mainly popularised by M. Friedman, the money income is a function of money supply. Whereas in the demand for money approach, money is the dependent variable and income, etc., the independent ones, in this approach income is the dependent variable and money the independent.

As we noted above, these variants of the quantity theory are basically the same but this classification will be convenient for the review of our statistical results.

5.1.1: VELOCITY OF MONEY APPROACH

Although the concept of velocity goes back to the mercantilist literature, the statistical work on it is of comparatively recent origin and mostly relating to the U.S. economy. A survey of literature in this connection has been provided by R. Selden (143). He finds that the income velocity of money has a downward secular trend. Whereas the earlier discussions of velocity tried to give institutional explanations for changes in velocity, Selden tries to give an explanation in terms of economic factors such as the cost of holding money, cost of substitutes, income, expectations, etc. He finds little support for the hypothesis that velocity movements are mainly a result of changes in the cost of holding money. The best explanation is 'the rise in real income *per capita* . . . aided perhaps by the decline in the cost of holding money' (Selden, op. cit.). This line of reasoning has been best developed in M. Friedman (42) and M. Friedman and Anna J. Schwartz (44). Basically the conclusion is that the money in real terms is a luxury and when 'permanent' real income increases, the demand for real money increases more than proportionately. Specifically, the income elasticity of demand for money is found to be 1·8 for the U.S. This means that over the period when the real income *per capita* was rising the real money demanded was rising more than proportionately and thus the income velocity was going down.* Friedman does not find any significant effect of rate of interest and rate of change of prices on velocity.

These results are contradicted by Latané (98, 99). He finds that the charts of income velocity (v) and the rate of interest (r) for the periods 1909–58 (annual figures) and 1949–59 (with r monthly and v quarterly) indicate a rather close and continuing relationship between v and r. The data for the period 1909–58 do not furnish evidence that there has been a shift over time in the schedule of

* It has been argued by J. Tobin (159) in a review of M. Friedman and Anna J. Schwartz (44) that this statement in terms of income elasticity of money being greater than unity is just another way of stating the declining velocity. It would have been, we feel, desirable if Friedman had buttressed his results from some cross-section study.

demand for proportionate cash balances. 'There is no significant evidence that financial intermediaries have increased the efficiency of cash balances nor is there evidence that cash balances are luxury goods' (Latané, op. cit.). Latané argues that Friedman's finding arises in part because the latter includes time deposits with money and time deposits have increased relative to demand deposits. Latané's findings support the Keynesian approach, and reduce the significance of the quantity theory of money.

In the Indian context also, several studies have been made. A. M. Khusro (89) tried to estimate the liquidity preference function for India by eliminating the money demanded for transaction purposes. V. C. Shah (149, 150) tried to test the relative efficiency of the quantity theory and the Keynesian income expenditure theory along the Friedman–Meiselman line (43) and came out in favour of the quantity theory of money. D. Biswas (16) also tried to estimate the demand function for money for the period 1935–55 and found that income and time are the prime determinants of total demand for money and the rate of interest is not an important variable. These results do not seem to reject our hypothesis. However, it seemed desirable to us to extend the period covered and to subject them to a more searching statistical investigation.

Our series cover the period 1901–02 to 1961–62. Our income-series refers to total income though for theoretical reasons it would have been desirable to exclude the non-monetary sector. We could not make this adjustment because no data were available for the purpose. Our money series excludes time deposits though their magnitude is small and their inclusion does not make much difference to the basic results. The income-velocity calculated from these is shown in Figure 5.1. From the figure it is obvious that there is a definite downward trend of income-velocity over the period. This agrees with the experience in the U.S. as noted by M. Friedman and others. However, there is no definite cyclical pattern in income-velocity as was found in the U.S. There are no known cyclical patterns of economic activity in India and income velocity does not apparently show any either. However, there are a few important breaks in the series, which deserve some attention. The years 1914–17 experienced an increase in income velocity which was followed by a relative stability (with a gentle downward trend) till 1929. The years 1930–31 and 1931–32 experienced a considerable fall in the velocity at which point it remained more or less stable till 1939. The years 1939–45 again experienced a steady fall in income-velocity which was followed by a period of rising velocity till 1950–51 at which point it remained stable (with minor fluctuations) till 1961–62. A detailed analysis of the behaviour of income-velocity will perhaps be quite

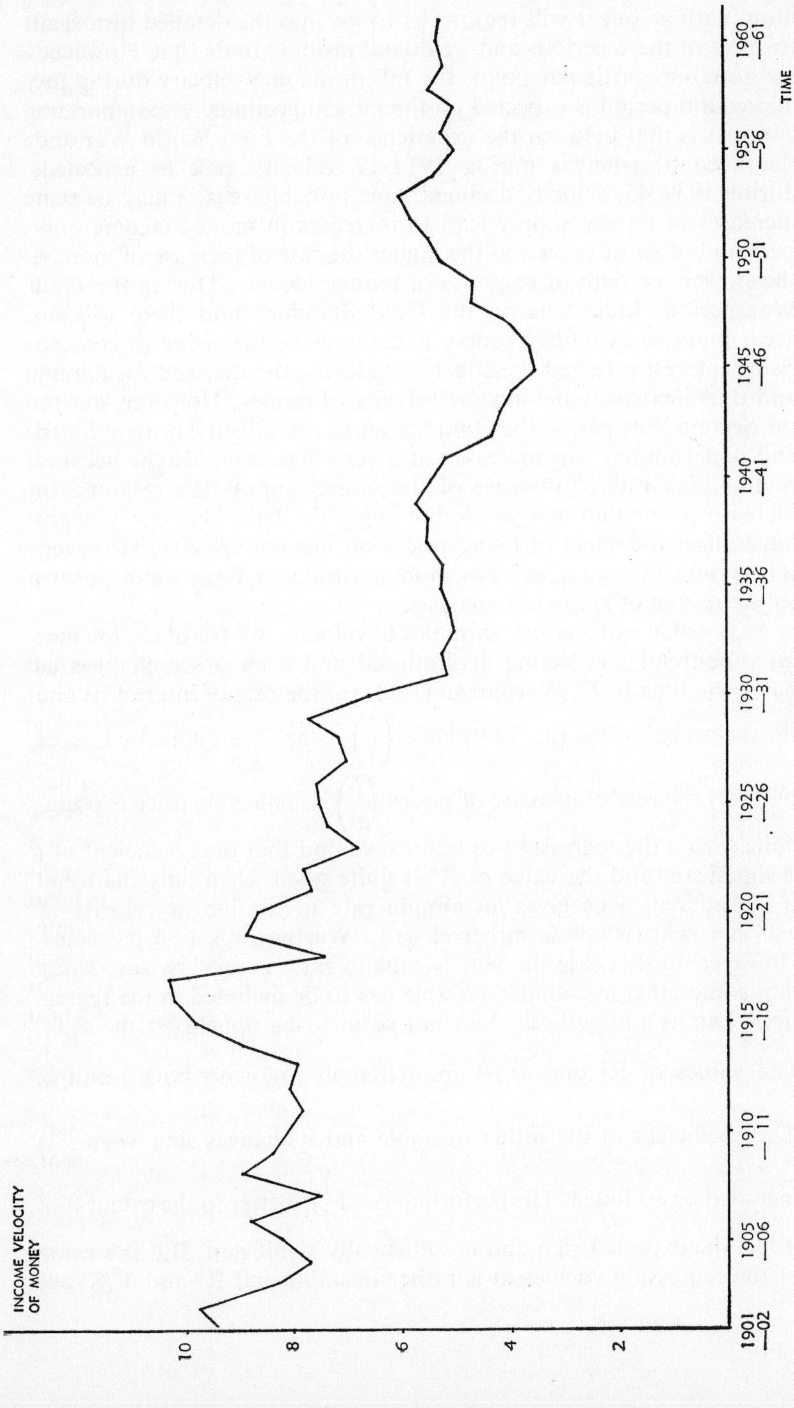
INCOME VELOCITY OF MONEY
10
8
6
4
2
1901 —02
1905 —06
1910 — 11
1915 —16
1920 —21
1925 —26
1930 —31
1935 —36
1940 —41
1945 —46
1950 —51
1955 —56
1960 —61
TIME

Figure 5.1

illuminating; but it will require us to go into the detailed historical features of these periods and we do not propose to do that. However, we note one particular point, the fall in income-velocity during the depression period is expected on theoretical grounds. The important contrast is that between the experience of the First World War and the Second: whereas during 1914–17 velocity rose as expected, during 1939–45, velocity declined. One possible reason may be that increases in money supply lead to increases in money income only over a number of years and the higher the rate of increase of money, the slower the path of response of money income. During the First War period, India was on the Gold Standard and there was no great increase in money supply and therefore the rising prices and rising interest rate had the effect of reducing the demand for money and thus increasing the income-velocity of money. However, during the Second War period the Gold Standard was effectively abandoned and paper money was increased at a very high rate. Maybe because of this high rate of increase of the money supply the response of increase in income was somewhat sluggish. Thus this effect might have offset the effect of rising prices on income velocity. However, this is only a rough guess. For more accurate analysis, we must turn to the results of statistical analysis.

As possible explanatory variables of velocity, we try the following: (*a*) time-trend t reflecting institutional and such other changes as has been done by C. Warburton (166); (*b*) the rate of interest (i) and the reciprocal of the rate of interest $\left(\frac{1}{i}\right)$ as has been done by Latané (99); (*c*) the rate of increase of prices $\left(\frac{\dot{p}}{p}\right)$ as reflecting price expectations. From the regression equations we find that the coefficient of t is significant and the value of $\bar{R}^2$ is quite good when only the trend is considered. This gives an annual rate of decline in velocity of 1·28 per cent (which is rather close to Warburton's 1·33 per cent). However, in this case the von Neumann ratio is too low suggesting that some other systematic variable has to be included in the regression. Latané's hypothesis does not seem to be upheld by the data. The values of $\bar{R}^2$ and δ^2/S^2 are extremely low with both i and $\frac{1}{i}$. The coefficient of i is rather unstable and it changes sign when $\frac{1}{i}$ is included or excluded. The performance of $\frac{1}{i}$ is better to the extent that it has the expected sign and is statistically significant. But the value of the regression coefficient is rather unstable and $\bar{R}^2$ and δ^2/S^2 are too low. On the other hand, the coefficient of t is highly stable and its F-value is very high. This suggests that there is a definite downward tendency in income-velocity and that is to be explained by a factor more or less continuous with time. We tried Friedman's hypothesis about the income-elasticity of demand for money. We took money both as including time deposits and as excluding time deposits, and took a five-year moving average of income as indicating 'permanent income'. However, in neither case was the regression coefficient of *per capita* real income at all significant. The main explanatory variable for the movements in real money demanded *per capita* was the time trend. The non-significant regression coefficient of income is of course surprising—in fact it is rather implausible. Maybe this is due to the statistical reason that, in this period, there was not much of an increase in real income *per capita.*

Thus we conclude that over the period studied income-velocity does not seem to have been influenced very much by factors such as the rate of interest, the rate of increase in prices, or *per capita* real income. The movements in income-velocity seem to be due to institutional and structural changes. The most important structural change that suggests itself is the changing degree of monetisation in the economy. As the non-monetised income flows are being drawn into the monetised sector, the money has to cover a wider area of economic transactions for the same level of income and consequently the income velocity of money goes down.

5.1.2: DEMAND FOR MONEY APPROACH

The demand for money approach was first popularised by the Cambridge school. In this original form, the demand for money was a fixed proportion of the money income: $M = k.(pY)$. Keynes accepted income as the main determinant of the demand for money for transactions and precautionary purposes but added the rate of interest as the determinant of speculative demand for money. In his version, we have $M = L_1(pY)+L_2(i)$ where $L_1(pY)$ is transaction cum precautionary demand for money and $L_2(i)$ is the speculative demand for money. However, in subsequent discussion, it has been clarified that the transactions demand for money may also be responsive to the rate of interest and that unless 'money illusion' is introduced in the speculative demand for money, it should also be dependent on prices and thus money income. Moreover, it is operationally difficult to separate the two types of demand for money. Thus it has become more popular to express the demand for money as $M = f(pY, i)$. Moreover, if we can assume that the demand function is homogeneous in pY, we have $\frac{M}{pY} = F(i)$. In this form, the equation can be used as a demand function for money as well as a determinant of the rate of interest.*

In our analysis, we consider the demand function for money in the form presented above $\frac{M}{pY} = F(i)$. We also consider the time trend (t), and the price expectations. Further, we also try to see if the rate of interest can be explained by $\frac{M}{pY}$, rate of price increase and the time trend. The results, as expected, are broadly similar to the results of the velocity approach. The coefficient of price expectations (indicated by the rate of increase of price) is found to be statistically insignificant. On *a priori* grounds, however, it seems plausible that price expectations will exert a significant influence on the demand for money. This suggests that the rate of increase of price $\left(\frac{\dot{p}}{p}\right)$ may not be a good indicator of price expectations. Following a suggestion in J. D. Sethi (147), we take the ratio of the forward price of gold to the spot price of gold as an indicator of price expectations. However, for this purpose we could not get data on gold prices except for the period 1950–51 to 1960–61. Obtaining the regression of money demanded on this variable for this period, we find that the coefficient of price expectations is still not very significant. Thus while recognising the importance of price expectations, we have to exclude it from our analysis. The coefficient of the rate of interest comes out with the right sign and it is also significant statistically. However, its value is rather unstable and when the rate of interest is the only explanatory variable of $\frac{M}{pY}$, the $\bar{R}^2$ is very low and so is δ^2/S^2. In order to test the importance of the rate of interest further, we carry out the regressions over three sub-samples: (I) the period 1901–02 to 1928–29; (II) the period 1929–30 to 1947–48; and (III) the period 1948–49 to 1961–62. The stability of the coefficients over sub-samples may be a further test of the importance of the variable concerned. By this test, the rate of interest fares even worse than it did in the complete sample. In Period I the $\frac{M}{pY} = f(i)$ equation gives wrong sign of the coefficient of i, very low F-value, and $\bar{R}^2$. When a time trend is included as an extra variable the sign of the coefficient of i is as expected but the coefficient is not statistically significant. In Period II the equation $\frac{M}{pY} = f(i)$ performs

* For an analysis of the latter aspect, see R. J. Ball (6).

better to the extent that the regression coefficient is of the right sign and statistically significant and $\bar{R}^2$ is slightly better. But here again, we find that the coefficient of i changes sign and becomes statistically insignificant when the time trend t is included. In Period III the coefficients of i in $\frac{M}{pY} = f(i)$ and $\frac{M}{pY} = f(i, t)$ are both statistically insignificant, though of the right sign. From these it seems that the rate of interest is not a significant determinant of the demand for money in the Indian context.

The most important variable for explanation of $\frac{M}{pY}$ comes out to be the time trend t. In the overall sample, its coefficient is highly significant and stable. The $\bar{R}^2$ is also quite high though the von Neumann ratio is not quite satisfactory. The coefficient of t is also significant in the sub-samples except in the sub-sample for Period III, where the variation in $\frac{M}{pY}$ itself is rather small. This result is naturally the same as obtained in velocity analysis and here again the main explanation that we can think of is the increasing degree of monetisation in the economy. Apart from the time trend, the other noticeable thing is that the constant term is highly significant both in the overall sample and in all the sub-samples. Thus, as in velocity analysis, so in this demand for money analysis, we come out with the conclusion that the ratio of money to income is stable except for a time trend, perhaps due to institutional changes.

We also tried to see if the Keynesian hypothesis of the rate of interest being determined by $\frac{M}{pY}$ is upheld by the data. Since $i = f\left(\frac{M}{pY}\right)$ is just the inverse function of $\frac{M}{pY} = f(i)$, the results are precisely the same as above. The coefficient of $\frac{M}{pY}$ is found to be of right sign and statistically significant for the period 1901–02 to 1961–62 but the values of $\bar{R}^2$ and δ^2/S^2 are very small. In the sub-sample for Period I the regression coefficient is statistically insignificant and of 'wrong' sign, and $\bar{R}^2$ and δ^2/S^2 are very small. In Period II the coefficient is of right sign and statistically significant and $\bar{R}^2$ is reasonably good. But here again δ^2/S^2 is small and the coefficient of $\frac{M}{pY}$ changes sign when t is included. In Period III also, the equation $i = f\left(\frac{M}{pY}\right)$ is rejected by all the statistical tests. We also tried to see if the results are improved when we include time deposits in our estimate of money supply. However, the results are not very different from the previous case.

5.1.3: MONEY INCOME GENERATION APPROACH

Lastly we come to the income generation approach of the quantity theory which has been popularised by Friedman and Meiselman (43). This seems to us to be the most promising line of approach for the quantity theory. This does not use a velocity concept which might appear to be rather mechanistic. Nor does it make the money a dependent variable which seems rather awkward when the quantity theory asserts that changes in money (exogenously determined) brings about changes in money income and prices. The income generation form emphasises that when money supply is increased it will create an excess supply of money to begin with. If the financial markets are not very developed, this discrepancy is sought to be corrected through increased expenditure on goods which increases money income. Whether the increased money income is the result of increased prices or increased output or both depends on effects of prices on output. In our context, output is determined by the supply of factors of production. So the increased money income will be mainly the result of increased price level.

In our statistical analysis, we start with the simple form $pY = f(M)$ and go on to more complicated hypotheses as problems are encountered. In the simple form, the value of $\bar{R}^2$ is quite high and the regression coefficient is highly significant. However, the von Neumann ratio is very low which suggests the need for some new variable. Introduction of the rate of interest does not help. The coefficient of i comes out with the wrong sign and the $\bar{R}^2$ and δ^2/S^2 do not improve significantly. Nor does the introduction of the time trend t serve any better. The coefficient of t is statistically insignificant and δ^2/S^2 does not improve.

Next, we try the lagged values of money. We take M_{-1} and M_{-2} as explanatory variables. However, these are highly collinear and the coefficients become highly unstable and statistically insignificant. In order to eliminate the problem of multi-collinearity and yet retain the lag hypothesis we try the distributed lag hypothesis with Koyck transformation. In this case, the results come out as statistically quite satisfactory. However, the coefficient of Y_{-1} is rather high (0·8005) and this leads to a long drawn process of adjustment of money income to money supply. In order to see if this result is due to our selection of an improper type of lag, we try various modifications of distributed lag hypothesis. To see if the lag distribution is skewed rather than monotonically declining, we try the method used by R. M. Solow and J. Kareken (152) in which Y_{-2} becomes an additional variable. However, the coefficient of Y_{-2} comes out as statistically insignificant. Thus there is no evidence of a skewed lag distribution though, of course, it is not possible to deny the possibility of a skewed distribution because of the multi-collinearity involved. Next, we try the log-linear relation between income, money supply and other variables. But here also the results are slightly inferior to the simple linear case. Lastly, we try a modified lag hypothesis where the lag coefficient is a function of the rate of change in the independent variable. Specifically, the lag distribution gives a slower rate of response when the rate of change in the independent variable is high. This modification seems intuitively plausible, but the statistical results are no better than in the simple hypothesis. The $\bar{R}^2$ is, in fact, a bit lower and the coefficient of $\log Y_{-1}$ comes out to be quite high. Thus it seems preferable to accept the simple case with distributed lag hypothesis. Thus we have:

$$(5.1.1) \qquad (pY) = \underset{(60{\cdot}35)}{115{\cdot}3565} + \underset{(0{\cdot}213)}{1{\cdot}14997M} + \underset{(0{\cdot}0478)}{0{\cdot}8005}\,(pY)_{-1}$$

$$\bar{R}^2 = 0{\cdot}992; \; \delta^2/S^2 = 2{\cdot}1472$$

The above results support our contention that in an under-developed country of the Indian type, the classical theory may be more likely to be applicable than the Keynesian theory. The Keynesian monetary theory may be said to imply that $i = f\left(\frac{M}{pY}\right)$ whereas the quantity theory requires $pY = \alpha + \beta M$. As we have seen above, the quantity theory equation gives a much better performance than the Keynesian equation. In the Friedman–Meiselman discussion of the comparative efficiency of the quantity theory and the Keynesian theory, the Keynesian theory is represented by the equation $pY = a + bE$ where pY is money income and E is autonomous expenditure. This, however, does not seem to us to be an appropriate contrast. In Keynesian theory, the autonomous expenditure determines via the multiplier, the level of *real* national income. The absolute prices are determined by the fixed money wages and the marginal productivity of labour at the level of employment determined by the effective demand. In other words, the quantity theory is concerned with the determination of money income (with real income determined by the supply of factors of production) whereas the Keynesian multiplier theory is concerned with the determination of real income (with money income dependent on the level of money wages, etc.). Thus it does not seem proper to contrast $pY = \alpha + \beta M$ with $pY = a + bE$. To us, it seems that the basic point at which the Keynesian theory of *money* departs from the classical theory of *money* is to make money demand and supply relevant only for the determination of the rate of interest. If the increased money supply does not affect the rate of interest, it will not have any effect on money income or prices in the Keynesian economics. Thus it seems that $i = f\left(\frac{M}{pY}\right)$ catches the Keynesian spirit better than $pY = a + bE$ *so far as the monetary theory is concerned.*

5.1.4: DETERMINANTS OF MONEY SUPPLY

In the above analysis we have assumed money supply to be an exogenous variable. In this respect, we are following the general tradition of macro-economics. However, it might reasonably be argued that the money supply is likely to be dependent on the rate of interest, the rate of change of prices and such other endogenous variables. In that case the regression of money stock on these variables gives rise to a problem of identification, as to whether the estimated equation indicates supply or demand condition or either at all. In fact it is sometimes argued that changes in money supply are only passive reflections of changes in demand for it, because of rising prices and incomes, and therefore the close relation between money and money income does not validate the quantity theory. This question of causality among statistically correlated variables is of course difficult to solve statistically. Some light on identification problems can be shed by the simultaneous equation estimation procedure. We do try this procedure in Chapter 7, but for the moment we confine ourselves to the single equation method and try to see if money supply is dependent on the endogenous factors referred to above or on exogenous factors alone.

The most obviously important determinant of money supply is what may be called high-powered money—i.e. the money issued by the Government and the Central Bank. In our context, this is indicated by notes and currencies. This may be regarded as exogenous to be determined by the Government decision. It is possible that even the Government's issuance of notes and currencies is dependent on the economic situation and it should be treated as an endogenous variable. However it is plausible to argue that the Government can control issuance of notes and currencies, if it wants to. At least, this is what seems implied in the discussions on the Government's decision about deficit financing in Plan documents and other official publications on the problem in India. Moreover, as we find in our statistical analysis, the supply of notes and currency is not significantly influenced by factors such as the rate of interest, or rate of change of prices. Thus for our purposes, notes and currency are treated as exogenously determined.

Given the amount of notes and currencies, the total money supply depends on the value of the 'money multiplier' which gives the ratio of total money to notes and currencies. As we have seen in Chapter 3, this multiplier depends on the public's propensity to deposit money in the banks, the banks' propensity to lend and the reserve requirements of the banks. These factors can be regarded as largely institutional and likely to change only slowly over time. In order to indicate their importance, we take a time trend (t). In the short run, moreover, the rate of interest and price expectations may have an important effect on the public's propensity to deposit and the banks' propensity to lend. For example, when the rate of interest is high, the public *might* economise in holdings of money in hand as well as in banks and buy other assets. This may reduce the deposits to a certain extent. On the other hand the higher rate of interest may induce the banks to stretch their lending capacity and thus increase the money supply. The net effect of these is difficult to determined *a priori*. Similarly, price expectations may have an influence on deposits.

Thus in our statistical analysis of the determinants of the money supply we consider the following variables: (*a*) notes and currency (C); (*b*) the rate of interest (i); (*c*) the rate of increase of prices $\left(\frac{\dot{p}}{p}\right)$ as indicating price expectations; (*d*) the time trend (t). We also consider the equation in three forms: (1) total money supply regressed on these variables, i.e. $M = f(C, i, \frac{\dot{p}}{p}, t)$; (2) the ratio between currency and the money $\left(\frac{C}{M}\right)$ as explained by the other factors, i.e. $\frac{C}{M} = f(i, \frac{\dot{p}}{p}, t)$; (3) the first differences in money (ΔM) as dependent on the first differences in currency (ΔC) and on other factors, i.e. $\Delta M = f(\Delta C, i, t)$. We consider these different forms in the hope that a good specification will satisfy the statistical tests in all the forms whereas a wrong specification may get caught in one or the other.

From the regression results we find that the coefficient of $\frac{\dot{p}}{p}$ is not statistically significant in any of the regressions and it can therefore be left out. The coefficient of the rate of interest is significant in form (1), but its value is rather unstable and it is not statistically significant in other forms of the equation. Thus it seems that the rate of interest may also be ignored in the present analysis. The most significant variable is currency (C). The regression coefficient is highly significant and very stable. Thus the money multiplier comes out to be about 1·5. In the first difference form also the coefficient of ΔC comes out to be remarkably stable and quite significant statistically. The marginal multiplier in this case, which can be regarded as the short run multiplier, comes out to be 1·4, which is very close to the earlier estimate of 1·5. The other significant variable is the time-trend. It is very highly significant in the form (2) where $\frac{C}{M}$ is the dependent variable. In form (1) the coefficient of t is significant when C is not included as an explanatory variable but it is not so highly significant when both C and t are present in the equation. This is because of the collinearity between C and t. However, the importance of t is indicated by the equation in the form (3) where the problem of multi-collinearity is not present. Moreover, since the regression coefficient of C in form (1) is not so different from that of ΔC in form (3), where multi-collinearity is not present, we can perhaps accept the regression of form (1) as reasonably accurate. Thus the relevant regression equations are the following:

$$(5.1.2) \qquad M = -59{\cdot}545 + 1{\cdot}466\,C + 1{\cdot}404\,t$$
$$(14{\cdot}260) \quad (0{\cdot}028) \quad (0{\cdot}85)$$
$$\bar{R}^2 = 0{\cdot}995;\ \delta^2/S^2 = 0{\cdot}213$$

$$(5.1.3) \qquad \frac{C}{M}(100) = 85{\cdot}328 - 0{\cdot}3505\,t$$
$$(0{\cdot}64) \quad (0{\cdot}0207)$$
$$\bar{R}^2 = 0{\cdot}8267;\ \delta^2/S^2 = 0{\cdot}4195$$

$$(5.1.4) \qquad \Delta M = 1{\cdot}0612 + 1{\cdot}359\,\Delta C$$
$$(1{\cdot}738) \quad (0{\cdot}053)$$
$$\bar{R}^2 = 0{\cdot}9171;\ \delta^2/S^2 = 1{\cdot}1163$$

As we have argued above, we can accept the equation (5.1.2) as a reasonable estimate. The main defect of this equation seems to be the evidence of auto-correlation shown by the low value of δ^2/S^2. However, in equation (5.1.4), where the auto-correlation is not present, the coefficient of ΔC is very close to the coefficient of C in equation (5.1.2). Thus it could perhaps be argued that in spite of the low value of δ^2/S^2, the regression coefficient of equation (5.1.2) does not appear to be seriously biased. This is of course on the presumption that the two types of equations should give the same result and this presumption may not be quite correct. Therefore we should search for some other variable which may improve the value of δ^2/S^2. But at the moment, we could not find any.

Lastly we test whether the currency itself is dependent on rate of interest and/or the rate of increase of prices. The results show that these factors are not in fact significant in explaining the movements in C. The only variable significantly related with C is the time trend. Thus it seems that we can regard C as an exogenous variable.

On the basis of the considerations above, we select the equation (5.1.2) as the equation showing the supply curve of money. We have:

$$(5.1.5) \qquad M = -59{\cdot}545 + 1{\cdot}466\ C + 1{\cdot}404\ t$$
$$(14{\cdot}260) \quad (0{\cdot}028) \quad (0{\cdot}85)$$
$$\bar{R}^2 = 0{\cdot}995; \ \delta^2/S^2 = 0{\cdot}213$$

5.2: MONEY WAGES AND PRICES

In keeping with most of the discussions of growth in the under-developed countries, we have assumed that the real wage in the non-agricultural sector remains roughly constant at the subsistence level in the early stage of economic growth. This situation is to be contrasted with that in developed economies where the real wage is found to be sensitive to the (marginal) productivity of labour, the degree of unemployment, the organisation of labour and such other factors. In this section we try to see whether this hypothesis is refuted by Indian data on the subject and to discuss the nature of the mechanism by which the changes in the cost of living are translated into the changes in money wages.

Data on money wages and the cost of living index since 1939 have been published by the Labour Bureau, Government of India. These data are, of course, subject to a number of limitations. They relate to only those who earn less than Rs. 200 per month. They refer to the earnings rather than wages. They include the valuation of several 'concessions' or payments in kind which might have been somewhat arbitrary. They have also varied in coverage over time because of partition and non-reporting. However, in spite of these defects, the broad tendency is clear. Over the period 1939–40 to 1960–61 real wages have tended to remain roughly constant with occasional fluctuations. About fluctuations again we note that whenever the rise in the cost of living index has been very rapid, the real wage has tended to fall. This suggests that the adjustment of money wages to the cost of living is not instantaneous but spread over a period. Thus there may be a distributed lag in wage-adjustment and we try this hypothesis in our statistical analysis later on.

It is difficult to get any definite evidence on wage movements before 1939. However, there are some scattered studies relating to particular periods. It was not found possible to build up a time-series by linking them together because of certain gaps in them. However, a review of these studies does give a broad picture and in the absence of anything better, this seems worth attempting.

The period between 1830 and 1860 witnessed the building of

railways, the establishment of tea and coffee plantations and the beginning of certain modern industries. According to D. H. Buchanan (17), there occurred during this period a doubling of wages throughout India. However, these are figures in money terms and since this period also witnessed increase in prices, this does not indicate the real income position of workers. From 1860 to 1895, 'wages were almost stationary with an advance of between five and ten per cent towards the end of this period' (op. cit.).

For the period 1897 to 1912, the data on wages are provided by K. L. Datta (27). The figures of average real wages in industries are as follows:

TABLE 5.1

TRENDS IN INDUSTRIAL REAL WAGE, 1897–1912

Year	*Average Real Wage Index in Industry 1892 = 100*
1897	85
1898	101
1899	107
1900	91
1901	99
1902	108
1903	114
1904	118
1905	109
1906	100
1907	98
1908	91
1909	102
1910	110
1911	110
1912	106

Source: K. L. Datta, *Report on Enquiry into Rises of Prices in India*, Volume III, Calcutta, 1914.

This table shows some fluctuations in real wage index; but on the whole it is difficult to detect any trend in it.

For the period 1914–35, we have tried to build up a rough All-India index from the data given by S. P. Saksena (139). In this paper, Saksena gives for 1914–35 the year by year figures of money wages and the cost of living index for a number of important industrial centres in India. We assume that the industrial centres represent the wage and cost of living indices of the provinces in which they were situated. In the cases where more than one industrial centre is located in any province, we take a simple average of the centres as representing the province. Further, we combine the state indices by the weights of employment in different states. For this purpose, we utilise the figures of average daily number of workers in employment by different industries in different states in 1935 as given in *Statistical Abstract of British India*, 14th issue. The results are shown in Table 5.2.

TABLE 5.2

TRENDS IN MONEY WAGES, COST OF LIVING AND REAL WAGES, 1914–1935

Year	*Index of Money Wages 1909–13 = 100*	*Index of Cost of Living 1909–13 = 100*	*Index of Real Wages 1909–13 = 100*
1914	103	114	90·35
1915	108	121	89·25
1916	112	123	91·05
1917	116	122	95·08
1918	122	136	89·70
1919	138	181	76·24
1920	164	192	85·41
1921	176	191	92·14
1922	178	178	100·00
1923	174	164	106·09
1924	175	165	106·06
1925	176	165	106·66
1926	173	176	98·29
1927	162	176	92·04
1928	163	171	95·32
1929	159	175	90·85
1930	162	154	105·19
1931	147	115	127·82
1932	147	109	134·86
1933	143	112	127·67
1934	139	106	131·13
1935	137	108	126·85

Source: Computed from S. P. Saksena 'Cost of Living Indices and Wages' in *Economic Problems of Modern India*, Vol. II, edited by R. K. Mukherjee and H. L. Dey, Macmillan & Co. Ltd., 1941.

From this table it seems that up to 1930 there is no trend in real wages, though there are some fluctuations. After 1930 there seems to be an upward trend in real wages. But obviously this was due to the falling prices during the Great Depression and it does not indicate any basic trend. It only illustrates our earlier point that changes in prices take a few years to be translated into changes in money wages. There is perhaps also an asymmetry in this respect. The adjustment of money wages in the downward direction is slower than that in the upward direction.

From the rough survey of wage movements it thus seems that on the whole there does not appear to be any significant trend in real wages in India. The hypothesis of constant real wages in the early stage of growth is thus not refuted by the data we have. Next we should try to examine the adjustment mechanism of the money wage response to changes in prices. For this purpose we utilise the figures of money wage and price movements over the period 1939–60. The various forms in which we have tried the relationship between money wages (W_i) and prices (p_c) are the following:

(5.2.1) $$W_i = \alpha + \beta p_c + \gamma t$$

(5.2.2) $$W_i = \alpha + \beta p_{c_{-1}} + \gamma t$$

(5.2.3) $$W_i = \alpha + \beta p_c + \gamma W_{i_{-1}}$$

(5.2.4) $$\log W_i = \alpha + \beta \log p_c + \gamma t$$

(5.2.5) $$W_i - W_{i_{-1}} = \alpha + \beta(p_c - p_{c_{-1}})$$

We tried our regressions for two periods 1939–40 to 1961–62 and 1948–49 to 1960–61 separately for two reasons: in the first place we wanted to maintain the conformity with our general study (which relates mostly to the period 1948–49 to 1960–61) and secondly we utilise the sub-samples as a means of choosing between alternative specifications. From the results we find that the form (5.2.5) gives poor results. The coefficient is not statistically significant and the $\bar{R}^2$ is extremely small in the case of the period 1948–49 to 1960–61. In the period 1939–40 to 1961–62 the coefficient of $(p_c - p_{c_{-1}})$ is statistically significant, but the $\bar{R}^2$ is still very small and the value of the coefficient of $(p_c - p_{c_{-1}})$ is very different from that in the period 1948–49 to 1960–61. The reason may be that the first difference form of the equation gives mainly the short run effect and as noted earlier money wages adjust to prices over a number of years. Similarly we find that in form (5.2.4) the regression coefficient is unstable over the sub-samples. For the period 1939–62, the value of β is $\underset{(0{\cdot}067)}{0{\cdot}607}$ whereas that for the period 1948–60, it is $\underset{(0{\cdot}129)}{0{\cdot}0702}$. The value for the latter period is statistically insignificant and economically implausible. Again the value of δ^2/S^2 is unstable between the two periods and extremely low for the period 1939–40 to 1961–62. Thus it seems that this specification also is not acceptable. On similar grounds form (5.2.1) may also be rejected. Equation (5.2.2) gives reasonably stable results; but the coefficient of $p_{c_{-1}}$ seems too low. In view of the information (obtained from the overall descriptive study above) that the real wage is roughly constant, the coefficient of 0·210 or 0·472 for $p_{c_{-1}}$ seems difficult to accept. The only remaining equation is that in the form of distributed lag hypothesis with Koyck transformation. This form gives a good statistical performance on every count. The coefficients are statistically significant and stable over the sub-samples. The $\bar{R}^2$ is high and so is δ^2/S^2. However, of the two equations relating to the two periods, we prefer the one relating to the former period. This is so on two grounds: in the first place, the results are better for statistical reasons to a certain extent and secondly, because the year 1948–49 was not a normal year in the sense that prices were abnormally high and real wages rather low. Moreover, the first period has a larger number of observations and a bigger sample is likely to give better results. Thus the equation that we finally choose is:

$$W_i = -2{\cdot}5414 + 0{\cdot}2683\, p_c + 0{\cdot}7702\, W_{i_{-1}}$$
$$(9{\cdot}57) \qquad (0{\cdot}0673) \qquad (0{\cdot}0562)$$
$$\bar{R}^2 = 0{\cdot}991;\ \delta^2/S^2 = 1{\cdot}8096$$

We also tried to see if the real wages are connected with the productivity of labour and the degree of unemployment. As indicator of productivity of labour, we took the index of marginal productivity of labour for the non-agricultural sector from the time-series data. The method of computation is explained in Appendix I. We find that the regression coefficient is not significant and the $\bar{R}^2$ and δ^2/S^2 are low. This suggests that productivity increases were not passed on to wage increases in the period under consideration. We could not test the relation between real wage and unemployment because no satisfactory time-series data on unemployment are available. But broadly speaking we know that over the period under study, unemployment increased wihout reducing real wages. This seems to support the idea of a reserve army of labour available at subsistence wages with real wages remaining at that level even when the reserve army or the productivity of labour increase.

5.3: MISCELLANEOUS PRICE EQUATIONS

Lastly, we come to the equations determining prices in the non-agricultural sector, the price of exports and several other types of price relations. As regards the prices of non-agricultural goods, our hypothesis is that they are determined by relations of the form $W_i = p_{im} . \frac{\delta Y_i}{\delta L_i}$ where money wages are already assumed to be determined by the real wage and the price of consumer goods, and the level of employment (L_i) is determined by the availability of the marketed surplus of agriculture. In other words, $p_{im} = W_i / \frac{\delta Y_i}{\delta L_i}$.

So we try the regression of p_{im} on $W_i / \frac{\delta Y_i}{\delta L_i}$. The simple correlation between the two is 0·83 but there is some auto-correlation. Therefore, we try the distributed lag hypothesis with the Koyck transformation. In this case, the values of $\bar{R}^2$ and δ^2/S^2 are reasonably high though the coefficients of $W_i / \frac{\delta Y_i}{\delta L_i}$ and $p_{im_{-1}}$ are not highly significant statistically. However, in the absence of anything better, we accept this equation as a reasonable one:

(5.3.1)
$$p_{im} = \underset{(19{\cdot}498)}{3{\cdot}105} + \underset{(23{\cdot}23)}{25{\cdot}26}\left[W_i / \frac{\delta Y_i}{\delta L_i}\right] + \underset{(0{\cdot}336)}{0{\cdot}7068}\, p_{im_{-1}}$$
$$\bar{R}^2 = 0{\cdot}742;\ \delta^2/S^2 = 1{\cdot}963$$

As regards export prices, one would expect, *a priori*, that they are influenced by internal prices and world demand situation. We regress the export price index on various internal prices—general price level (p), agricultural price index (p_a), manufactured goods price index (p_{im}), etc. However, none of these prices can explain export prices at all satisfactorily. All the statistical criteria —$\bar{R}^2$, δ^2/S^2, F-values of the coefficients—indicate poor results. The main reason for this result seems to be that exportable commodities form a small group of the total of agricultural and manufactured goods and perhaps this group does not always move in unison with the others. Perhaps the world demand situation which did not affect the internal prices so much was the more powerful determinant of the export prices. As indicators of world demand we consider four variables—world exports (X_w), world export prices (p_{xw}), exports of underdeveloped countries (X_{wu}), and price of exports of underdeveloped countries (p_{xu}). The regression equation with internal general price index (p) and price of exports of underdeveloped countries (p_{xu}) gives the best results. So we select this equation:

(5.3.2)
$$p_x = \underset{(54{\cdot}6526)}{-219{\cdot}7205} + \underset{(0{\cdot}4120)}{1{\cdot}2599}\, p + \underset{(0{\cdot}3123)}{1{\cdot}9791}\, p_{xu}$$
$$\bar{R}^2 = 0{\cdot}7935;\ \delta^2/S^2 = 2{\cdot}085$$

In this case, the values of $\bar{R}^2$ and δ^2/S^2 are quite satisfactory. The regression coefficients have the right signs and they are statistically quite significant. The magnitudes of the coefficients may seem a bit too large. Actually, perhaps the result only indicates that the price of exports of Indian goods has been rising faster than the internal general price level in India and the world price of the exports of the underdeveloped countries.

The remaining price equations are mainly statistical approximations. To a certain extent, they are true by definition. For example, the index of consumer prices is by definition a weighted average of food prices and prices of other consumer goods. Similarly, the price index of investment goods is a weighted average of the price of manufactured goods, wages and prices of imported machines. However, not all the prices included in the definition of these indices are included in our model. So we have to take some sort of rough approximation to the prices included in our model. Thus we regress the consumer goods price index on the price of agricultural goods only. The regression coefficient of p_a is statistically significant but the $\bar{R}^2$ and δ^2/S^2 are low. Maybe it is with a lag that agricultural prices influence the prices of food and other wage goods. Therefore, we try a distributed lag hypothesis with Koyck transformation and this gives reasonably satisfactory results.

For the explanations of p_{inv} we obtain reasonably satisfactory results by regressing it on W_i and p_{im}. Lastly, we regress the price index of the non-agricultural sector on p_{im} to tie up the system. The fit in this case is not very good, but in view of the definitional character of the equation and its minor place in our system, we accept this equation. Thus we have:

(5.3.3)
$$p_c = -20{\cdot}7097 + 0{\cdot}37629\, p_a + 0{\cdot}84368\, p_{c_{-1}}$$
$$(16{\cdot}196) \quad (0.1212) \quad (0.1495)$$
$$\bar{R}^2 = 0{\cdot}852; \ \delta^2/S^2 = 1{\cdot}70628$$

(5.3.4)
$$p_{inv.} = -3{\cdot}0835 + 0{\cdot}7858\, p_{im} + 0{\cdot}2354\, W_i$$
$$(5{\cdot}2083) \quad (0{\cdot}0785) \quad (0{\cdot}0314)$$
$$\bar{R}^2 = 0{\cdot}9927; \ \delta^2/S^2 = 2{\cdot}1384$$

(5.3.5)
$$p_i = 73{\cdot}1858 + 0{\cdot}27133\, p_{im}$$
$$(8{\cdot}0036) \quad (0{\cdot}07257)$$
$$\bar{R}^2 = 0{\cdot}5533; \ \delta^2/S^2 = 0{\cdot}8183$$

In connection with these price equations, one point deserves mention. It may seem strange that we do not consider the price of raw materials or the level of indirect taxes in price determination, as is usually done. Actually this is so because we are not considering retail prices or even wholesale prices. The prices in our context are the national income deflators for different sectors. This, in its turn, is necessary for maintaining the national income identity according to which the price multiplied by the real national income is equal to money national income. In a more detailed model where intermediate goods and the Government sector are considered in greater detail, we could include other prices as well. But at our level of aggregation, we have to be satisfied with only a few prices.

CHAPTER 6

Investment and Foreign Trade

In this chapter we consider the statistical estimation of the parameters of the investment functions (Sections 6.1 and 6.2) and the foreign trade equations (Section 6.3).

6.1: INVESTMENT IN THE AGRICULTURAL SECTOR

6.1.1: TIME-SERIES ANALYSIS

Our first hypothesis was that investment depends on current and past trends in disposable agricultural income, the weights of past incomes declining in a geometric series. We tried the hypothesis with investment (I'_a) and income (Y'_{da}) *at current prices* and the agricultural price index. With a Koyck transformation, the estimated equation was:

$$(6.1.1) \qquad I'_a = \underset{(59{\cdot}02)}{70{\cdot}71} + \underset{(0{\cdot}0185)}{0{\cdot}0345}\, Y'_{da} - \underset{(101{\cdot}52)}{161{\cdot}71}\, p_a + \underset{(0{\cdot}2176)}{0{\cdot}525}\, I'_{a_{-1}}$$

$$\bar{R}^2 = 0{\cdot}8746; \; \delta^2/S^2 = 2{\cdot}19$$

where I'_a, Y'_{da} are respectively investment and disposable income in the agricultural sector at current prices.

In this case the over-all fit is reasonably good. The residuals are randomly distributed. The regression coefficients of the main variables, namely income and lagged investment, are statistically significant and economically plausible. The long-term solution of the equation is obtained by putting $I'_a = I'_{a_{-1}} = \ldots = $ a constant. In that case, we have:

$$I'_a(1-0{\cdot}525) = 70{\cdot}71 + 0{\cdot}0345\, Y'_{da} - 161{\cdot}71\, p_a$$

or

$$I'_a = 148{\cdot}86 + 0{\cdot}0726\, Y'_{da} - 340{\cdot}4\, p_a$$

This result seems very similar to that obtained by regressing investment on current disposable income and price without considering any lag. The estimated equation is:

$$(6.1.2) \qquad I'_a = \underset{(70\cdot377)}{109\cdot59} + \underset{(0\cdot011)}{0\cdot0736}\, Y'_{da} - \underset{(94\cdot79)}{322\cdot8765}\, p_a$$
$$\bar{R}^2 = 0\cdot81;\ \delta^2/S^2 = 1\cdot65$$

In this case, the over-all goodness of fit and the von Neumann ratio are not very different from the lagged case whereas the standard errors of the regression coefficients are considerably lower. Thus from the point of view of statistical efficiency, it seems better to work with the unlagged hypothesis as giving the long run investment function. The closeness between the regression coefficients implies that the neglect of the lag hypothesis does not introduce any serious error in the long-run investment function. Moreover, it becomes very difficult to operate with a distributed lag when more than one variable is involved unless we can assume the same lag pattern for all the variables. For these reasons, we decided to drop the lag considerations and work with the unlagged income hypothesis.

Having disposed of the question of lags, we come to the estimation of the investment equation as presented in Chapter 3. Here the investment figures deflated by the investment cost index is a function of disposable income ($p_aY_a - T_a$) in agriculture deflated by the investment cost index ($p_{inv.}$) (denote it by Y_{da}) and the relative prices of agricultural output and investment goods. In addition, we also consider the effect of government developmental expenditure in agriculture. The regression equations thus obtained are:

$$(6.1.3) \qquad I_a = \underset{(102\cdot01)}{39\cdot94} + \underset{(0\cdot023)}{0\cdot0262}\, Y_{da} - \underset{(164\cdot3)}{78\cdot80}\frac{p_a}{p_{inv.}} + \underset{(0\cdot187)}{0\cdot2676}\, G_a$$
$$\bar{R}^2 = 0\cdot789;\ \delta^2/S^2 = 1\cdot891$$

$$(6.1.4) \qquad I_a = \underset{(62\cdot95)}{159\cdot71} + \underset{(0\cdot012)}{0\cdot055}\, Y_{da} - \underset{(57\cdot61)}{300\cdot357}\, \frac{p_a}{p_{inv.}}$$
$$\bar{R}^2 = 0\cdot762;\ \delta^2/S^2 = 1\cdot36$$

Comparing the above two results, we find that the correlation coefficient is slightly higher in the former case but the t-values of the regression coefficients are much lower. Thus though it seems intuitively desirable to include the variable G_a, the statistical results are unsatisfactory. So we choose the latter equation as being more satisfactory. In this equation the marginal propensity to invest (which by our argument is the same as the marginal propensity to save) is 5·5 per cent. At the low level of *per capita* income that characterises the Indian agriculture, this figure does not seem unreasonable. Apparently, the coefficient on the terms of trade may seem unusually large, but actually this might be so because the terms of trade are expressed as ratio and not as percentage. Again, it may seem strange that the terms of trade have a negative coefficient which might imply that an improvement in the terms of trade of agriculture reduces investment in agriculture. Actually, however, we have to take into account the effect of terms of trade on income as well. If terms of trade improve by 1 per cent, the value of Y_{da} also increases by Y_{da} (0·01). In the year 1960–61, the value of Y_{da} was Rs. 6813 crores. Thus the net effect of improvement in terms of trade by 1 per cent is an increase in net investment by

$$\begin{aligned} \Delta I_a &= (0{\cdot}055 \times 6813 \times 0{\cdot}01 - 300{\cdot}357 \times 0{\cdot}01) \text{ (Rs. crores)} \\ &= (3{\cdot}75 - 3{\cdot}00) \text{ (Rs. crores)} \\ &= 0{\cdot}75 \text{ (Rs. crores).} \end{aligned}$$

We have argued in Chapter 3 that demand is not a limiting factor in production and thus the acceleration theory of investment is unlikely to be applicable to the Indian agriculture. Let us now test this hypothesis using net investment at constant prices as the dependent variable and the increase in output at constant prices as the independent variable. We get:

$$(6.1.5) \qquad \begin{aligned} I_a &= \underset{(10{\cdot}95)}{128{\cdot}9875} + \underset{(0{\cdot}043)}{0{\cdot}0217} (Y_a - Y_{a_{-1}}) \\ R &= 0{\cdot}157; \ \delta^2/S^2 = 0{\cdot}275 \end{aligned}$$

Here we find that all the statistical tests, namely F-value of the regression coefficient, the correlation coefficient, and the von Neumann ratio, go against the acceleration hypothesis.

We have also ignored the rate of interest in our investment equation. Intuitively, it seems plausible that credit conditions will exert considerable influence on investment in Indian agriculture. To a certain extent, the influence of credit position is included in our analysis in so far as the supply of funds with the village money lenders is influenced by agricultural income. Beyond that, it was found difficult to obtain any other indicator of credit conditions or rate of interest. The rate of interest in the rural sector is known to be high but there are no figures of year-to-year variations in the rate of interest. To a large extent the rural rate of interest is determined by the degree of monopoly and the risk element in rural credit transactions. Since these factors are unlikely to change from year to year to a significant extent, the interest rate may not change from year to year either and thus we can ignore it in explaining the investment time-series. If the rural rate of interest varies at all, it might be expected to vary in response to the changes in the rate of interest in the organised sector. Therefore, in the absence of any better indicator, we take the yield on 3 per cent bonds (i) as a proxy for the interest rate in the rural sector. Taking income and price as other independent variables, we get:

(6.1.6) $$I_a = -215{\cdot}27 + 0{\cdot}0311\, Y_{da} - 88{\cdot}1\, p_a + 79{\cdot}83\, i$$
$$(92{\cdot}41) \quad (0{\cdot}0146) \quad (93{\cdot}8) \quad (20{\cdot}01)$$
$$\bar{R}^2 = 0{\cdot}9227;\ \delta^2/S^2 = 2{\cdot}093$$

Here we find that the regression coefficient of the rate of interest is quite significant statistically, but its sign is the opposite of the expected. Since it seems difficult to think of any reason why increase in interest can favour investment, we ignore this variable as well.

6.1.2: CROSS-SECTION ANALYSIS

For this purpose, we utilise two sources of data; the Farm Management Studies Report on Bombay for the year 1955–56 and the National Sample Survey Report on the 2nd and the 3rd Round. The Farm Management Report gives figures of gross and net investment per farm for two districts in Bombay, namely, Ahmednagar and Nasik. For each district, there are two types of samples —a cost accounting sample and a survey sample. In order to see whether the two districts and the two techniques give basically the same result, we put all these data together and use dummy variables for both the place and the technique of survey. We use dummy variables for the constant term in the equation only which implies that the slope of the function is assumed to be the same for both the places and the techniques of survey. It is possible to allow for varying slope as well (see, for example, Klein–Ball, *et al.* (92)), but since we are using the dummy variables only to test the homogeneity of the data, no attempt was made to incorporate this sophistication.

The regression of gross investment in income and the dummy variables gives the following result:

(6.1.7) $$GI_a = 7{\cdot}9076 + 0{\cdot}186\, Y_a - 6{\cdot}686\, D_1 - 146{\cdot}67\, D_2$$
$$(74{\cdot}28) \quad (0{\cdot}037) \quad (63{\cdot}95) \quad (62{\cdot}5)$$
$$\bar{R}^2 = 0\ 474;\ \delta^2/S^2 = 1{\cdot}523$$

where GI_a = gross investment
Y_a = income
D_1 = dummy variable for place
and D_2 = dummy variable for technique of survey.

The regression coefficient of the dummy variable for place (D_1) is not significantly different from zero but that for the technique of survey is. This implies that the results of the two techniques of survey are significantly different from each other and we should fit two separate functions to the data yielded by them.

Assuming that the above result applies to net investment as well as gross investment, we fit two different functions to the data from the two sources with respect to gross as well as net investment. The results are:

Cost Accounting Sample

(6.1.8) $$GI_a = 24{\cdot}176 + 0{\cdot}0507\ Y_a$$
$$(38{\cdot}54) \quad (0{\cdot}026)$$
$$\bar{R}^2 = 0{\cdot}15;\ \delta^2/S^2 = 1{\cdot}34$$

(6.1.9) $$NI_a = 44{\cdot}39 - 0{\cdot}042\ Y_a$$
$$(25{\cdot}88)\ (0{\cdot}018)$$
$$\bar{R}^2 = 0{\cdot}236;\ \delta^2/S^2 = 1{\cdot}235$$

Survey Sample

(6.1.10) $$GI_a = -116{\cdot}43 + 0{\cdot}2889\ Y_a$$
$$(73{\cdot}42) \quad (0{\cdot}049)$$
$$\bar{R}^2 = 0{\cdot}6897;\ \delta^2/S^2 = 1{\cdot}7795$$

(6.1.11) $$NI_a = -168{\cdot}21 + 0{\cdot}2678\ Y_a$$
$$(73{\cdot}53) \quad (0{\cdot}049)$$
$$\bar{R}^2 = 0{\cdot}654;\ \delta^2/S^2 = 1{\cdot}95$$

These results, however, do not yield a simple conclusion. The regression coefficient of income is significant in all the cases (except 6.1.8), thus suggesting that income exerts an important influence on private investment in Indian agriculture. This corroborates our time-series finding. However, the values of the regression coefficients of Y_a are widely divergent in the above equations (6.1.8)–(6.1.11), and they do not agree with the time-series coefficient of Y_{da}. As against the marginal propensity to invest of about 5 per cent in time-series, we get here a marginal propensity to net investment of —4 per cent and 27 per cent in the above cases. Some difference in the regression coefficients can of course be expected. For one thing, income in time-series refers to the total agricultural income which includes income of the moneylenders, etc., whereas income in the cross-section refers to farm income only—the effect of borrowing is not included. Secondly, the time-series study includes the effect of government outlays on private investment, whereas the cross-section study does not. But the actual difference between the two types of estimates seems much more than can be rationalised in this way. Because of the instability of the two estimates and because of the sketchiness of the data in the Farm Management Studies, we reject the Farm Management cross-section results without any further attempt at reconciliation. It may, however, be of interest whether the result improves if the problem of heteroscedasticity is resolved by taking weighted least squares estimates.

The second source of data for our cross-section study is provided by the 2nd and 3rd Rounds of the National Sample Survey. The 2nd round related to the period June 1950 to May 1951, and the 3rd round to the period October 1950 to September 1951. The investment figures refer to net investment and include investment in land, houses, wells, tanks, implements, etc. Unfortunately, there are no figures on income in the N.S.S. reports. Only the figures of total expenditure are given. However, it may be assumed that total expenditure is a function of income and we may use total expenditure as a proxy for income. Since in the Indian context, a large proportion of income is likely to be spent, it may not introduce any significant change in the regression coefficient either. Another problem with the N.S.S. data is that they are presented for only a small number of groups and for statistical reasons, it seems necessary to pool together the results of the two rounds. In order to test whether the two rounds are basically similar in this respect, we use a dummy variable (which is 0 for the 3rd round and 1 for the 2nd round). The result of the regression is:

(6.1.12)
$$NI_a = \underset{(27{\cdot}9)}{-7{\cdot}99} + \underset{(0{\cdot}017)}{0{\cdot}028}\,C - \underset{(10{\cdot}59)}{9{\cdot}87}\,D_1$$
$$\bar{R}^2 = 0{\cdot}092;\ \delta^2/S^2 = 2{\cdot}45$$

where C = expenditure
D_1 = dummy variable.

The result indicates that the coefficient of the dummy variable is not significantly different from zero. Thus the pooling together of the two rounds seems justified. Therefore, we carry out the regression without the dummy variable. The result is:

(6.1.13)
$$NI_a = \underset{(27{\cdot}76)}{-8{\cdot}246} + \underset{(0{\cdot}0168)}{0{\cdot}0254}\,C$$
$$\bar{R}^2 = 0{\cdot}1038;\ \delta^2/S^2 = 2{\cdot}39$$

In this case, $\bar{R}^2$ is very small and the regression coefficient is less than twice its standard error. However, the comparison of the value of regression coefficient obtained above with the regression coefficient in the time-series suggests an interesting methodological point. The cross-section estimate does not include the influence of government activity on private investment. Thus the coefficient shows the effect of increases in income alone. In the time-series results, we find that when the government expenditure is taken as a separate variable, the regression coefficient of income comes out to be 0·0262. This is remarkably close to the estimate obtained above. The cross-section result may be helpful in choosing between the competing specifications in the time-series study. Thus if the cross-section result were statistically satisfactory, we could have preferred the specification $I_a = f(Y_{da}, \frac{p_a}{p_{inv.}}, G_a)$ to the equation $I_a = f(Y_{da}, \frac{p_a}{p_{inv.}})$ in time-series study even though on purely time-series results, the latter is superior to the former. However, as the matters stand, the cross-section result above is not statistically satisfactory and therefore it does not provide a basis for selection amongst the time-series specifications.

To summarise, the cross-section results provide qualitative support for our hypothesis about agricultural investment at the micro level, even though the quantitative results are rather different. The regression result that we finally accept is:

$$(6.1.14) \qquad I_a = \underset{(62{\cdot}95)}{159{\cdot}71} + \underset{(0{\cdot}012)}{0{\cdot}055}\, Y_{da} - \underset{(57{\cdot}61)}{300{\cdot}357}\, \frac{p_a}{p_{inv.}}$$

$$\bar{R}^2 = 0{\cdot}762;\ \delta^2/S^2 = 1{\cdot}36$$

6.2: INVESTMENT IN NON-AGRICULTURAL SECTOR

As in the agricultural sector, so in the non-agricultural sector, we rely mainly on the aggregative time-series data for investment, income, profit, etc., for the non-agricultural sector. These data are not available in the ready-made form suitable for our use and we had to process them to a certain extent. Apart from these, we have utilised the time-series data of net investment in certain particular industries (cement, paper, sugar, iron and steel, and cotton) as given in G. Rosen (134). We have also utilised the figures of growth in paid-up capital of joint stock companies as given in *The Progress of Joint-Stock Companies in India* (60). Lastly, apart from these time-series data, we have utilised the cross-section data on investment in public limited companies as given in the *Reserve Bank of India Bulletin*, September 1962 (131).

In connection with the non-agricultural investment function, our first task is to find out the relative importance of the three theories referred to in Chapter 3. In this connection, we have to consider the profit index, the rate of change of output and the rate of interest. As the indicator of profits in the non-agricultural sector, we take the industrial profit index (π), which is constructed from the profits figures of public limited companies in different industries. To test the acceleration principle, we take the rate of change in output in the non-agricultural sector, every year. Lastly, as regards the rate of interest, we take the long-term rate of interest (indicated by the yield on 3 per cent government bonds). Apart from these variables, we have also to consider other relevant factors like government control (GC), and the rate of increase of prices $\left(\frac{\dot{p}}{p}\right)$. The introduction of a government control variable is necessary because the Government has been exerting an important influence on actual investment during this period through its policy of licensing, and sanctioning capital issues. In our analysis the variable (government control) is indicated by the figure of capital issues sanctioned by the controller of capital issues. We also tried the figures of foreign exchange reserves and of the changes in foreign reserves, as explanatory variables indicating the necessity for government control; but poor results were obtained. We also consider the rate of change of prices because this may influence profit expectations and because our investment figures include investment in inventories and this type of investment may be considerably influenced by price expectations—which can be assumed to be roughly indicated by the rate of increase of prices. As for prices, we take the general wholesale price index as the relevant price variable. We experiment with these variables in three forms: without any lag, with a lag of one period and a geometrically declining distributed lag with the Koyck transformation.

The coefficient of $I_{i_{-1}}$ as an explanatory variable in equation for I_i, comes out to be negative in all cases. This suggests alternatively positive and negative weights in a geometrically declining series and this does not seem plausible in our context. Therefore we have to reject the distributed lag hypothesis of Koyck type as being unsuitable for our purposes. We also find that the unlagged values of the variables give better results than the lagged ones. This is indicated by the higher correlation coefficient and F-values of the regression coefficients with unlagged values than with the lagged ones. Therefore, we concentrate on the unlagged values of the variables only.

As regards the three competing hypotheses of the determination of investment, we find the interest rate hypothesis least promising. The simple correlation coefficient of investment with the rate of interest is positive (its value is 0·65). The partial regression coefficient of the interest rate (i) in the equations $I_i = f(\pi, \Delta Y_i, i)$ and $I_i = f(\pi, \Delta Y_i, i, \frac{\dot{p}}{p})$ also turns out to be positive (the opposite of what we should expect on theoretical grounds) and it is also statistically insignificant at a 95 per cent level of significance. So we feel that we can also omit the interest rate as a useful variable in the investment function, when we are considering aggregate investment in non-agricultural sector as a whole. However, as we note below, the interest rate fares better in other cases such as the analysis of paid-up capital figures of the Joint Stock Companies.

The choice between the profit hypothesis and the acceleration hypothesis is difficult. Individually, both seem to perform well. Simple correlation coefficients of profit index and the rate of change of income with respect to the investment are reasonably high (the values are 0·77 and 0·64 respectively; and F-values of the regression coefficients of π and ΔY_i indicate a statistically significant contribution of each of the variables to the explanation of the investment I_i.* However, when both the variables are included in the regression equation, problems arise. F-values of the regression coefficients of both the variables are reduced considerably, though the F-value of π is much better than that of ΔY_i. This would suggest that the profit hypothesis is better than the acceleration hypothesis. However, we also find that the equation $I_i = f(\Delta Y_i, GC)$ gives better results than $I_i = f(\pi, GC)$ and this indicates that the acceleration hypothesis is superior to the profit hypothesis. Thus we find that a clear cut choice between the two hypotheses is not possible on the basis of the aggregative data. We cannot take both the variables, because in that case the regression coefficient of neither variable is significant. Nor is it possible to choose one of these variables because neither is consistently better than the other in all the regressions, though the profit hypothesis is slightly better than the acceleration hypothesis. Thus clearly we must consider some other evidence to be able to make a choice in this respect.

In this connection we consider three types of data: the net investment figures of some selected industries, the paid-up capital figures of joint-stock companies, and the cross-section data on public limited companies. The figures of investment in some selected industries are obtained from G. Rosen (134). We have tried to test the validity of the profit hypothesis, the interest rate hypothesis, the acceleration hypothesis and the Chenery hypothesis. Unfortunately, the results are not very encouraging. Except in the case of the cement industry, none of the variables considered explain investment at all satisfactorily. The value of $\bar{R}^2$ is generally low, though the von Neumann ratio is satisfactory in most of the cases. However, it is interesting to note that the acceleration principle in general gives better results than the profit hypothesis. We also note that Chenery hypothesis gives better results than the acceleration principle in the form presented by Chenery. The contrast between the aggregate and industry-wise data suggests an interesting hypothesis. Generally it is supposed that either of these principles should be valid both at the aggregate and at the industry level. However as our results suggest, both these hypotheses might be valid at different levels. It is possible that profit level determines aggregate investment whereas the distribution of this total amongst industries is guided by technological factors underlying the acceleration principle. The shifting of funds from one industry to another is quite possible when the same financial group controls several industries, as was the case with Managing Agencies in India. Another interesting point is that the interest rate

* It is interesting to note that Chenery hypothesis (20) fares worse than the simple acceleration hypothesis.

has generally the expected negative sign and the t-values of its coefficients are above 3 in the case of cement industry and between 1 and 2 in the case of other industries. However, it is difficult to see how this result at the industry level can be reconciled with the result at the aggregative level, where the rate of interest comes out with a positive coefficient. While considering these reconciliations it is important to note that the samples in the two cases relate to two different periods and the remarks on reconciliation are applicable only on the assumption that there has been no change in the basic structure during the two periods.

Next, we analyse the figures of paid-up capital of joint stock companies. We experiment with the following variables: (1) profit index of the industrial sector; (2) increase in output of the industrial sector; and (3) the yield on 3 per cent bonds. We also try the distributed lag hypothesis with a Koyck transformation. The fit, in general, is rather poor. The coefficient of profit (π) comes out to be negative. The coefficient of the rate of increase of output (ΔO) is positive but again not significant at the 95 per cent level. The interest rate performs well. The lag coefficient is also statistically significant and meaningful. The *relative* efficiency of the interest rate rather than profit or change in output is an interesting finding. We suggest the following line of reconciliation with our earlier findings. Increase in the paid-up capital of companies is primarily a financial phenomenon and the issue of new shares and their acceptance by the public are very much influenced by conditions in financial market represented by the rate of interest. Thus from the analysis of our results we come to the following conclusion about investment behaviour. The physical investment at the aggregate level depends primarily on the total profit situation in the economy; the distribution of this total among individual industries depends primarily on the acceleration principle; and the issue of equities and their acceptance depend primarily on the financial situation represented by the rate of interest.

Lastly we analyse the cross-section investment figures of Public Limited Companies for the year 1959 presented in the *Reserve Bank of India Bulletin*, September 1962. Here we analyse the investment in four forms: (*a*) gross fixed investment, (*b*) total net investment, (*c*) percentage increase in gross fixed capital, (*d*) percentage increase in total assets. The first two are taken to see if the behaviour of fixed and inventory investment is significantly different. The later two are taken in order to eliminate the heteroscedasticity introduced in the cross-section data because of the variance in the size of the companies in different industries. As explanatory variables, we take profits and sales. Interest rate is assumed to be the same for the different industries in the cross-section and is thus omitted. As regards profits, again we take the figures for the current year as well as the previous year. Moreover in explanation of gross investment, we take the figures of profits retained plus depreciation allowances; in the explanation of total net investment, the figures of profits retained only, and in the case of the percentage increase of capital, the figures of profits after tax as percentages of net worth. As regards sales, we take the increase in sales in the current year and two previous years. Here again, when we consider the percentage increase in assets, we take the increase in sales as a percentage of total sales in 1956.

The results of this cross-section analysis are not very satisfactory especially in the cases where the scale effect is eliminated. In the cases where the scale effect is not eliminated, the profit hypothesis on the whole performs better and it is the current profit rather than the previous year's profit that is more significant. In the cases where the scale effect is eliminated neither hypothesis gives a satisfactory result. Thus it seems that these data do not help in our study of investment.

On the basis of the above discussion, we would choose the profit index as an explanatory variable in our investment equation. Apart from the slight statistical superiority of the profit hypothesis, it is also intuitively more plausible. In a newly developing economy, where supply constraints are more important than the demand constraint, the profit hypothesis, emphasising the importance of the supply of investible funds, may be more relevant for the determination of investment than the acceleration hypothesis which concentrates attention on the demand side only. However, one statistical difficulty is presented from the point of view of determination of profit within the system. The profit index that we have been using so far is the industrial profit index and as such it refers only to a part of the non-agricultural sector as a whole. It was not found possible to determine the profit index from within our system. Nor is there any other index available for the profits of the non-agricultural sector as a whole. Therefore as an alternative indicator of saving potentiality and the supply of investible funds, we consider the disposable income of the non-agricultural sector. Subtracting taxation from the value of income in the non-agricultural sector and dividing through by the investment price index, we have $\frac{p_1Y_1-T_1}{p_{inv.}}$ as the relevant variable. This variable gives a reasonably good fit in the investment equation.

Next we consider the importance of the rate of change of prices in our investment equation. As we have already noted our investment figures include investment in inventories and because of the suspected importance of the speculative element in commodity hoarding, we should consider the impact of price changes on investment. We take the general national income deflator as an indicator of the overall price situation. The rate of change of this price index is taken as a determinant of price expectations. This variable has a statistically significant coefficient and the plausible positive sign. This indicates that when the rate of increase of prices increases, investment also increases perhaps because of speculative investment in commodities and because of high profit expectations. This hypothesis is further confirmed from the rough figures of inventory investment available from the C.S.O. publication *Estimates of Gross Capital Formation in India* (51). Here, using inventory investment as the dependent variable, we find that the regression coefficient of the rate of change of price is statistically significant. However, in view of the sketchiness of the data in this respect, we do not disaggregate our investment analysis any further and concentrate on the total investment figures only.

Lastly, we consider the influence of government control (GC) on private investment in the non-agricultural sector. To begin with, we consider this variable as one of the explanatory variables of investment in a straightforward regression equation. The results in this case are not very encouraging. The simple correlation between I_i and GC is 0·53. The sign of the correlation coefficient is as expected but the value is rather low. Nor are the F-values of the regression coefficients to be considered at all satisfactory. The regression coefficient of GC is only around 2–3 and this seems to limit implausibly the scope of government control. Therefore we try another variant of the equation. Assuming that GC indicates the influence of government on total non-agricultural investment we can say that realised investment is a product of investment demand (I_i^d) and the proportion of this demand permitted by the Government to fructify (GC). Thus, we have $I_i = GC.I_i^d$. In this case the relevant variable to be explained is investment demand, $\frac{I_i}{GC}$. Here again, we find that the distributed lag hypothesis with Koyck transformation does not improve the results. Unlagged values of $\frac{p_iY_i - T_i}{p_{inv.}}$ and $\frac{\dot{p}}{p}.100$ give a reasonably good fit, though $\bar{R}^2$ is less than that in the equation

$$I_i = f\left(\frac{p_iY_i - T_i}{p_{inv.}}, \frac{\dot{p}}{p}100, GC\right).$$

This, of course, is not a fair comparison. For this purpose, we must transform the variable $\frac{I_i}{GC}$ to the original form of I_i. However, in this transformed equation, there arises a problem of definition of R^2

In this form, the residuals do not sum up to zero and the total variance cannot be partitioned between the explained variance and the residual variance. If we take the ratio of the variance of the predicted values to the variance of the original values as an approximation to R^2 in this case we find that the explanatory power of the transformed equation is not very much reduced. Even better results are obtained from the equation of the form:

$$(6.2.1) \qquad I_i = GC\left(\alpha + \beta\frac{p_iY_i - T_i}{p_{inv.}} + \gamma\frac{\dot{p}}{p}.100\right)$$

$$= \alpha GC + \beta\frac{p_iY_i - T_i}{p_{inv.}}GC + \gamma\frac{\dot{p}}{p}.100.GC$$

In this case, we obtain the regression of I_i on GC, $\frac{p_iY_i - T_i}{p_{inv.}}GC$ and $\frac{\dot{p}}{p}100.GC$ suppressing the constant term. However, we find that the sum of residuals in this case is nearer to zero than in the previous case. The values of R^2 as defined by the ratio of the predicted variance to total variance is higher in this case than in the other, and the regression coefficients are quite satisfactory statistically. Thus we select this form as the best equation for the explanation of investment in the non-agricultural sector. We have:

$$(6.2.2) \qquad I_i = \frac{GC}{100}\left[\underset{(525{\cdot}77)}{-1219{\cdot}723} + \underset{(0{\cdot}1105)}{0{\cdot}3633}\frac{p_iY_i - T_i}{p_{inv.}} + \underset{(9{\cdot}143)}{20{\cdot}0242}\frac{\dot{p}}{p}100\right]$$

$$\delta^2/S^2 = 2{\cdot}8533$$

$\bar{R}^2 = 0{\cdot}7751$ when the R^2 is defined as the ratio of predicted variance to total variance, and $\bar{R}^2 = 0{\cdot}9357$ when R^2 is defined as the ratio of the sum of squares of predicted values to that of the actual values.

6.3: FOREIGN TRADE SECTOR

A number of attempts has already been made to obtain the foreign trade elasticities for India. J. J. Polak (119) obtained these elasticities from the Indian data of the period 1923–39. V. N. Murti and V. K. Sastry (109) estimated the elasticities of demand for certain Indian imports and exports from the data relating to the period 1927–37. N. V. A. Narasimham in his planning model for India (112) estimated the import function of India from the data for the period 1923–38. H. Banerji (7) analysed the import demand of India for the inter-war period 1920–39. More recently, M. Dutta (32, 33) has analysed the import and export functions of India from the data for the period 1950–60. He has also analysed the import structure of India over the period 1900–46 (34). Some estimates of price elasticities in exports of certain commodities from India have also been made by B. Cohen (23). Most of these studies, however, differ from ours in respect of the time period covered and/or the level of aggregation used. Thus while noting their results in our discussions, we could not take any of these estimates straight away.

6.3.1: EXPORT FUNCTION

In theoretical discussions, as well as statistical estimates, two explanatory variables are generally used for exports: (*a*) the level of economic activity in the rest of the world; and (*b*) relative prices. In our discussion also, we consider these variables. Various authors have used various indicators of the level of economic activity of the rest of the world. Polak worked with an index of world trade. Murti and Sastry used an index of world income while Dutta has used 'world industrial output'. In our investigations we have preferred to use the index of world income as the best indicator of economic activity. Dutt's argument that most Indian exports are 'used to feed industrial output of the world', does not seem entirely convincing in view of Table 6.1 given below.

TABLE 6.1

PERCENTAGE DISTRIBUTION OF INDIAN EXPORTS, 1962–63

Principal Exports	*Per cent*
1. Jute manufactures	22·2
2. Tea	18·8
3. Cotton manufactures	6·8
4. Oil cakes	4·6
5. Leather and leather manufactures	3·3
6. Iron ore and concentrates	2·9
7. Cashew kernel	2·8
8. Tobacco	2·8
9. Cotton (raw)	2·5
10. Spices	2·0
11. Hides and skins (undressed)	1·6
12. Mica	1·5
13. Manganese ore	1·2
14. Wool (raw including wool tops)	1·0
15. Others	26·0
	100·0

Source: *India: Pocket Book of Economic Information*, Government of India, 1963.

From the above table it is obvious that a considerable part of exports consists of consumer goods (tea, cashew kernels, spices, cotton manufactures, etc.) and it seems better to take the income variable which of course includes industrial output as well. Similarly, it seems to us that world trade is a derived figure and explaining Indian exports by world exports is only explaining the part by the whole. The income variable is more basic than the trade variable and the world income elasticity of exports ties up better with the Engel elasticities than does the world trade elasticity of exports. For these reasons, we used the variable Y_w, which stands as a world income index at constant factor cost.

Another variable of theoretical importance is the terms of trade. In this connection, Dutta (32) has used a variable constructed on the basis of ratios between the wholesale price index of the particular area to which Indian goods are exported and the export price index of India. Cohen used the ratio of the Indian prices and the prices of India's chief competitors in particular commodities. Further, in his explanation of exports of tea, Dutta (33) has used the prices of tea from Ceylon, the price of substitute product coffee, as well as the price of Indian tea. Our analysis is at a fairly aggregative level and we have not been able to consider the prices of competing products and competing countries in any detail. At an aggregative level, we tried three definitions of relative prices: (*a*) terms of trade of India which is obtained by dividing the price index of Indian exports by the price index of Indian imports $\frac{p_x}{p_m}$; (*b*) the ratio of the price index of Indian exports and the price index of world exports $\frac{p_x}{p_{xw}}$; and (*c*) the ratio of the price index of Indian exports and the export price index of the underdeveloped countries $\frac{p_x}{p_{xu}}$, which may be regarded as India's competitors in the world market. All the variants of relative prices have the right sign (negative) in the regression equations but the values are not very highly significant statistically (t-values are all less than 3). However, on *a priori* grounds, it seems that the terms of trade should not be very important in the Indian context, where there is very little substitution between exported and imported commodities. Moreover, the prices of competitors are likely to be more significant in India's case than those of the world as a whole. Therefore we select $\frac{p_x}{p_{xu}}$ as the indicator of the price effect in our export equation.

Apart from these variables, it might have been desirable to consider some variable indicating the domestic retention of exportables. It is sometimes argued that as industrialisation proceeds, more and more exportables will be used domestically and less and less will be left for exports. Actually, however, there seems no reason to believe that exports should be regarded as residuals, after domestic demand has been met. It seems more appropriate to assume that both domestic and foreign demand impinge simultaneously on the supply of exportables. Thus the line of causation through which home demand should make itself felt is through bidding up prices and this effect has already been taken into account when we considered the price variable.

In view of the considerations above, we choose the following equation for exports:

$$(6.3.1) \qquad \underset{}{X} = \underset{(146{\cdot}7855)}{575{\cdot}3957} + \underset{(0{\cdot}8764)}{2{\cdot}0848}\, Y_w - \underset{(115{\cdot}4744)}{208{\cdot}5028}\, \frac{p_x}{p_{xu}}$$

$$\bar{R}^2 = 0{\cdot}3476; \; \delta^2/S^2 = 2{\cdot}2753$$

The coefficient of correlation in the above equation is low. But in fact the variation in exports over this period has been so small that it is difficult to expect high correlation. However, the t-value of the income coefficient is quite satisfactory (more than 2) though that of the price variable is only 1·8. The value of δ^2/S^2 is quite good indicating the randomness of the residuals.

The above equation yields an elasticity of demand for Indian exports with respect to world income (taken at the mean of the sample, $e_{Yw} = \frac{dX}{d_{Yw}} \cdot \frac{\bar{Y}_w}{\bar{X}}$) of 0·3513. This is as expected because India's exports consist mostly of primary goods for which the income elasticity is likely to be low according to Engel's law. The values of the elasticity obtained by Murti and Sastry (e = 1·12) and by Dutta (32) (e = 2·66) do seem too high and no convincing explanation has been given by them. Polak's estimate of an export elasticity with respect to world trade (e = 0·45) seems more plausible and is closer to our estimate. The price elasticity at the mean of the sample

$$e_p = \frac{d(X)}{d\left(\frac{p_x}{p_{xu}}\right)} \cdot \frac{\left(\frac{p_x}{p_{xu}}\right)}{\bar{X}}$$

as given by our equation is —0·4417. This compares with the price elasticity of —0·78 obtained by Murti and Sastry. The price elasticity yielded by our equation is rather low but not unexpected in view of the nature of Indian exports. Our estimates support the general belief that Indian exports are inelastic with respect to world income as well as the relative price of India and her competitors. The estimate of price elasticity suggests that a unilateral devaluation by India will not increase her export earnings.

6.3.2: IMPORT FUNCTION

Traditionally domestic income and terms of trade are the two important variables in the explanation of imports. For domestic income various authors have used various indices. Narasimham used disposable income in current rupees, Murti and Sastry used an index of industrial activity, Dutta used an index of industrial output. In his more detailed study, Dutta (32) uses exports, and indices of industrial activity as explanatory variables. As regards relative prices, Narasimham ignores them 'because of the predominance in imports of consumer durables and investment goods which cannot be produced at home' (op. cit.). Murti and Sastry considered a price variable and reported an insignificant coefficient and price elasticity of (—0·38). Dutta (32) constructed a variable taking the ratios of the Indian domestic wholesale price index and the import price index but found the coefficient of this variable to be insignificant. For an earlier period 1900–1946, however, Dutta (34) found a significant coefficient on the relative price variable in the case of total imports and the imports of intermediate goods. Apart from these it may be necessary in the Indian context, to consider a government control variable finding its expression in investment programmes and import licence policies. We may also consider a time trend to find out if there is any tendency towards effective import substitution as the Indian economy grows.

We begin with the consideration of government control. Intuitively, it seems that actual imports in India are determined not by the propensity to import but by the capacity to import which is determined by the foreign exchange position. However, while accepting the importance of this factor it is difficult to find a variable which can take this effect into account at all satisfactorily. Historically, India had a large foreign exchange reserve at the beginning of our sample period and it has been dwindling as the economy has been industrialising. However, the volume of imports has been rising over time, and in this respect promises of aid and loans might be as helpful as the actual foreign reserves. Thus if we take a regression of imports on foreign reserves we find a negative correlation—imports have been rising as reserves have been falling. Thus, as a functional relationship it will imply that when foreign exchange reserves fall, imports rise as a result, and this does not seem plausible. Nor is the situation improved if we take the decline in foreign reserves with or without a lag as the explanatory variable. One way may be to take exports as the explanatory variable. But this does not seem plausible *a priori*. In the first place, over the period exports have been roughly stagnant and imports have been rising mainly through drawing down the sterling balances and foreign loans and aid. Therefore, so far as the movement of imports over the sample is considered, it cannot be explained by exports. Secondly, if exports are a source of foreign exchange, it is better to include them in a foreign exchange constraint equation rather than as an explanatory variable for imports. In our case, we got a coefficient of exports equal to 3·0426, meaning that if exports increase by one unit, imports increase by 3·0426 and this seems hardly plausible. Therefore, while recognising the importance of the foreign exchange situation in determining actual imports, we have to think of other ways of introducing it. We therefore introduce another equation giving the foreign exchange constraint which determines the import capacity of the country.

Apart from the foreign exchange constraint, we consider income and investment as determining import requirements. Regressing imports on income as well as investment in the non-agricultural sector* we find that the coefficients are not meaningful. The coefficient of income comes out to be negative. This seems due to multi-collinearity. Fortunately some data on the imports of capital goods and consumer goods and raw materials are separately available and we make use of this additional information to bypass the problem of multi-collinearity. As regards the imports of capital goods we find that the coefficient of investment is statistically significant and economically meaningful. Taking the time trend we find that over the sample period at least there has been no significant import substitution so far as capital goods are concerned. However, there is an element of collinearity between $(I_i + G_i)$ and t and it is possible that this has vitiated the estimate of the time coefficient. In order to overcome this problem, we take the import of capital goods as a ratio of total investment and regress it on t. However, even in this modified form, the coefficient of t comes out to be positive and statistically insignificant. Thus we take the import of capital goods as dependent on total investment in the non-agricultural sector. We did not consider the price variable because most of the capital goods are not substitutable with home goods and as such the importance of price is likely to be negligible.

Next we consider the imports of raw materials and consumption goods. We exclude from these figures the import of food-grains, because these are in the nature of an exogenous variable depending

* We consider only non-agricultural investment because import content of agricultural investment is small.

on climate and foreign aid available. Some other imports not specified are also excluded. As explanatory variables of import of consumer goods (M_c) we consider three variables: (1) income in the non-agricultural sector (Y_i) at 48–49 prices; (2) the relative price of imports and domestic manufactures $\left(\frac{p_m}{p_{im}}\right)$; and (3) a time trend. The results show that the relative price variable does not have a significant coefficient and it comes out with the 'wrong' sign. The income variable and the time trend are correlated. So their simultaneous presence leads to rather large standard errors. Therefore, we try the variable $\frac{M_c}{Y_i}$ which indicates the average propensity to import with respect to non-agricultural income. Here again we find that the price effect is not important; the time trend comes out with the right sign and a statistically significant coefficient. Thus we find that there seems to be a tendency towards import substitution so far as consumer goods are concerned. Thus our equations are:

(6.3.2)
$$M_k = \underset{(41{\cdot}771)}{59{\cdot}9567} + \underset{(0{\cdot}0535)}{0{\cdot}2778}\,(I_i + G_i)$$
$$\bar{R}^2 = 0{\cdot}6840; \; \delta^2/S^2 = 1{\cdot}7515$$

(6.3.3)
$$\frac{M_c}{Y_i} = \underset{(0{\cdot}00315)}{0{\cdot}05523} - \underset{(0{\cdot}000445)}{0{\cdot}00227}\,t$$
$$\bar{R}^2 = 0{\cdot}6758; \; \delta^2/S^2 = 2{\cdot}4966$$

6.3.3: THE FOREIGN SECTOR AS A WHOLE

In the above two sub-sections we have considered the export and import functions. In considering imports we have omitted the determinants of the imports of food-grains and miscellaneous imports. We have argued that the imports of food-grains are exogenous for two reasons: they depend on the domestic climate and they depend on the availability of foreign aid for food-grains imports. Both of these variables are exogenous to our system. Thus we have:

(6.3.4)
$$MT = M_k + M_c + M_o$$

where MT = the total imports at constant prices
M_o = the imports of food-grains and other unspecified goods at constant prices.

Lastly we have to consider the foreign exchange constraint on imports. According to this constraint the value of imports cannot exceed the value of exports by more than the inflow of capital (FC). In our definition of FC, we include not only actual foreign investment but such other items as invisibles, errors, and omissions, etc. (for details see Appendix I). This foreign exchange constraint is defined by the equation:

(6.3.5) $$p_m M = p_x . X + FC$$

The sub-system of equations given by equations (6.3.1) to (6.3.5) determines the five variables: X, $I_i + G_i$, MT, M_c and M_k, while the rest of the variables in this sub-system are either predetermined in other sub-systems or are exogenous variables to the system as a whole.

CHAPTER 7

Summary of the Results

In the preceding three chapters we have considered separately the statistical estimates of the various equations in our model. In the course of this discussion we have utilised subjective judgment as well as objective statistical criteria to choose particular specifications as better than others. In this chapter we pool the chosen equations (Section 7.1) and consider their statistical performance in comparison with other similar models (Section 7.2). We also consider the results of applying simultaneous equation methods to two sub-systems in our model (Section 7.3).

7.1: THE MODEL

The estimated form of our model is as follows:

(7.1.1) $$\log Y_a = \underset{(0{\cdot}575)}{2{\cdot}9142} + \underset{(0{\cdot}0785)}{0{\cdot}6543} \log K_a - \underset{(0{\cdot}0228)}{0{\cdot}0347} \log R_2$$
$$\bar{R}^2 = 0{\cdot}7204;\ \delta^2/S^2 = 1{\cdot}8622$$

(7.1.2) $$F_a = \underset{(675{\cdot}611)}{-3836{\cdot}183} + \underset{(0{\cdot}1360)}{2{\cdot}0699}\, Y_a$$
$$\bar{R}^2 = 0{\cdot}951;\ \delta^2/S^2 = 1{\cdot}175$$

(7.1.3) $$L_i = \underset{(279{\cdot}154)}{1803{\cdot}044} + \underset{(0{\cdot}0392)}{0{\cdot}3347}\, F_a + \underset{(0{\cdot}3044)}{1{\cdot}1844}\, (M-X)_a$$
$$\bar{R}^2 = 0{\cdot}8697;\ \delta^2/S^2 = 2{\cdot}3674$$

(7.1.4) $$\log Y_i = -0{\cdot}4407 + \underset{(0{\cdot}0734)}{0{\cdot}5599} \log K_i + \underset{(0{\cdot}0628)}{0{\cdot}4401} \log L_i$$
$$\bar{R}^2 = 0{\cdot}8675;\ \delta^2/S^2 = 0{\cdot}7095$$

(7.1.5) $$Y = Y_a + Y_i$$

(7.1.6) $$M = \underset{(14{\cdot}260)}{-59{\cdot}545} + \underset{(0{\cdot}028)}{1{\cdot}466}\, C + \underset{(0{\cdot}850)}{1{\cdot}404}\, (t+48)$$
$$\bar{R}^2 = 0{\cdot}995;\ \delta^2/S^2 = 0{\cdot}213$$

(7.1.7) $$(pY) = \underset{(60{\cdot}35)}{115{\cdot}3565} + \underset{(0{\cdot}213)}{1{\cdot}14997}\, M + \underset{(0{\cdot}0478)}{0{\cdot}8005}\, (pY)_{-1}$$
$$\bar{R}^2 = 0{\cdot}992;\ \delta^2/S^2 = 2{\cdot}1472$$

(7.1.8) $$p = p_a \frac{Y_a}{Y} + p_i \frac{Y_i}{Y}$$

(7.1.9) $$p_c = \underset{(16{\cdot}196)}{-20{\cdot}7097} + \underset{(0{\cdot}1212)}{0{\cdot}3763}\ p_a + \underset{(0{\cdot}1490)}{0{\cdot}8437}\ p_{c_{-1}}$$
$$\bar{R}^2 = 0{\cdot}852;\ \delta^2/S^2 = 1{\cdot}7063$$

(7.1.10) $$p_i = \underset{(8{\cdot}0036)}{73{\cdot}1858} + \underset{(0{\cdot}0726)}{0{\cdot}2713}\ p_{im}$$
$$\bar{R}^2 = 0{\cdot}5413;\ \delta^2/S^2 = 0{\cdot}8183$$

(7.1.11) $$p_{im} = \underset{(19{\cdot}448)}{3{\cdot}105} + \underset{(23{\cdot}23)}{25{\cdot}26}\ \frac{W_i}{\frac{\delta Y_i}{\delta L_i}} + \underset{(0{\cdot}3360)}{0{\cdot}7068}\ p_{im_{-1}}$$
$$\bar{R}^2 = 0{\cdot}742;\ \delta^2/S^2 = 1{\cdot}963$$

(7.1.12) $$p_{inv.} = \underset{(5{\cdot}2083)}{-3{\cdot}0835} + \underset{(0{\cdot}0785)}{0{\cdot}7858}\ p_{im} + \underset{(0{\cdot}0314)}{0{\cdot}2354}\ W_i$$
$$\bar{R}^2 = 0{\cdot}9927;\ \delta^2/S^2 = 2{\cdot}1384$$

(7.1.13) $$W_i = \underset{(3{\cdot}16)}{-0{\cdot}829} + \underset{(0{\cdot}080)}{0{\cdot}318}\ p_c + \underset{(0{\cdot}0565)}{0{\cdot}7697}\ W_{i_{-1}}$$
$$\bar{R}^2 = 0{\cdot}990;\ \delta^2/S^2 = 1{\cdot}814$$

(7.1.14) $$I_a = \underset{(62{\cdot}95)}{159{\cdot}71} + \underset{(0{\cdot}012)}{0{\cdot}055}\ \frac{p_a Y_a - T_a}{p_{inv.}} - \underset{(57{\cdot}61)}{300{\cdot}357}\ \frac{p_a}{p_{inv.}}$$
$$\bar{R}^2 = 0{\cdot}762;\ \delta^2/S^2 = 1{\cdot}360$$

(7.1.15) $$I_i = \frac{GC}{100}\left[\underset{(525{\cdot}77)}{-1219{\cdot}723} + \underset{(0{\cdot}1105)}{0{\cdot}3633}\ \frac{p_i Y_i - T_i}{p_{inv.}} + \underset{(9{\cdot}143)}{20{\cdot}9242}\ \frac{\dot{p}}{p}100\right]$$
$$\bar{R}^2 = 0{\cdot}7751;\ \delta^2/S^2 = 2{\cdot}8533$$

(7.1.16) $$p_x = \underset{(54{\cdot}6526)}{-219{\cdot}7205} + \underset{(0{\cdot}4120)}{1{\cdot}2599}\ p + \underset{(0{\cdot}3123)}{1{\cdot}9791}\ p_{xu}$$
$$\bar{R}^2 = 0{\cdot}7935;\ \delta^2/S^2 = 2{\cdot}085$$

(7.1.17) $$X = \underset{(146{\cdot}7855)}{575{\cdot}3957} + \underset{(0{\cdot}8764)}{2{\cdot}0848}\ (Y_w) - \underset{(115{\cdot}4744)}{208{\cdot}5028}\ \frac{p_x}{p_{xu}}$$
$$\bar{R}^2 = 0{\cdot}3476;\ \delta^2/S^2 = 2{\cdot}2753$$

(7.1.18) $$p_m(MT) - p_x.X = FC$$

(7.1.19) $$M_k = \underset{(41{\cdot}771)}{59{\cdot}9567} + \underset{(0{\cdot}0535)}{0{\cdot}2778}\ (I_i + G_i)$$
$$\bar{R}^2 = 0{\cdot}6840;\ \delta^2/S^2 = 1{\cdot}7515$$

(7.1.20) $\dfrac{M_c}{Y_i} = 0{\cdot}05523 - 0{\cdot}00227\, t$
$(0{\cdot}00315)\ (0{\cdot}000445)$
$\bar{R}^2 = 0{\cdot}6758;\ \delta^2/S^2 = 2{\cdot}4966$

(7.1.21) $MT = M_k + M_c + M_o$

(7.1.22) $G_i = (I_i + G_i) - I_i$

(7.1.23) $K_a = \dfrac{K_a{}^{\circ} + K_a{}^{\circ} + G_a + I_a}{2}$

(7.1.24) $K_i = \dfrac{K_i{}^{\circ} + K_i{}^{\circ} + G_i + I_i}{2}$

The meaning of the symbols in the above equations has already been explained in Chapter 3. The figures in the brackets indicate as usual the standard errors of the coefficients. The system consists of 24 equations, of which 17 are real equations and 7 definitions, constraints or identities.

7.2: THE TEST STATISTICS

One indicator of the adequacy of the model is provided by the standard test statistics, namely, R, δ^2/S^2 and t-values of the estimated parameters. We cannot always rely on these tests mechanically and we have to take into account various subsidiary statistical and economic considerations in choosing particular equations. Thus, on several occasions, we have accepted a particular equation on *a priori* grounds even when its statistical results were not very good. This applies particularly to some price equations, which we have introduced to close the system. Similarly, we accepted the money supply equation even though the value of δ^2/S^2 was unduly low when we found that the parameters of the equations are not significantly altered even when we obtain them by taking the first differences of the variables (where the problem of auto-correlation is not present). However, in spite of these qualifications, a summary of the test statistics* will provide a rough indicator of the goodness of the model, in comparison with similar other models. In particular, we compare our results with those of four other models—(i) the Narasimham model for India (112), (ii) the Klein–Shinkai model for Japan (93), (iii) the Klein–Goldberger model for the U.S. (91), and (iv) the Klein–Ball–Hazlewood–Vandome model for the U.K. (92). These models, of course, differ in the methods of estimation, in the size of the sample, in the size of the system and in the nature of the data. However, a comparison of test statistics will provide at least a rough indicator of the comparative efficiency of our model.

* The idea of this type of summary was taken from J. Johnston (78).

We begin with a consideration of the standard errors of the parameters. This is a very important statistic of the model and it has been provided by all the models under consideration. We take the t-values of the coefficients of variables (omitting those of the constant terms in the equation) and arrange them in four groups. The results are given in Table 7.1.

TABLE 7.1

t-VALUES OF THE REGRESSION COEFFICIENTS IN VARIOUS MODELS

	t-values in the range				
	Below 1	*1–1·99*	*2–2·99*	*3–*	*Total*
1. Our model:					
(*a*) Number of coefficients	0	4	3	23	30
(*b*) %	(0)	(13·3)	(10·0)	(76·7)	(100·0)
2. Narasimham Model (India):					
(*a*) Number of coefficients	0	1	2	17	20
(*b*) %	(0)	(5·0)	(10·0)	(85·0)	(100·0)
3. Klein–Shinkai Model (Japan):					
(*a*) Number of coefficients	0	3	10	22	35
(*b*) %	(0)	(8·6)	(28·6)	(62·9)	(100·0)
4. Klein–Goldberger Model (U.S.):					
(*a*) Number of coefficients	2	11	6	17	36
(*b*) %	(5·6)	(30·6)	(16·7)	(47·2)	(100·0)
5. Klein–Ball *et al.* Model (U.K.):					
(*a*) Number of coefficients	41	30	20	72	163
(*b*) %	(25·2)	(18·4)	(12·3)	(44·2)	(100·0)

From the above table it is obvious that the comparative performance of our model in terms of t-values of the coefficients is quite good. In fact our model fares better than most others except the Narasimham model (which, however, fares much worse in other respects).

Next we consider the values of the von Neumann ratio. Using the table given in Ezekiel and Fox (37), we find out the number of equations in which the hypothesis of zero auto-correlation of residuals is accepted or rejected in various models. The results are given in Table 7.2.

Here again we find that our model fares quite well in comparison with others. In particular, we note that Narasimham model which fared better than our model in respect of t-values fares much worse in this respect.

Lastly we consider the values of the coefficient of multiple correlation. This is, of course, a rather weak test and the Klein–Goldberger model does not give this statistic at all. There is also a problem of

TABLE 7.2

THE EVIDENCE OF AUTO-CORRELATION OF RESIDUALS IN VARIOUS MODELS

	The hypothesis of zero auto-correlation of residuals is accepted at 5% *level of significance*	1% *level of significance*	*The hypothesis rejected at either level*	*Total*
1. Our Model:				
(*a*) Number of equations	13	1	3	17
(*b*) %	(76·5)	(5·9)	(17·6)	(100·0)
2. Narasimham Model (India):				
(*a*) Number of equations	4	1	6	11
(*b*) %	(36·4)	(9·1)	(54·5)	(100·0)
3. Klein–Shinkai Model (Japan): The statistics not given				
4. Klein–Goldberger Model (U.S.):				
(*a*) Number of equations	10	1	3	14
(*b*) %	(71·4)	(7·1)	(21·4)	(100·0)
5. Klein–Ball *et al.* Model (U.K.):				
(*a*) Number of equations	10	5	17	32
(*b*) %	(31·3)	(15·6)	(53·1)	(100·0)

comparison here: the Klein–Shinkai model gives the values of R^2, the Klein–Ball *et al.* model gives those of $\bar{R}$ whereas we have been using the values of $\bar{R}^2$. However, in view of the rough nature of this comparison and the weakness of the statistic itself, we did not think it worth while to recompute them for bringing them to a common definition. We are taking the values of R in our case as well as in the cases of the Klein–Shinkai model and the Narasimham model, whereas in the case of the Klein–Ball *et al.* model we are taking the values of $\bar{R}$. The results are given in Table 7.3.

In the light of the above statistic also, our model does not fare too badly. In fact, so far as the test statistics go, the comparative performance of our model is quite good. However, one important problem with our model is that our equations are estimated by the method of ordinary least squares whereas the other models considered above, except the Narasimham model, have been obtained by simultaneous equation methods. In Chapter 3 we noted some of the reasons why OLS may not be altogether unsuitable in our context. However, we also promised to compare the OLS results with those of the simultaneous equation methods, especially Two-stage Least Squares and Limited Information Maximum-likelihood method. It is to this task that we turn now.

TABLE 7.3

THE VALUES OF MULTIPLE CORRELATION IN VARIOUS MODELS

	Values of R* *in the range*					
	Below 0·75	*0·75– 0·79*	*0·80– 0·89*	*0·90– 0·99*	*0·99–*	*Total*
1. Our Model:						
(*a*) Number of equations	1	1	5	6	4	17
(*b*) %	(5·9)	(5·9)	(29·4)	(35·3)	(23·5)	(100·0)
2. Narasimham Model (India):						
(*a*) Number of equations	1	1	4	5	0	11
(*b*) %. . . .	(9·1)	(9·1)	(36.4)	(45·5)	(0)	(100·0)
3. Klein–Shinkai Model (Japan):						
(*a*) Number of equations	1	1	1	10	2	15
(*b*) %	(6·7)	(6·7)	(6·7)	(66·7)	(13·3)	(100·0)
4. Klein–Goldberger Model (U.S.): The statistics not given						
5. Klein–Ball *et al.* Model (U.K.):						
(*a*) Number of equations	3	0	6	18	5	32
(*b*) %	(9·4)	(0)	(18·8)	(56·3)	(15·6)	(100·0)

* In the case of Klein–Ball *et al.* model, the values are of $\bar{R}$.

7.3: RESULTS OF SIMULTANEOUS EQUATION METHODS

One difficulty that we face in applying the simultaneous equation methods in a straightforward way is that presented by a lack of sufficient degrees of freedom. Our model contains 13 exogenous variables and 7 predetermined variables, whereas our sample has only 12 common observations on all the variables (though we have particular series extending over a longer period). Thus it is quite impossible to apply a simultaneous equation method to the model as a whole. Fortunately, our model is capable of subdivision among sub-models with fewer exogenous variables.

We try two such sub-models. The first consists of the first four equations in our model and they are concerned with the determination of income and employment in the two sectors. The second is concerned with the determination of the absolute price and money supply. We are not considering the rest of the equations of the model partly because our exercise in simultaneous equation methods is mainly exploratory and partly because the rest of the equations do not lend themselves to any neat grouping.

There is another problem with the first set of equations. Some of these are in non-linear form and as such present difficulties. To make them more easily amenable to TSLS and LIML methods, we linearise these equations. The equations in the linearised form are:

$$\text{Set A}\begin{cases} (7.3.1) & Y_a = \alpha_{1\cdot 0} + \alpha_{1\cdot 1}K_a + \alpha_{1\cdot 2}R_2 + u_1 \\ (7.3.2) & F_a = \alpha_{2\cdot 0} + \alpha_{2\cdot 1}Y_a + u_2 \\ (7.3.3) & L_i = \alpha_{3\cdot 0} + \alpha_{3\cdot 1}F_a + \alpha_{3\cdot 2}(M-X)_a + u_3 \\ (7.3.4) & Y_i = \alpha_{4\cdot 0} + \alpha_{4\cdot 1}K_i + \alpha_{4\cdot 2}L_i + u_4 \end{cases}$$

For the monetary sector, the equations are:

$$\text{Set B}\begin{cases} (7.3.5) & (pY) = \alpha_{5\cdot 0} + \alpha_{5\cdot 1}M + \alpha_{5\cdot 2}(pY)_{-1} + u_5 \\ (7.3.6) & M = \alpha_{6\cdot 0} + \alpha_{6\cdot 1}C + \alpha_{6\cdot 2}t + u_6 \end{cases}$$

The first set of equations (call it set A) contains four endogenous variables—Y_a, F_a, L_i, Y_i—and four exogenous variables—K_a, R_2, $(M-X)_a$, K_i. The system is thus determinate, subject of course to the usual conditions of independence and consistency of the equations. Each of the equations also satisfies the *order* condition of identification which states that the number of predetermined variables excluded from the relation must be *at least* as great as the number of endogenous variables included less one. Similarly the set B consists of two endogenous variables—(pY) and M and three predetermined ones—$(pY)_{-1}$, C and t. This system is also determinate and each of the equations satisfies the *order* condition of identification.

It is interesting to find that the results of OLS and TSLS are remarkably similar. The only significant difference is in the equation (7.3.4) of Set A, where, as we have already noted, the multi-collinearity vitiates the estimates completely. The closeness of the results from these two methods is rather reassuring and it seems that our OLS estimates may not be altogether misleading in our context. As regards LIML, the estimates of equation (7.3.3) in Set A and equation (7.3.5) in Set B are similar to those obtained by OLS and TSLS. The estimates of equation (7.3.4) in Set A by LIML are rather different from those obtained by OLS and that is to be expected in view of the multi-collinearity we have already noted. Thus it seems from this exercise in comparative estimates by OLS, TSLS, and LIML methods that in our context at least, the OLS does not produce any very significantly biased estimates and since, as noted in Chapter 3, OLS has many other advantages of flexibility of sample size, etc., we have no reason to reject OLS estimates. One reason for the above results seems to be that our model has a large element of one-way causality and as has been shown by H. Wold and L. Jureen (167) and F. M. Fisher (40), the problem of consistency of OLS estimates is considerably reduced in such cases. However, when we try to solve the system for forecasting and policy discussions, we have to use the predicted values of the current and lagged endogenous variables (rather than their actual values) and it remains to be seen how much the predicted values will differ in this case from those obtained by ordinary least squares. We consider this aspect in the next chapter.

CHAPTER 8

Applications of the Model: A Simulation Approach

In this chapter we consider the possible applications of our model. We begin with a methodological point about the merits of simulation approach (Section 8.1). In Section 8.2 we utilise this approach for prediction within and beyond the sample period. Then in Section 8.3 we utilise our model for determination of optimum capital–labour ratio and the allocation of investment in the context of planning in underdeveloped countries. Lastly, in Section 8.4, we analyse the effects of variation in exogenous variables on the system.

8.1: A NOTE ON SIMULATION APPROACH

In the case of an econometric model which is linear in variables, it is conventional to present the solution of the system by giving the endogenous variables as explicit functions of the exogenous variables. This reduced form is convenient for prediction and policy considerations. Even when certain non-linearities are present in the form of ratios, products, etc., an attempt is made to linearise them by taking the partial derivatives of the function at the mean value of the variables in the sample (see, for example, A. S. Goldberger (46)). Our model contains certain non-linearities and it was not found possible to solve the system explicitly in terms of the exogenous variables. Nor did we think it proper to linearise the system on the basis of certain unrealistic assumptions. Instead, we tried to simulate our model on the computer.

For this purpose, we introduce the simplifying assumption that capital entering into the production functions is capital at the beginning of the year and not mid-year capital. With this, we find that the first six equations (equations (7.1.1) to (7.1.6) in Chapter 7) can be solved one by one. The price equations (equations (7.1.8) to (7.1.13)) present a block of six simultaneous equations which have to be solved simultaneously. The rest of the equations are also solved one by one. Thus we find that once we specify our exogenous variables, we can obtain the solutions of all the variables and the model moves from year to year under the impact of dynamic elements contained in it. The simulation approach seems to us to be more promising than the 'reduced form' approach. The 'reduced form' requires linearisation when in fact we suspect that non-linearities exist in real life. Since computers now available can easily tackle the non-linearities, there seems to be no important reason to sacrifice them in model-building. Of course, with the simulation approach, we do not get complete solutions but only the solutions for particular values of the exogenous variables. However, in most real problems, we are concerned with variations in policy instruments within narrow limits so that this defect of the simulation approach may not be a serious one. In any case, if sufficient computer time is available, we may experiment with as many variations in policy instruments as we choose. Another advantage of the simulation approach is that we do not have to confine ourselves to 'impact multipliers' of variation in exogenous variables. We have the whole year-to-year movement of the system before us and we can find the impact of a change in an exogenous variable up to any number of years we want.

Of course, we have not fully exploited the potentiality of the simulation approach in our simple model. Many of the problems of aggregation and estimation can be minimised if we are in a position to simulate large systems on computers. Instead of taking, for example, the aggregate investment functions we can take the figures for sectors which might be available from sample surveys, sectoral studies, etc. We can bring in a much greater amount of external information and constraints in our model if we are not constrained by the desire for explicit solution of the model with the techniques available. We could bring in multiple constraints not all of which apply at a particular time. Thus in consideration of the employment function in Chapter 2, we might have liked to introduce the double constraint of wage-goods and capital, but for purposes of explicit solution, we had to concentrate on one main restraint, namely, wage-goods. Similarly in output determination, it might have been desirable to consider the double constraint of 'effective demand' and supply of factors of production. It seems that if we are simulating a system on the computer, it might be possible to come much closer to reality in these respects. This is one direction in which our model could be expanded in future.

8.2: PREDICTION WITHIN AND BEYOND THE SAMPLE

In econometric literature, two types of forecasts are generally considered: the *ex post* forecast and the *ex ante* forecast. In an *ex post* sense, we insert the observed values of the exogenous variables and compute the values of the endogenous variables as predicted by the model. These predicted values of the endogenous variables are then compared with the actual values of the endogenous variables. This does not give any information about the future but it is quite useful for testing the behaviour of the model outside the sample. In the *ex ante* forecast, the values of the exogenous variables have to be assumed on *a priori* information or some simple extrapolation. Then, the endogenous values are calculated from the model. This seems a very weak test of the quality of the model because the deviation of the forecast value from the actual may be as much due to wrong assumptions about the exogenous variables as to the defect of the model. However, while *ex ante* forecasting may not be very suitable from the point of view of testing the model, it may be very useful for policy considerations when we want to know the effects of changes in the exogenous variables on the endogenous variables in the future.

Our sample terminates with the year 1960–61. Since then the values of most of the variables have been available but unfortunately the values of some crucial variables like investment are not yet available. So, for the time being, we have to confine ourselves to prediction within the sample period. This is not the same thing as obtaining the predicted values of the variables within the sample from the individual equations. In the simulation approach, the predicted values emerge from the simultaneous equation system and it should indicate the extent of error due to our following a single equation approach. Moreover, the system is also using the predicted, instead of the actual, values of lagged endogenous variables, and the simulation results over a number of years should indicate how the errors accumulate over time in the use of the model.

In this connection, one problem is presented by the disturbance terms in the equations. Theoretically, if each equation is disturbed by a random term with zero mean, in prediction the random term will be zero and we can ignore it. Of course, in a non-linear structural model this procedure will not be justified. For as Klein and Goldberger (91) (p. 75) point out, 'Although disturbances are individually zero on the average, their covariation need not be zero on the average. . . . The forecast equations will depend on non-linear functions of the separate disturbances, and, in general, the estimated covariances of these disturbances will have to be taken into account.' However, on the basis of some experimental calculations, Klein and Goldberger found that the estimated covariances had no perceptible effect on the forecasts and they decided to ignore the disturbances. A more important problem in assuming error terms to be zero in forecasting is that the error terms may be serially correlated. In order to solve this problem, Klein and Goldberger adopted the following procedure:

'Our preferred procedure is to compute the residuals of all structural equations and make a special study of their time patterns in a recent period, say, the last five years in annual models. Persistent biases are investigated. These would be indicated by a series of four or five consecutive residuals of the same sign and similar magnitude for the test observation periods. If there is *independent* information to confirm the existence of a bias and if we think it will continue into the forecast period, we use the latest estimate of the residuals as a positive or negative additive constant in the equation system in place of the zero value for the disturbance.' (op. cit., p. 77). While we also favour this type of flexible technique of econometric forecasting in contrast to any mechanical method, we were unable to use it because of the absence of any *independent* information. In our context, there is an additional reason for ignoring the random element. We want to use the alternative runs of the simulation to find out the effects of tax measures, currency variation, etc. But if random elements are present in the equations, it will be difficult to decide what part of the variation in the endogenous variable is due to the variation in exogenous variable and what part due to the variation in random element. Therefore, after some preliminary explorations, we decided to ignore the disturbance terms in our equations.

It is easy to see that the results of the simulation will depend to a certain extent on the year with which our simulation begins. If we start with a 'bad' year where the prediction is poor, all the subsequent years might have poor predictions as well. Thus not knowing the extent of this type of accumulation of errors, we choose by turn all the years of our sample as initial years and carry out the simulation for the subsequent years. We have to start with the year 1949–50, because some of our equations contain lagged values and our data begin from 1948–49. Thus we computed with the help of our 'Simulation Programme' 78 sets of values for the endogenous variables—1 set for the year 1949–50, 2 sets for 1950–51, and so on up to 12 sets for 1960–61.

How should we judge whether the predictions are good or not? In the absence of any known theoretical statistic for judging the goodness of fit of a model as a whole, we construct a simple intuitive statistic for the purpose. We find out the percentage by which the predicted values deviate from the actual values in the case of each variable and then take the mean of the absolute values of these percentage deviations. If the fit is perfect the value of this statistic will

TABLE 8.1

AVERAGE PERCENTAGE DEVIATION OF THE PREDICTED VALUES FROM THE ACTUAL VALUES (d)

$$d = \frac{1}{n}\sum_{i=1}^{n}\left|\frac{\hat{Y}_i - Y_i}{Y_i}100\right|$$

where $\hat{Y}_i$ = the predicted value of the variable i

and Y_i = the actual value of the variable i.

Initial year of the process	*Predicted value for the year*											
	1949–50	*1950–51*	*1951–52*	*1952–53*	*1953–54*	*1954–55*	*1955–56*	*1956–57*	*1957–58*	*1958–59*	*1959–60*	*1960–61*
1949–50	10·37	35·77	8·53	21·19	10·03	4·31	9·19	9·22	10·02	8·31	14·55	11·41
1950–51		29·70	9·54	21·98	11·35	3·88	9·77	9·61	10·11	8·29	14·41	11·34
1951–52			11·80	20·49	8·92	4·82	8·98	8·94	9·81	8·14	14·27	11·08
1952–53				23·19	10·03	4·71	9·53	9·15	9·76	8·02	14·02	10·78
1953–54					11·57	4·00	9·87	9·49	9·49	7·39	13·26	10·20
1954–55						6·92	11·41	10·50	9·00	6·43	11·68	8·34
1955–56							4·51	8·08	9·76	8·25	15·06	11·65
1956–57								7·58	9·83	8·12	14·99	11·66
1957–58									9·13	5·73	11·74	8·66
1958–59										5·66	9·96	7·44
1959–60											7·80	6·01
1960–61												5·80

be zero and it will go on increasing as the quality of the model worsens. Of course, this is a very rough type of criterion. For one thing, not all the variables are of equal importance in an economic sense and a simple average may be misleading. On the other hand, it is not easy to suggest any wholly satisfactory set of weights to be used in this case. Secondly, there is the problem as to how much deviation can be regarded as tolerable. Much would, of course, depend on the nature of the economy under consideration and the rate of growth and amplitude of fluctuations of the variables. It should perhaps be possible to define the tolerance limits for deviation in a model but so far no such statistic seems to have been devised.

The results of this exercise are given in Table 8.1. The mean value of these deviations is 10·59 per cent. This result is not very encouraging but it is difficult to say how the similar other models will fare in this respect. One important aspect that deserves attention is that there is some, but not very great, accumulation of error as the system moves on.

It may be desirable to supplement the above analysis of the average movement of all the variables by an analysis of the movements of a few particular variables. We select 7 out of the 22 endogenous variables in our model. The selected variables are: agricultural output (Y_a), non-agricultural output (Y_i), general price level (p), money wage rate (W_i), private agricultural investment (I_a), private non-agricultural investment (I_i) and the exports (X). The selection of these variables is of course a matter of subjective judgment. However,

TABLE 8.2

PERCENTAGE DEVIATION OF THE PREDICTED VALUES FROM THE ACTUAL VALUES IN THE CASE OF SOME IMPORTANT VARIABLES

	Variables						
Year	Y_a	Y_i	p	W_i	I_a	I_i	X
1949–50	4·56	4·01	−3·44	−3·55	18·6	23·2	5·52
1950–51	5·88	6·32	−6·82	4·04	30·8	71·1	−8·39
1951–52	4·37	2·47	−5·68	2·35	4·55	−13·4	11·2
1952–53	4·78	−0·226	−1·99	−0·621	10·9	−49·2	−0·065
1953–54	−0·763	−2·79	−3·01	1·80	23·1	−32·1	8·72
1954–55	1·69	−3·49	6·97	3·86	13·5	9·27	3·76
1955–56	3·92	−3·48	6·07	0·324	9·11	−17·5	−9·05
1956–57	0·800	−2·38	−0·681	−0·465	−10·6	−44·5	−3·45
1957–58	13·1	1·80	−4·37	−4·29	3·58	25·6	−6·39
1958–59	4·42	3·55	−7·06	−5·22	6·78	−9·89	−9·13
1959–60	7·84	4·68	−6·64	−7·99	−8·77	50·0	0·339
1960–61	4·03	−1·01	4·40	−12·5	10·7	26·3	8·68

the importance of these variables in the context of our model is obvious. The movements of these variables are presented in Table 8.2. We consider only the estimates obtained from continuous simulation for 12 years starting from the year 1949–50. The results in Table 8.1 suggest that in our case the estimates are not likely to be significantly different even if we vary our initial year. The results of Table 8.2 confirm our earlier conclusion that there does not seem to be any significant tendency towards an accumulation of errors over time. The agricultural output shows upward deviation in the first few years and this is perhaps the reason why the deviations are on the whole predominantly in the positive direction. The general price level shows the opposite tendency, partly because of the upward tendency of agricultural output which in its turn also influences non-agricultural output. The private investment in the agricultural sector as well as that in the non-agricultural sector shows considerable deviation, mostly in the upward direction. This also seems to be partially due to the upward deviation in agricultural output. But here again there is no tendency towards accumulation of errors over time. The deviations in the rest of the variables are more or less random without any considerable accumulation of errors, though the deviations in the case of non-agricultural private investment are quite large.

Another way of testing the goodness of the model as a whole may be to calculate the standard statistics like $\bar{R}^2$ and δ^2/S^2 for the values predicted by the simulation for the sample period. However, in this case, there is a problem with the definition of R^2. Here the residuals do not sum up to zero and the total variance is not partitionable between predicted variance and residual variance and R^2 defined as the ratio of the predicted variance to the total variance may be greater than unity. Since it is difficult to interpret a value of R^2 greater than unity or to compare it with those obtained from single equation estimates, we decided to reject this statistic. Instead, we construct a simple intuitive statistic to indicate the deviation of the predicted values from the actual. We take the average of the absolute values of the percentage deviation of the predicted values from the actual values. We also calculate the values of δ^2/S^2, which are done in the usual manner. These values are obtained from three types of predicted values. In the first place, we take the values predicted by single equations in the system. Secondly, we take the values predicted by our simulation programme when we use the actual values of lagged endogenous variables for every year of the period 1949–50 to 1960–61. Thirdly, we take the values predicted by the simulation programme when we use the predicted values of lagged endogenous variables, rather than the actual values. The comparison between the second and the first set of predicted values shows the effects of simultaneity in the system whereas that between the third and the second shows the effects of lagged endogenous variables in the system.

TABLE 8.3

COMPARISON OF THE ESTIMATES OBTAINED FROM SINGLE EQUATION METHOD, ANNUAL SIMULATION AND CONTINUOUS SIMULATION

	Percentage deviation of the predicted values from the actual			δ^2/S^2		
Variables	*Single equation estimates*	*Estimates from simulation for every year*	*Estimates from continuous simulation for 12 years 1949–60*	*Single equation estimates*	*Estimates from simulation for every year*	*Estimates from continuous simulation for 12 years 1949–60*
	(1)	(2)	(3)	(4)	(5)	(6)
Y_a	3·31	3·21	4·68	1·93	1·99	0·830
F_a	2·99	6·67	9·13	0·976	1·58	0·829
L_i	2·15	2·81	3·68	2·39	0·649	0·351
Y_i	1·72	3·02	3·02	0·726	0·906	0·818
M	2·10	2·07	2·07	0·483	0·454	0·454
p	3·53	3·61	4·76	3·19	1·51	0·622
p_c	2·07	3·33	6·54	1·71	1·75	0·205
p_i	0·999	1·28	1·81	0·818	1·29	0·639
p_{im}	1·96	2·28	3·61	1·96	2·06	0·506
$p_{inv.}$	0·456	2·28	3·43	2·08	1·83	0·463
I	2·30	2·47	3·92	2·57	2·26	0·370
I_a	7·55	9·54	12·6	1·37	1·13	0·787
I_i	26·2	30·3	31·0	2·85	2·98	1·83
p_x	4·72	5·87	6·44	1·92	1·20	1·04
X	5·32	5·86	6·23	2·41	2·91	2·48
M_c	12·0	12·6	12·6	2·24	2·19	2·17
(I_i+G_i)	28·5	23·1	23·3	2·04	1·96	1·65

The results of these computations are presented in Table 8.3. We present the results only of those variables which are obtained from real equations in our system, thus omitting those which are obtained from definitions or constraints. It should be noted that in some cases, the values of the von Neumann ratio as presented in Table 8.3 differ from those in the summary statement of the model in Chapter 7. This is so because in our original estimates, we have used varying sizes of sample and various transformations of original variables to make the estimates better. In Table 8.3. however we are, for the sake of comparison, computing the necessary statistics from the same sample size and the same form of predicted values. Comparing the first three columns, we find that the errors of prediction accumulate as we use more and more of the predicted values in the system. However, except in the case of F_a, p_c, $p_{inv.}$, I_a, the accumulation of error does not appear to be very great. The values of δ^2/S^2 are not so different between columns (4) and (5) except in the case of F_a. However, when we take continuous simulation, the values of δ^2/S^2 get much worse. Except in the case of last five variables, all the others show serial correlation of residuals. This is, of course, not unexpected. In a continuous simulation the errors of prediction in one year influence predictions in the next year so far as the lagged endogenous variable is used in prediction. Thus we find that deviations not only tend to become somewhat larger as simulation proceeds to distant years, they also tend to lose their random character and become biased in one direction or another.

What does the above simulation analysis show about the behaviour of our model within the sample? It is difficult to give a simple answer. However, on the whole it seems that though there does occur some accumulation of errors and bias in the system as simulation is carried over a number of years, the magnitude of errors is not very great and we should be able to use the model for a period of, say, five years, with reasonable confidence.

Next we might try to use our model for prediction outside the sample. In this case, the main difficulty is related to the prediction of the exogenous variables. It might be possible to construct a separate sub-model to predict the values of these variables, but we do not propose to enter that sphere. Instead, we consider a hypothetical case where exogenous variables are kept at the level reached by them at the end of the sample. We then try to see how the system will move in that context. For this purpose, we again utilise our simulation programme and the results of this exercise are presented in Table 8.4. There is perhaps not much point in going into the details of this hypothetical prediction. We only note that this yields a growth of 15 per cent in agricultural output and of 18 per cent in non-agricultural output over a period of four years. In a subsequent section, we will consider how the results will differ if we vary the exogenous variables one by one.

8.3: PLANNING FOR A TARGET RATE OF GROWTH

In this section, we would try to see how our model could be utilised for planning in underdeveloped countries. In mixed economies of the Indian type, the Government is mainly concerned with

TABLE 8.4

MOVEMENT OF THE SYSTEM WITH EXOGENOUS VARIABLES AT A FIXED LEVEL

Variables	*1960–61*	*1961–62*	*1962–63*	*1963–64*	*1964–65*
Y_a	5713	5924	6136	6349	6562
F_a	7988	8425	8864	9305	9747
L_i	4891	5037	5184	5332	5480
Y_i	6725	7025	7331	7639	7950
Y	12437	12949	13466	13988	14513
M	2892	2894	2895	2896	2898
p	111·02	111·95	111·75	110·76	109·21
p_a	117·60	119·19	118·25	115·55	111·68
p_c	127·99	132·13	135·27	136·90	136·81
p_i	105·43	105·84	106·31	106·77	107·18
p_{im}	118·86	120·37	122·08	123·79	125·29
$p_{inv.}$	126·59	129·12	131·73	134·17	136·19
W_i	154·10	159·80	165·18	169·84	173·41
I_a	168·78	179·49	189·39	198·19	205·86
I_i	776·14	816·80	853·37	898·39	952·67
p_x	114·11	115·27	115·03	113·77	111·83
X	564·04	561·55	562·08	564·75	568·89
MT	953·06	956·25	955·57	952·14	946·71
M_c	188·22	180·69	171·90	161·80	150·34
M_k	399·03	410·66	418·76	425·44	431·46
(I_i+G_i)	1071·76	1099·20	1119·91	1136·98	1152·38
G_i	295·62	282·39	266·54	238·59	199·71

investment planning. This in its turn involves three important problems: (*a*) how much to invest, (*b*) in which sector to invest, and (*c*) what type of techniques to adopt in each sector. The question of the optimum rate of saving (and investment) has received a considerable amount of theoretical attention ever since Frank Ramsey's classic paper on the problem. However, basically it seems to be a political decision about the relative utility of present and future and we do not propose to enter into it. We would, however, try to find out the necessary rate of investment for a target rate of growth. The question of investment allocation has been approached from two points of view: the point of view of consistency and that of optimality. A large body of literature based on input–output analysis has been developed in order to answer the question as to how the different sectors should be developed so that they can meet the demand for their products at the time required. The problem of optimality seems to have received somewhat lesser theoretical attention. In the Indian context, Mahalanobis's two-sector model (102) does consider the problem of allocation from the point of view of optimal growth. However, no optimal solution for the allocation parameter is obtained from the set of equations. The growth equation does emphasise that the higher the allocation to the investment goods sector, the higher will be the rate of growth of income after a certain time period has elasped. However, when the actual choice of allocation parameter is considered, it is chosen on intuitive basis as $\lambda_K = \frac{1}{3}$ stating that it did not seem possible to go beyond that value of λ_K (see Mahalanobis (102)).

In the field of choice of techniques, the earlier discussions suggested the desirability of choosing labour intensive techniques on the ground that the opportunity cost of labour is zero when there is a huge amount of disguised unemployment. N. S. Buchanan (18) and J. J. Polak (118) are the most well-known supporters of this criterion. Subsequently it was recognised that the opportunity cost of labour may not be zero and it led to the Social Marginal Productivity criterion of A. E. Kahn (81). The opposite extreme of the Buchanan–Polak criterion was reached by W. Galenson and H. Leibenstein (45) who emphasised the extra demand generating aspect of extra employment. Assuming that the wage earners do not save they were led to the conclusion that the labour-intensive method will lead to a fall in the saving-income ratio and thus to a lower rate of growth of income. Thus they came to a paradoxical conclusion that even in the midst of huge unemployment and capital shortage, the underdeveloped countries should adopt the most capital-intensive techniques. Essentially similar conclusions were reached by A. K. Sen (144).

Galenson and Leibenstein are perhaps right in emphasising the extra demand generating aspect of extra employment but they go too far in assuming that fiscal policy cannot regulate the rate of saving at all. Our position is that while fiscal policy cannot regulate the demand for necessities (mainly food), it can regulate the demand for luxuries (all products of the non-agricultural sector in our model). Thus in our model the choice of techniques influences the allocation between the agricultural and non-agricultural sector but not necessarily the rate of saving. Labour is not costless in our model as it is in the Buchanan–Polak model, but the cost of labour is now expressible in terms of capital. In our case the choice of techniques can be made independently of the decision about the rate of saving. Galenson and Leibenstein tie up the question of rate of saving so tightly with that of choice of techniques that the two are no longer independent decisions. The same defect seems to be present also in Mahalanobis's model. It can be seen quite easily as follows:

Mahalanobis's basic equations are:

$$I_{t+1} - I_t = \lambda_K . \beta_K I_t$$
$$C_{t+1} - C_t = \lambda_C . \beta_C I_t$$

From these two, it follows:

$$(8.3.1) \qquad \frac{\Delta I_{t+1}}{\Delta C_{t+1}} = \frac{\lambda_k \beta_k I_t}{\lambda_c \beta_c I_t} = \frac{\lambda_k \beta_k}{\lambda_c \beta_c}$$

Since the right hand side does not contain any timed variable w can drop the time subscript on the left as well. Assuming, as Mahalanobis does, that saving and investment are equal, we have the marginal income-saving ratio as:

$$(8.3.2) \qquad \frac{\Delta Y}{\Delta S} = \frac{\Delta C + \Delta S}{\Delta S} = \frac{\Delta C}{\Delta S} + 1 = \frac{\lambda_c \beta_c}{\lambda_k \beta_k} + 1$$

Since β's are constant, the marginal saving-income ratio is given uniquely by λ_k (which is equal to $1 - \lambda_c$). Thus the question of investment allocation is no longer a decision independent of the decision about the rate of saving. In our model we try to answer the question of choice of techniques and investment allocation independently of the decision about the rate of saving.

An important aspect of our analysis is that labour in the non-agricultural sector is, in a way, a produced means of production. The release of labour from the agricultural sector is possible only when the marketed surplus of food is increased, which in its turn requires extra capital. In the context of our simplified hypothesis, we find that when capital in agriculture is increased, output of agriculture and food-grains is increased, and this permits an increase in employment in the non-agricultural sector. Thus the cost of labour in the non-agricultural sector can be expressed in terms of capital. The problem of the allocation of capital is solved by making the marginal productivity of capital equal in both the sectors. In our previous analysis, investment in the two sectors is largely non-substitutable. However, for the purpose of considering the question of allocation of investment at all, we have to assume substitutability, at least at the margin. We have emphasised in Chapter 2 that industrialisation is essential for sustained growth. Therefore we assume that the increase in agricultural output is not desired for its own sake, but only in so far as it is necessary for releasing labour for the non-agricultural sector. In that case, we get a very convenient rule for the allocation of investment. The relevant productivities to compare in that case are:

$$\frac{\delta Y_i}{\delta K_i} \text{ and } \frac{\delta Y_i}{\delta K_a}$$

Now, $\dfrac{\delta Y_i}{\delta K_a} = \dfrac{\delta Y_i}{\delta L_i} \cdot \dfrac{\delta L_i}{\delta F_a} \cdot \dfrac{\delta F_a}{\delta Y_a} \cdot \dfrac{\delta Y_a}{\delta K_a}$

In an optimum situation, the two marginal productivities should be the same. Thus, we should have:

$$\frac{\delta Y_i}{\delta K_a} \Big/ \frac{\delta Y_i}{\delta K_i} = 1$$

Making the necessary substitutions, we get:

$$\text{(8.3.3)} \qquad \frac{K_i}{L_i} = B_o K_a^{1-\alpha_1}$$

where B_o is a constant depending on the various parameters of our model.

Putting in the numerical estimates of the parameters we have, the optimum capital–labour ratio:

$$\text{(8.3.4)} \qquad \frac{K_i}{L_1} = 0{\cdot}1522\ K_a^{0\cdot3457}$$

The above equation enables us to determine the optimum capital–labour ratio in the non-agricultural sector. Indirectly this formula also determines something about investment allocation. For in our model, an increase in employment requires an increase in agricultural output and thus additional investment in agriculture. Let us assume that the desired rate of growth in the non-agricultural sector (say, 10 per cent per annum) is given exogenously and we are concerned with finding out the optimum techniques (capital–labour ratio) and the investment allocation. In our model, this is obtained by solving the following system of equations:

$$\text{(8.3.4)} \qquad \frac{K_i}{L_i} = 0{\cdot}1522\ K_a^{0\cdot3457}$$

$$\text{(8.3.5)} \qquad \log (L_i) = \log (Y_i) + 0{\cdot}4407 - 0{\cdot}5599 \log \left(\frac{K_i}{L_i}\right)$$

$$\text{(8.3.6)} \qquad F_a = \frac{1}{0{\cdot}3347}[L_i - 1803{\cdot}044 - 1{\cdot}1844\ (M-X)_a]$$

$$\text{(8.3.7)} \qquad Y_a = \frac{1}{2{\cdot}0699}[F_a + 3836{\cdot}183]$$

$$\text{(8.3.8)} \qquad \log (K_a) = \frac{1}{0{\cdot}6543}[\log Y_a - 2{\cdot}9142 + 0{\cdot}0347 \log R_2]$$

$$\text{(8.3.9)} \qquad K_i = \frac{K_i}{L_i}.L_i$$

$$\text{(8.3.10)} \qquad K_a = \exp (\log K_a)$$

$$\text{(8.3.11)} \qquad \Delta K_a = K_a - K_{a_{-1}}$$

$$\text{(8.3.12)} \qquad \Delta K_i = K_i - K_{i_{-1}}$$

Given the rate of growth of Y_i and the exogenous variables—$(M-X)_a$, R_2, $K_{a_{-1}}$, $K_{i_{-1}}$—this system of 9 equations determines 9 unknowns. We know the answer to the choice of techniques and investment allocation from one single set of simultaneous equations.

Computationally, it was found convenient to solve the above system on the computer by the method of iteration. Briefly speaking, the programme proceeds as follows. We start with the given capital in agriculture (K_a) for the previous year and work out the system which gives a value of K_a for the current year. Since the marginal productivity of K_a at the level of the previous year is likely to be different from that in the current year, this does not give the correct magnitude of the optimum capital–labour ratio. Thus if $\left|\frac{K_a-K_{a_{-1}}}{K_{a_{-1}}}\right|>0{\cdot}001$ we instruct the computer to take the mean of $K_{a_{-1}}$ and K_a and start the process all over again. The iteration is continued till variation in capital at the beginning and the end of the process is less than or equal to 0·1 per cent of the initial capital. The solution gives us the optimum values of K_a and K_i for a given Y_i. Subtracting the values of K_a and K_i from those of the last year, we get the optimum investment required in each sector.

TABLE 8.5

OPTIMUM GROWTH PATH FOR 10 PER CENT GROWTH PER ANNUM IN NON-AGRICULTURAL SECTOR

	Years					
Variables	*1960–61*	*1961–62*	*1962–63*	*1963–64*	*1964–65*	*1965–66*
$\frac{K_i}{L_i}$	3·50	3·66	3·82	4·00	4·17	4·36
L_i	5272	5656	6069	6513	6992	7508
ΔK_a	1277	1199	1351	1520	1710	1922
ΔK_i	−605	2248	2517	2818	3156	3533
$\Delta K=\Delta K_a+\Delta K_i$	672	3447	3868	4338	4866	5455
$\lambda_a=\frac{\Delta K_a}{\Delta K_a+\Delta K_i}$		0·3478	0·3492	0·3503	0·3514	3523
Y_a	6262	6816	7412	8054	8745	9490
Y_i	6840	7524	8276	9104	10014	11016

In our exercise with this model, we assumed that 10 per cent per annum growth is desired in the non-agricultural sector. The computer was instructed to chart out the path of the relevant variables for 6 years and the results are given in Table 8.5. Some interesting aspects of the results may be noted briefly. For 1960–61, with the output in the non-agricultural sector given, we come out with a negative investment for the non-agricultural sector. This would suggest that in 1960–61 there was slight over-capitalisation in the non-agricultural sector. This may have been due to the excessively capital intensive projects of the Second Five Year Plan. The capital–labour ratio is increasing over time. Thus it seems that we should start with fairly labour-intensive techniques and then switch over to capital intensive techniques as capital accumulation proceeds. This seems more reasonable than the Galenson–Leibenstein idea of starting off with capital-intensive projects. Another interesting—rather intriguing—feature of our results is that the allocation to agriculture does not decline—in fact it increases slightly as time goes on. This may be due to certain limitations of our model. For one thing, if the economy develops considerably the employment function of our model will change significantly. In fact, as we have noted in our theoretical analysis of Chapter 2, the whole model will be different once the economy passes from Stage I to Stage II of its career. That is why we are limiting ourselves to projections for only 6 years from 1960 by which time the Indian economy is unlikely to cross over to Stage II. Another important defect of our model is of course its inability to take into account the importance of technical progress. The importance of this factor is very much emphasised in our theoretical scheme. But unfortunately, we could not devise a sensible way of including it in our model at the empirical level. These limitations should be borne in mind while considering the policy implications of our model.

8.4: ANALYSIS OF THE EFFECTS OF VARIATION IN EXOGENOUS VARIABLES

After having obtained the desired path of growth, we have to answer the question: how to attain this path? We have seen how the system will move if exogenous variables were kept where they are. This will be a sort of *laisser faire* solution with the Government just keeping its tax and spending levels at their original values. Our results in Table 8.4 show that the rate of growth of non-agricultural output is likely to be rather low and for a target rate of growth higher than this, we must vary the exogenous variables.

In our analysis in Chapter 3, we have noted that two of the exogenous variables (R_2, and t) are quite outside our control. The Government can control six exogenous variables, namely, C, T_a, T_i, GC, G_a and M_o, and we would try to see the effects of variation in these on the endogenous variables in our system. Two other exogenous variables, namely, $(M-X)_a$ and FC which are under the control of the foreign countries could perhaps be influenced by the political efforts of the domestic Government. We would therefore study the effects of variation in eight exogenous variables, C, T_a, T_i, GC, G_a, M_o, $(M-X)_a$ and FC. Of these again we would consider two forms of variation in $(M-X)_a$. In the first case $(M-X)_a$ is increased and there is no other variation in the exogenous variables. In the second case, an increase in $(M-X)_a$ of 100 is associated with an increase in C of 20, which is *roughly* equal to half the price of importing 1 million tons of food-grains at the price of 1962–63.

A well-known analysis of the effects of fiscal measures in the framework of an aggregative model has been provided by A. S. Goldberger (46). He considers impact multipliers, intermediate run responses as well as long-term dynamic effects of changes in exogenous policy variables. In a linearised version of the reduced form, he uses the following relation for his computation of impact (one-year) multipliers:

$$\dot{y} = \pi_0 \dot{z}$$

where $\dot{y}$ is the vector of rate of change in endogenous variables,
$\dot{z}$ is the vector of the rate of change of exogenous variables,
π_0 is the matrix obtained from the partial derivatives of endogenous variables with respect to the exogenous variables at the mean value of the variables.

In connection with the discussion of intermediate run responses, the variables are timed and the vector of exogenous variables is partitioned into an exogenous vector $\dot{v}_t$ and a lagged endogenous vector $\dot{y}_{t-1}$ and the coefficient matrix π_0 is correspondingly partitioned. The reduced form then becomes:

$$\dot{v}_t = \pi_1 \dot{v}_t + \pi_2 \dot{y}_{t-1}$$

With initial conditions and the time path of exogenous variables specified, the time paths of the endogenous variables are traced out by repeated use of the above formula.

As we have noted above, we preferred to simulate our model on the computer rather than follow the reduced form approach. Thus we do not have to linearise the system and we get the time path of the endogenous variables by a single programme on the computer. The results could be easily predicted for any number of years; but we preferred to stop at the 5th year. This is the period for which our Plans are formulated and moreover our model is built mainly on the experience of 13 years and perhaps it is not safe to use it for prediction over a very long run.

As noted above we consider the effects of variation in 8 exogenous variables, C, T_a, T_i, GC, G_a, M_o, $(M-X)_a$ and FC. The amount of variation considered is just illustrative. In the case of taxes, T_a and

T_i, we assume a once for all increase of Rs. 100 crores which will yield Rs. 100 crores every year. In the case of currency creation, however, the Government gets Rs. 100 crores every year if it creates additional Rs. 100 crores every year. GC is assumed to have been reduced by 10 points. M_o is reduced by 100. $(M-X)_a$ is increased by 100. In another form $(M-X)_a$ is increased by 100 and at the same time C is increased by 20. Lastly FC is assumed to have been increased by 100. The results of simulations with these variations in the exogenous variables are given in Table 8.6. A comparison with the movement of the system without any change in the exogenous variables will show the effects of variation in the exogenous variable concerned. Let us briefly consider the effects of variation in the various variables

In the first year, currency creation does not affect output and employment in either sector. Prices are of course increased, and the amount of private investment in both sectors is also increased. The volume of exports is lower than it would have been otherwise; but because of price inelasticity, export earnings and consequently imports are higher. By the 5th year of the simulation, all the endogenous variables are different from what they would have been in the absence of any change. In general, the change is in a desirable direction. The real wages are however lower than they would have been. In the absence of any change $\frac{W_i}{p_c}$ would have been 126·75 in the 5th year of the simulation whereas with currency creation it is only 116·78.

The variation in T_a affects only agricultural private investment to begin with. By the fifth year of the simulation, most of the variables are affected. However, the main effect is a reduction in agricultural output and investment. The impact on the rest of the economy is rather small. Of course, the taxation could be utilised for increasing agicultural investment by the Government which would more than counterbalance the adverse effects of agricultural taxation on agriculture, as shown by the differential effects of variation in G_a.

The variation of T_i has a very limited effect in our model. It affects only the distribution of total non-agricultural investment between the private and public sector. Since total investment in the non-agricultural sector in our model is determined by the import of capital goods, it is not affected by T_i. Thus even by the 5th round of simulation the only differential effects of T_i are on the distribution of total non-agricultural investment between the private and public sectors. The effects of variation in GC are similar. Here again the only variables affected are I_i and G_i.

Import of food-grains unaccompanied by money creation increases non-agricultural employment and output in our model. The general price level is lower than it would have been otherwise but the terms of trade of agriculture are also worsened. Private investment in agriculture is lower than what it would have been otherwise but non-agricultural private investment is higher. Because of the lower prices, the quantity of exports is higher but export earnings lower. Consequently, the total non-agricultural investment is lower. If, however, the import of food-grains is accompanied by creation of money to a certain extent (to the extent of half the value of imports in our experiment) there is an upward pressure on prices. The private agricultural investment is higher and so is total as well as private non-agricultural investment. Moreover, if we consider the effects of extra public investment in the agricultural sector permitted by the import of food-grains, the effects would be still better.

The effects of an increase in the inflow of foreign capital and a reduction in the import of miscellaneous imports (with capital inflow constant) are naturally quite beneficial. The growth of total output is higher, prices are lower and non-agricultural investment is higher. The interesting thing to note is that the effects on the agricultural sector are rather insignificant. There is only a marginal effect on the terms of trade between the agricultural and non-agricultural sectors and consequently private agricultural investment is not affected significantly.

From the above brief review, it seems that simulation analysis can provide useful information as to the effects over time of various policy instruments. However, it is also obvious that our results are only illustrative. The model has to be expanded very considerably before it can yield results directly useful for policy-makers.

TABLE 8.6

EFFECTS OF VARIATION IN EXOGENOUS VARIABLES: 1960–61

Endogenous Variables	Variation in Exogenous Variables									
	No change	$\Delta C = 100$ *every year*	$\Delta T_a = 100$	$\Delta T_i = 100$	$\Delta(M-X)_a' = 100$	$\Delta(M-X)_a = 100$ *and* $\Delta C = 20$	$\Delta FC = 100$	$\Delta M_o = -100$	$\Delta GC = -10$	$\Delta G_a = 100$
Y_a	5713	5713	5713	5713	5713	5713	5713	5713	5713	5713
F_a	7988	7988	7988	7988	7988	7988	7988	7988	7988	7988
L_i	4891	4891	4891	4892	5010	5010	4891	4891	4891	4891
Y_i	6725	6725	6725	6725	6796	6796	6725	6725	6725	6725
Y	12437	12437	12437	12437	12508	12508	12437	12437	12437	12437
M	2892	3039	2892	2892	2892	2922	2892	2892	2892	2892
p	111·02	112·38	111·02	111·02	110·39	110·66	111·02	111·02	111·02	111·02
p_a	117·60	120·52	117·60	117·60	116·15	116·74	117·60	117·60	117·60	117·60
p_c	127·99	129·09	127·99	127·99	127·45	127·67	127·99	127·99	127·99	127·99
p_i	105·43	105·45	105·43	105·43	105·54	105·55	105·43	105·43	105·43	105·43
p_{im}	118·86	118·94	118·86	118·86	119·27	119·28	118·86	118·86	118·86	118·86
$p_{inv.}$	126·59	126·73	126·59	126·59	126·87	126·90	126·59	126·59	126·59	126·59
W_i	154·10	154·45	154·10	154·10	153·92	193·99	154·10	154·10	154·10	154·10
I_a	168·78	169·09	164·43	168·78	168·60	168·66	168·78	168·78	168·78	168·78
I_i	776·14	800·03	776·14	747·79	783·28	788·03	776·14	776·14	697·58	776·14
p_x	114·11	115·82	114·11	114·11	113·31	113·65	114·11	114·11	114·11	111.41
X	564·04	560·41	564·04	564·04	565·73	565·01	564	564·04	564	564·04
MT	953	958	953	953	951	952	1039	953	953	953
M_c	188	188	188	188	190	190	188	188	188	188
M_k	400	405	400	400	396	397	485	500	400	400
I_i+G_i	1072	1084	1072	1072	1061	1063	1290	1327	1072	1072
G_i	296	284	296	324	278	275	514	551	374	296

TABLE 8.6 (*continued*)

EFFECTS OF VARIATION IN EXOGENOUS VARIABLES: 1961–62

Endogenous Variables	*No change*	$\Delta C = 100$ *every year*	$\Delta T_a = 100$	$\Delta T_i = 100$	$\Delta(M-X)_a = 100$	$\Delta(M-X)_a = 100$ *and* $\Delta C = 20$	$\Delta FC = 100$	$\Delta M_o = -100$	$\Delta GC = -10$	$\Delta G_a = 100$
	Variation in Exogenous Variables									
Y_a	5924	5924	5921	5924	5923	5923	5924	5924	5924	5972
F_a	8425	8425	8421	8425	8425	8425	8425	8425	8425	8425
L_i	5037	5038	5036	5037	5156	5156	5037	5037	5037	5071
Y_i	7025	7028	7024	7025	7095	7096	7068	7075	7025	7046
Y	12949	12951	12946	12949	13019	13019	12992	12999	12949	13018
M	2894	3187	2894	2894	2894	2952	2894	2894	2894	2894
p	111·95	115·57	111·98	111·95	111·35	112·07	111·58	111·52	111·95	111·36
p_a	119·19	127·00	119·25	119·19	117·74	119·30	118·50	118·38	119·19	117·83
p_c	132·13	136·0	132·15	132·15	131·12	131·90	131·87	131·82	132·13	131·62
p_i	105·84	105·94	105·84	105·84	106·01	106·03	105·78	105·77	105·84	105·87
p_{im}	120·37	120·72	120·36	120·37	121·00	121·07	120·15	120·11	120·37	120·46
$p_{inv.}$	129·12	129·75	129·12	129·12	129·51	129·64	128·93	128·89	129·12	129·15
W_i	159·80	161·30	159·80	159·80	159·34	159·64	159·71	159·70	159·80	159·63
I_a	179·49	180·93	175·13	179·49	179·14	179·42	179·38	179·36	179·49	181·65
I_i	816·80	851·13	817·02	789·0	835·33	842·26	824·35	825·63	732·12	811·76
p_x	115·27	119·84	115·31	115·28	114·52	115·43	114·81	114·73	115·28	114·53
X	561·55	551·84	561·48	561·55	563·16	561·23	562·54	562·71	561·55	563·10
MT	956·25	968·2	956·34	955·25	954·19	956·65	1040·49	954·77	956·25	954·2
M_c	180·69	180·75	180·67	180·69	182·49	182·50	181·79	181·98	180·69	181·22
M_k	410·66	422·56	410·77	410·66	406·80	409·25	493·80	507·90	410·66	408·09
I_i+G_i	1099·20	1129·63	1099·47	1099·20	1089·31	1095·58	1311·79	1347·83	1099·20	1092·60
G_i	282·39	278·50	282·46	310·19	253·98	253·32	487·44	522·20	365·06	280·87

TABLE 8.6 (*continued*)

EFFECTS OF VARIATION IN EXOGENOUS VARIABLES: 1962–63

Endogenous Variables	*Variation in Exogenous Variables*									
	No change	$\Delta C = 100$ *every year*	$\Delta T_a = 100$	$\Delta T_i = 100$	$\Delta(M-X)_a = 100$	$\Delta(M-X)_a = 100$ *and* $\Delta C = 20$	$\Delta FC = 100$	$\Delta M_o = -100$	$\Delta GC = -10$	$\Delta G_a = 100$
Y_a	6136	6137	6132	6136	6135	6136	6136	6136	6136	6232
F_a	8864	8868	8856	8864	8864	8864	8864	8864	8864	9063
L_i	5184	5185	5182	5184	5303	5303	5184	5184	5184	5251
Y_i	7331	7339	7329	7331	7400	7401	7414	7428	7331	7371
Y	13466	13476	13460	13466	13535	13537	13550	13564	13466	13602
M	2895	3335	2895	2895	2895	2893	2895	2895	2895	2895
p	111·75	118·23	111·80	111·75	111·18	112·47	111·06	110·95	111·75	110·63
p_a	118·25	132·16	118·37	118·25	116·82	119·60	117·01	116·79	118·25	115·68
p_c	135·27	143·76	135·33	135·27	133·88	135·58	134·58	134·46	135·27	133·87
p_i	106·31	106·58	106·30	106·31	106·51	106·56	106·15	106·12	106·31	106·36
p_{im}	122·08	123·09	122·07	122·08	122·82	123·02	121·49	121·39	122·08	122·28
$p_{inv.}$	131·73	133·43	131·73	131·73	132·12	132·46	131·20	131·11	131·73	131·75
W_i	165·18	169·04	165·21	165·18	164·39	165·16	164·90	164·85	165·18	164·61
I_a	189·39	192·93	185·04	189·39	188·89	189·60	189·15	189·11	189·39	193·30
I_i	853·37	886·17	853·26	826·13	871·83	878·60	876·81	880·78	767·0	855·98
p_x	115·03	123·19	115·09	115·03	114·31	115·93	114·16	114·02	115·03	113·62
X	562·08	544·72	561·95	562·08	563·61	560·15	563·93	564·23	562·08	565·08
MT	955·57	976·51	955·73	955·57	953·62	958·02	1038·71	952·81	955·57	951·71
M_c	171·90	172·10	171·86	171·90	173·52	173·57	173·86	174·19	171·90	172·84
M_k	418·76	439·50	418·97	418·76	415·19	419·55	499·96	513·72	418·76	413·97
I_i+G_i	1119·91	1172·95	1120·45	1119·91	1110·78	1121·93	1327·5	1362·7	1119·91	1107·65
G_i	266·54	286·77	267·19	293·79	238·95	243·3	450·72	481·94	352·91	251·67

TABLE 8.6 (*continued*)

EFFECTS OF VARIATION IN EXOGENOUS VARIABLES: 1963–64

Endogenous Variables	*No change*	$\Delta C = 100$ *every year*	$\Delta T_a = 100$	$\Delta T_i = 100$	$\Delta(M-X)_a = 100$	$\Delta(M-X)_a = 100$ *and* $\Delta C = 20$	$\Delta FC = 100$	$\Delta M_o = -100$	$\Delta GC = -10$	$\Delta G_a = 100$
Y_a	6349	6351	6343	6349	6348	6349	6349	6349	6349	6491
F_a	9305	9310	9292	9305	9304	9305	9305	9305	9305	9600
L_i	5332	5334	5328	5332	5450	5450	5332	5332	5332	5431
Y_i	7639	7659	7637	7639	7707	7712	7761	7782	7639	7698
Y	13988	14010	13979	13988	14056	14060	14110	14130	13988	14189
M	2896	3483	2896	2896	2896	3014	2896	2896	2896	2896
p	110·76	120·45	110·82	110·76	110·22	112·15	109·80	109·64	110·76	109·19
p_a	115·55	136·22	115·71	115·55	114·17	118·30	113·86	113·58	115·55	111·97
p_c	136·90	151·84	137·01	136·90	135·21	138·19	135·68	135·47	136·90	134·37
p_i	106·77	107·37	106·77	106·77	106·97	107·09	106·48	106·43	106·77	106·84
p_{im}	123·79	125·99	123·78	123·79	124·53	124·97	122·71	122·53	123·79	124·05
$p_{inv.}$	134·17	137·72	134·18	134·17	134·48	135·19	133·18	133·02	134·17	134·08
W_i	169·84	177·57	169·90	169·84	168·70	170·24	169·24	169·14	169·84	168·60
I_a	198·19	204·66	193·86	198·19	197·58	198·89	197·85	197·79	198·19	203·47
I_i	898·39	918·22	897·91	871·64	917·63	921·94	938·01	944·72	807·46	909·34
p_x	113·77	1259·80	113·86	113·77	113·10	115·53	1125·68	112·37	113·77	111·80
X	564·75	538·78	564·57	564·75	566·18	561·01	567·31	567·74	564·75	568·96
MT	952·14	983·11	952·38	952·14	950·27	956·93	1034·30	948·23	952·14	996·61
M_c	161·80	162·21	161·75	161·80	163·25	163·33	164·38	164·82	161·80	163·04
M_k	425·44	456·00	425·73	425·44	422·13	428·70	505·02	518·51	425·44	418·68
I_i+G_i	1136·98	1215·1	1137·7	1136·98	1128·51	1145·32	1340·46	1375·0	1136·98	1119·69
G_i	238·59	296·91	239·82	265·34	210·89	223·38	402·45	430·25	329·52	210·36

TABLE 8.6 (*continued*)

EFFECTS OF VARIATION IN EXOGENOUS VARIABLES: 1964–65

Endogenous Variables	*Variation in Exogenous Variables*									
	No change	$\Delta C = 100$ *every year*	$\Delta T_a = 100$	$\Delta T_i = 100$	$\Delta(M-X)_a = 100$	$\Delta(M-X)_a = 100$ *and* $\Delta C = 20$	$\Delta FC = 100$	$\Delta M_o = -100$	$\Delta GC = -10$	$\Delta G_a = 100$
Y_a	6562	6568	6554	6562	6561	6562	6562	6562	6562	6750
F_a	9747	9758	9730	9747	9745	9748	9746	9746	9747	10136
L_i	5480	5484	5474	5480	5598	5599	5480	5480	5480	5610
Y_i	7950	7986	7947	7950	8018	8025	8109	8136	7950	8026
Y	14513	14553	14501	14513	14579	14588	14671	14698	14513	14776
M	2898	3631	2898	2898	2898	3044	2898	2898	2898	2898
p	109·21	122·30	109·30	109·21	108·71	111·32	108·03	107·84	109·21	107·26
p_a	111·68	139·35	111·87	111·68	110·37	115·89	109·64	109·30	111·68	107·29
p_c	136·81	159·84	136·98	136·82	134·90	139·49	135·02	134·72	136·81	133·03
p_i	107·18	108·28	107·17	107·18	107·36	107·58	106·73	106·66	107·18	107·24
p_{im}	125·29	129·35	125·28	125·29	125·95	126·77	123·64	123·37	125·29	125·52
$p_{inv.}$	136·19	142·50	136·20	136·19	136·36	137·63	134·65	134·39	136·19	135·86
W_i	173·41	186·67	173·50	173·41	171·91	174·56	172·37	172·20	173·41	171·25
I_a	205·86	215·86	201·54	205·86	205·19	207·25	205·46	205·39	205·86	212·18
I_i	952·67	948·09	951·78	926·31	973·27	972·67	1008·89	1018·41	856·24	973·06
p_x	111·83	128·32	111·93	111·83	111·20	114·48	110·34	110·09	111·83	109·37
X	946·71	988·42	947·01	946·71	944·92	954·09	1027·96	941·75	946·71	939·64
MT	946·71	988·42	947·01	946·71	944·92	954·09	1027·96	941·75	946·71	939·64
M_c	150·34	151·01	150·28	150·34	151·62	151·76	153·35	153·85	150·34	151·78
M_k	431·46	472·51	431·83	431·46	428·40	437·43	509·72	522·99	431·46	422·97
I_i+G_i	1152·38	1257·33	1153·31	1152·38	1144·54	1167·64	1352·48	1386·43	1152·38	1130·66
G_i	199·71	309·25	201·53	226·07	171·27	194·98	343·59	368·02	296·14	157·60

Chapter 9

A Note on India's Third Five Year Plan

In this chapter we utilise our model to comment on some aspects of India's Third Five Year Plan. Of course, we have to remember that in reality Plans have to be formulated in the light of many economic, social, political and military considerations, and our model, as it stands, does not consider non-economic aspects of planning at all. Even in purely economic matters, our model is highly aggregative and thus incapable of yielding any detailed Plans which of course are necessary in practice. In spite of these limitations, it might be desirable to draw up a plan in the light of our model and if we find that the actual plans diverge too much from our estimates, there is, we could say, a *prima facie* case for re-examining the priorities of the Plan.

We begin with a statement of the objectives of the Third Five Year Plan. They were stated to be:

'(1) To secure a rise in national income of over 5 per cent per annum, the pattern of investment being designed also to sustain this rate of growth during subsequent Plan periods;

'(2) to achieve self-sufficiency in food-grains, and increase in agricultural production to meet the requirements of industry and exports;

'(3) to expand basic industries like steel, and chemicals, fuel and power and establish machine-building capacity, so that the requirements of further industrialisation can be met within a period of 10 years or so mainly from the country's own resources;

'(4) to utilise to the fullest possible extent the manpower resources of the country and to insure a substantial expansion in employment opportunities; and

'(5) to establish progressively greater equality of opportunity and to bring about reduction in disparties in income and wealth and a more even distribution of economic power.' (*Third Five Year Plan* (69), p. 48.)

In our context, there is no variable to indicate income distribution and therefore we cannot consider the objective (5) above. Nor do we consider the expansion of employment opportunities as an objective in itself. The objective (3) is also rather qualitative in character and our model is not sufficiently disaggregative to take into account different types of industries. However, we have postulated the maximisation of non-agricultural output as our objective in determination of investment allocation and this takes into account, to a certain extent, the objective (3) above. The two objectives that we can consider in our model explicitly are those about the rate of growth of income and self-sufficiency in food-grains. The objective of a rise in national income of 'over 5 per cent' per annum is rather vague. From the other statements in the *Third Five Year Plan* (69) it seems that the objective can be stated as a rise in national income of 6 per cent per annum. We take this figure as the objective in our exercise. There is also some vagueness about the pattern by which self-sufficiency in food-grains is to be achieved by the end of the Third Plan. We assume that the amount of net imports of food-grains in 1960–61 is to be linearly reduced over the period of the Third Plan so that by the year 1965–66 the net imports are zero.

TABLE 9.1

OPTIMUM PLAN ACCORDING TO OUR MODEL

Variables	*1961–62*	*1962–63*	*Years* *1963–64*	*1964–65*	*1965–66*
Y_a	6494	6905	7336	7787	8260
Y_i	7015	7414	7481	8299	8790
Y	13509	14319	15177	16086	17050
K_i/L_i	3·5656	3·6833	3·8030	3·9249	4·0492
L_i	5350	5551	5767	5997	6242
ΔK_a	1773	902	977	1056	1142
ΔK_i	28	1374	1485	1606	1736
$\Delta K = \Delta K_a + \Delta K_i$	1801	2276	2462	2662	2878

With these objectives given, our computer programme yields the optimum values of such variables as capital–labour ratio, employment in the non-agricultural sector, investment in the agricultural and the non-agricultural sector, food-grains output and agricultural and non-agricultural output. The computer programme in Chapter 8 started with a target rate of growth in the non-agricultural sector. However, with a slight modification of the programme we can also, start with a given rate of growth in national income as a whole. The results of this exercise are presented in Table 9.1.

The above table gives the annual investment targets for achieving the target rate of 6 per cent per annum growth in national income. One interesting thing that deserves mention is that in this scheme the first year of the Plan comes out as a 'consolidation' or rather 'correction' year. During this year net investment in non-agricultural sector is very small. Almost the whole of the net investment goes to the agricultural sector. This suggests that in 1960–61, agriculture had, in the light of our model, inadequate capital, and the non-agricultural sector was over-capitalised. After the initial correction has taken place, investment in the non-agricultural sector is in absolute terms greater than that in the agricultural sector, though both are increasing over time.

Next, we compare the above results with the actual plans as given in *The Third Five Year Plan*. The comparative picture is given in Table 9.2.

TABLE 9.2

A COMPARISON BETWEEN THE THIRD PLAN AND THE PLAN YIELDED BY OUR MODEL

	Our Model	*Third Plan*
1. Increase in agricultural output over the period 1961–66	40%	30%
2. Investment in agriculture	Rs. 5850 crores (at 48–49 prices)	Rs. 2110 crores
3. Investment in non-agriculture	Rs. 6229 crores (at 48–49 prices)	Rs. 8290 crores
4. Total investment	Rs. 12079 crores (at 48–49 prices)	Rs. 10400 crores
5. Increase in employment in non-agricultural sector	12·3 millions	10·5 millions
7. Incremental capital–labour ratio	Rs. 5064 (at 48–49 prices)	Rs. 7895

From the above table, it seems that in comparison with our model there was inadequate provision for investment in the agricultural sector in the Third Plan. Of course, we have to be careful in comparing these investment figures. For one thing, our investment figures are in 48–49 prices of investment goods, whereas the Plan figures are presumably at current prices. However, if our investment figures were expressed in current prices, they are likely to be only higher. Secondly, we have to remember that our agricultural sector is defined as vertically integrated; so that investment in fertiliser production for instance should, according to our model, be included in the agricultural sector, whereas in the Plan figures such investment would have been treated as non-agricultural investment. Thirdly, our model is a simplified one and it does not take into account the questions of technical progress, external economies of development of basic industries, etc. Lastly, our model does not consider political and military reasons which might have exerted some influence in determination of Plans. In spite of these qualifications, it seems that if the basic logic of our analysis is correct, there is at least a *prima facie* case for the re-examination of the priorities of our Plans. Our results also suggest that if the national income is to grow at 6 per cent per annum total investment has to be higher than that postulated in the Third Plan. Conversely, the investment proposed in the Third Plan is unlikely to yield the target rate of growth of national income. This implies that the production functions underlying the calculations of the Planning Commission over-estimate the productivity of capital. Lastly we find that our strategy will lead to a greater increase in employment than expected in the Third Plan and that the incremental capital–labour ratio implicit in the Plan is higher than the optimum yielded by our model. Inflating our incremental capital–labour ratio by the price index of the investment goods of 1960–61, we come out with a figure of Rs. 6611 at 60–61 prices. Assuming that the corresponding Plan figure of Rs. 7895 is at 60–61 prices, it is about 19 per cent higher than our optimum.

We can also utilise our model to determine the import requirements of the Plan. The import of capital goods is determined by the equation (7.19) (see Chapter 7) once the investment in non-agricultural sector is given. Similarly, given the income in the non-agricultural sector we can find out the import of raw materials and consumer goods from the equation (7.20) of Chapter 7. There is some difficulty about the determination of M_o which includes imports of miscellaneous goods and food-grains. In view of the assumption of self-sufficiency in food-grains by 1965–66, we would perhaps assume that M_o will decline over the period 1961–62 to 1965–66 to zero in a linear fashion. However M_o also includes miscellaneous goods and as an alternative, we can assume that M_o remains at the level of 1960–61. The above considerations will determine the value of MT for every year. There is, however, a further problem of prices of import goods over the Plan period. As a simplification, we assume that the prices in the Third Plan will remain the same as those in the year 1960–61. On the basis of these assumptions, we calculated from our our model the import requirements of Rs. 5471 crores (if we assume M_o = constant at the level of 1960–61) and of Rs. 3583 crores (if we assume M_o declining linearly to zero by 1965–66). By comparison, the Third Plan estimates the total import requirements to be Rs. 5750 crores. This does not differ very much from our first estimate and can be accepted as plausible. The level of exports in our model depends mainly on exogenous factors such as world income and export prices of underdeveloped countries. Since our model does not predict these exogenous variables, we refrain from any computation of possible export earnings.

Next we consider the monetary and price aspects of the Plan. As regards prices, the Third Plan states '. . . it is essential to ensure that there is no accentuation of inflationary pressures in the course of the Third Plan and that the levels of living of the more vulnerable classes in society are safeguarded' (op. cit., p. 119). Assuming that the phrase 'no accentuation of inflationary pressures' means that the general price level within the Third Five Year Plan period be the same as that in 1960–61, we can find out the amount of deficit financing permissible in the Third Plan period.

The Third Plan suggests a deficit financing of the amount of Rs. 550 crores. The final document does not explain the rationale of this figure but some argument is presented in *Third Five Year Plan: A Draft Outline* (68). The argument runs as follows: 'On a broad consideration of the trends in aggregate output, one might assume that money supply could increase by about 33 per cent in the third plan period without causing excessive pressure on prices. On the basis of an estimated quantum of money supply by the end of the second plan, the additional money creation permissible in the third plan might be of the order of Rs. 950 crores—if it is assumed that money supply and aggregate output would be approximately in balance at the end of the second plan. Part of the increase in money supply comes about through the banking system. Allowing for this, the amount of budgetary deficits that could be considered permissible for the Third Plan is taken at Rs. 550 cores' (op. cit., p. 49).

The basic logic of the above argument is similar to ours. However, with the help of our estimated equations we can make a more precise and more explicit computation of the permissible amount of deficit financing—which is defined as the same as currency creation. *Assuming that the aggregate output increases at the target rate*, and price level (p) is to be kept at the level of 1960–61, we can find out the safe amount of money supply and currency from the equations (7.6) and (7.7) of Chapter 7. The results of these computations are given in Table 9.3.

From this table, we find that the permissible amount of deficit financing according to our model is Rs. 706 crores over the Third Plan period. This is somewhat higher than the estimate given in the Third Plan.

Among other sources of financial resources, the Plan considers direct and indirect taxation, surplus from state-owned enterprises, public borrowings, etc. These are mostly presented as rough estimates of the potentialities of the various sources and there is no adequate

TABLE 9.3

DETERMINATION OF DEFICIT FINANCING

Year	M_t	C_t	ΔC_t
1960–61	2730	1956	
1961–62	3095	2093	137
1962–63	3287	2223	130
1963–64	3490	2361	138
1964–65	3706	2507	146
1965–66	3934	2662	155
			Total 706

analysis of the optimality or the procedure of these estimates, in the Plan. Our model considers only the direct taxation under the headings of agricultural taxation (T_a) and non-agricultural taxation (T_i). However, these are exogenous variables in our model and we have no basis of estimating the potentialities of these revenues in the context of our model. We have analysed the effects of variation in T_a and T_i on various endogenous variables; but in the absence of any welfare function dependent on endogenous variables, we have not been able to suggest any optimal tax policy. Our model has to be considerably expanded, before we can consider these problems.

In the above analysis we have been able to comment only on some aggregative aspects of India's Third Five Year Plan. However, it does suggest how econometric model building could be helpful for planning in underdeveloped countries. One important problem is presented by the lack of suitable data. We could not even find the annual figures of net investment in different sectors over the period under study. Similarly, in spite of the importance of a marketed surplus of agriculture, no systematic data on it are available. Nor are annual figures of employment in different sectors of the economy published. The coverage of figures on wages and profits is also very limited. To the extent that the assumptions made in the compilation of the data are inaccurate, the results yielded by our model have to be taken cautiously, though our model retains its importance as an exercise in methodology. It seems that if econometric model building is to serve its rightful purpose in planning, much more effort has to be devoted to the collection and publication of statistics along the lines suitable for econometric uses.

APPENDIX I

The Compilation of the Data

In recent years there has been a considerable growth in the volume of official economic statistics in India. However, in spite of this, we could not get all the data necessary for our model from the published sources. Inevitably, we had to build up many series ourselves on the basis of many scattered sources of information, and we had to introduce various assumptions in the process. This was over and above the fact that the published data are themselves based upon very many assumptions and on rather inaccurate reporting at the primary stage of data collection. Thus the data that emerged finally and the statistical estimates based on them cannot be regarded as fully accurate. However, in spite of these difficulties, this type of exercise seems worthwhile to us. In the first place, however inadequate the data may be, the policy-makers have to take quantitative decisions and it is better to base them on some rough data than on pure intuition. Secondly, this type of exercise may emphasise the particular directions in which the existing data are deficient so that in future attempts might be made to improve them. The sources used for the compilation of our data are noted below.*

I.1: AGRICULTURAL PRODUCTION FUNCTION

I.1.1: TIME-SERIES DATA

Y_a: net agricultural outout (value added) at 1948–49 prices (in Rs. crores)

The estimates for the years 1948–49 to 1960–61 were obtained from *Estimates of National Income 1948–49 to 1961–62* (52)

The estimates for the years 1920–21 to 1947–48 were obtained from K. Mukerji (105).

K_a: mid-year capital in agriculture at 48–49 prices (in Rs. crores)

* For details of the computations involved in this compilation, the interested reader is again referred to the author's Ph.D. thesis.

(i) For the years 1948–49 to 1960–61 our procedure was to start with the estimates of capital in agriculture at the beginning of the year 1950–51 and then to build up the capital series for other years by adding or subtracting the net investment figures of the relevant years. The main sources utilised for this purpose are:

M. Mukherjee and N. S. R. Sastry (107), *Reserve Bank of India Bulletin*, January, 1963, *Estimates of Gross Capital Formation in India 1948–49 to 1960–61* (C.S.O.), *Estimates of National Income* (C.S.O.), and *Economic Survey of Asia and Far East* (163).

(ii) For the years prior to 1948–49 no official statistics on capital formation are available. We had to build up a very rough series in the following way. The principal components of agricultural capital as given by Mukherjee and Sastry (107) are the following: livestock, agricultural implements, private irrigation, public irrigation and plantations. Our method was to try to build up indices for each of these components for a period as far back as we could go. Then utilising Mukherjee and Sastry figures of capital in March 1956, we built up the complete series for capital in value terms. The main sources of information in this connection are *Livestock Censuses* and *Statistical Abstracts of British India.*

R_2: rainfall as an indicator of climate

As discussed in Chapter 3, the climate is indicated in our model by the percentage deviation of the actual rainfall from the normal rainfall. The main sources are: *The Statistical Abstracts*, *Monthly and Annual Rainfall* (57) and *Agricultural Situation in India* (47).

L_a: number of workers in agriculture (in 10,000)

The figures of workers in agriculture for Census years were obtained from B. R. Kalra (83).

LD: net area of land sown (in 100,000 acres)

These figures were obtained from the various issues of *Statistical Abstracts* and *Indian Agricultural in Brief* (55).

I.2: FOOD-GRAINS PRODUCTION FUNCTION

F_a: production of food-grains (in 10,000 metric tons)

The figures were obtained by using *Statistical Abstract, 1961*, *Indian Agriculture in Brief* (6th edition) and J. P. Bhattacharjee (14).

Y_a: net agricultural output (value added) at 48–49 prices (Rs. crores)

Already explained in (I.1).

I.3: EMPLOYMENT FUNCTION IN NON-AGRICULTURAL SECTOR

L_i: employment in the non-agricultural sector (number of workers in 10,000)

The figures for the years 1948–49 to 1950–51 were taken straightaway from the *Final Report of the National Income Committee* (53).

The figures for the years 1951–52 to 1960–61 had to be obtained by the combined use of the information provided in the *Digest of Indian Labour Statistics* (50) for the years 1960 and 1963 and the *Census of India* 1961, Paper No. 1.

F_a: production of food-grains (in 10,000 metric tons)

Explained above in (I.2).

$(M-X)_a$: net import of food-grains (in 10,000 metric tons)

For the years 1950–51 to 1960–61, the figures of imports and exports of food-grains were obtained from *Indian Agriculture in Brief* (6th edition) (55). For the years 1948–49 and 1949–50 the figures were obtained from J. P. Bhattacharjee (14).

I.4: NON-AGRICULTURAL PRODUCTION FUNCTION

I.4.1: GENERAL TIME-SERIES DATA

Y_i: output (value added) in the non-agricultural sector at 1948–49 prices (in Rs. crores)

These were obtained from the *Estimates of National Income 1948–49 to 1961–62* (52).

K_i: mid-year capital in the non-agricultural sector at 48–49 prices (in Rs. crores)

The procedure of its compilation was basically the same as that followed in the compilation of K_a in (I.1).

L_i: employment in the non-agricultural sector (number of workers in 10,000)

Already explained in (I.3).

I.4.2: CENSUS OF MANUFACTURING INDUSTRIES (C.M.I.) TIME-SERIES DATA (1946–58)

Y_i: value added in manufacturing industries (in Rs. millions)

These figures were obtained from various issues of *Statistical Abstracts of India.*

L_i: total number of employees in manufacturing industries (in thousands)

These were taken from *Statistical Abstracts.*

K_i: capital in manufacturing industries (in Rs. millions)

The original figures were again obtained from the *Statistical Abstracts*. However, for our purposes we had to process them to a certain extent. The original capital figures are at book-values. In order to use them in our production function analysis, we had to reduce them to constant investment cost prices.

I.4.3: C.M.I. CROSS-SECTION DATA

The data in this connection refer to those for 29 industries in 1958. The values for Y_i, K_i and L_i were all taken from the *Statistical Abstract, 1961.*

I.4.4: ANNUAL SURVEY OF INDUSTRIES (A.S.I.): CROSS-SECTION DATA

In this case, the data on value added, man hours worked and productive capital were taken from *Annual Survey of Industries, 1960*, Vol. I (48).

I.5: MONEY SUPPLY FUNCTION

C: notes and currency with the public (in Rs. crores)
M: money supply with the public (in Rs. crores) defined as notes and currency with the public plus demand deposits of the public with the banks.

Our series of C and M relate to the years 1901–02 to 1961–62. There is no official series on money supply over this period. We had to build up a series on the basis of scattered information and a good many assumptions. The main source was:

Banking and Monetary Statistics of India (128), Reserve Bank of India, 1954.

I.6: MONEY-INCOME DETERMINATION EQUATION

pY: net national income at current prices (in Rs. crores)

The figures for the years 1948–49 to 1961–62 were obtained from the *Estimates of National Income 1948–49 to 1960–61* (52).

The main sources were K. Mukerji (105) and *Statistical Abstracts*.

i: the rate of interest indicated by the annual average yield on Government of India securities (3% conversion loans, 1986 or later)

Banking and Monetary Statistics of India (128) gives these figures for every month over the years 1901 to 1952. We obtained the annual average by taking the average of 12 months of the fincial years over the period, 1901–02 to 1951–52. From 1952–53 to 1961–62, the figures were obtained from the annual *Reports on Currency and Finance*, Reserve Bank of India.

N: population of India (in crores)

The figures for the years prior to 1948–49 were taken from K. Mukerji (105). For the years 1948–49 to 1961–62, they were calculated from the figures of total national income and the *per capita* income as given by C.S.O. *Estimates of National Income*.

I.7: PRICE EQUATIONS

p: general price level given by the implicit price deflator of the national income (base 1948–49 = 100)

p_a: price of agricultural goods, indicated by the implicit price deflator of the agricultural income (base 1948–49 = 100)

p_i: price of non-agricultural sector, indicated by the implicit price deflator of the non-agricultural income (base 1948–49 = 100)

p_{im}: price of the manufacturing sector, indicated by the implicit price deflator of the mining, manufacturing and small enterprises in national income statistics (base 1948–49 = 100)

All these price indices were computed from the *Estimates of National Income, 1948–49 to 1961–62.*

p_c: working class cost of living index (base 1948–49 = 100)

W_i: index of earnings of factory workers (base 1948–49 = 100)

The figures for the years 1939–51 for p_c and W_i were obtained from *Indian Labour Gazette*, November 1955, and those for the years 1951–62 from the *Digest of Indian Labour Statistics*, 1964.

$\frac{\delta Y_i}{\delta L_i}$: marginal productivity of labour in non-agricultural sector

These were obtained from the estimated production function of the non-agricultural sector and the values of capital and labour in the non-agricultural sector for every year. The marginal product thus obtained in terms of constant 48–49 prices was then expressed in terms of indices with base 1948–49 = 100. This was done in order to make it comparable with the wage index.

$p_{inv.}$: investment cost index (base 1948–49 = 100)

The original data were obtained from two sources. For the years 1938–39 to 1949–50, the investment cost index was obtained from Mukherjee and Sastry (107). For the years 1949–50 to 1960–61 another investment cost index was obtained from *Reserve Bank of India Bulletin*, January 1963. These two indices were then chained and transferred to the base 1948–49 = 100.

I.8: INVESTMENT FUNCTION IN THE AGRICULTURAL SECTOR

I.8.1: TIME-SERIES DATA

I_a: private investment in the agricultural sector at 48–49 prices (in Rs. crores)

The source of data for this variable are already explained in connection with the explanation of K_a in (I.1).

T_a: taxation in agriculture (in Rs. crores)

This refers to land revenue only. The figures were obtained from the *Estimates of National Income, 1948–49 to 1961–62*, C.S.O. (52).

I.8.2: CROSS-SECTION DATA

The data in this connection were obtained from *Studies in the Economics of Farm Management* (67), *National Sample Survey Reports* on second round (June 1950 to March 1951) and third round (October 1950 to September 1951).

I.9: PRIVATE INVESTMENT FUNCTION IN THE NON-AGRICULTURAL SECTOR

I.9.1: TIME-SERIES DATA

I_i: net private investment in the non-agricultural sector at constant 48–49 prices (in Rs. crores)

The method of compiling I_i is already explained in connection with explanation for compiling K_i in (I.4).

GC: percentage of the applications for capital issues for which consent was given by the Controller of capital issues

This was obtained from the various issues of the *Report on Currency and Finance*, Reserve Bank of India.

T_i: taxation in the non-agricultural sector (in Rs. crores)

This was defined to include corporation tax and income tax only. The indirect taxes are ignored because they do not enter into the estimates of value added that we are using. The figures were obtained from *Estimates of National Income, 1948–49 to 1960–61* (52).

II: industrial profit index at constant prices (with base 1948–49 = 100)

Progress of Joint Stock Companies in India (60), Government of India, gives the industrial profit index with base 1939 = 100 for the years 1928 to 1953. *Statistical Abstract*, 1961, gives the index of industrial profits with base 1951 = 100 for the years 1951 to 1958. *Reserve Bank of India Bulletin, June 1962*, gives the figures of profits after tax of 1001 selected public limited companies for the years 1955 to 1960, from which we built an index of profits with base 1955 = 100.

We utilised the indices given above to obtain our series for π.

I.9.2: INVESTMENT IN SELECTED INDUSTRIES

Figures of capital formation, production and capacity were all taken from G. Rosen (134). Indices of profits were taken from *Progress of Joint Stock Companies in India* and they were deflated by the investment cost index for particular industries also given by G. Rosen.

I.9.3: CHANGES IN PAID-UP CAPITAL IN JOINT STOCK COMPANIES

Paid-up capital figures for companies registered and at work in India were obtained from *Progress of Joint Stock Companies in India* (160).

Indices of industrial profit were again those obtained from *Progress of Joint Stock Companies in India* and they were deflated by the investment cost index in the same way as were the figures of changes in capital.

Indices of industrial activity (base 1935 = 100) were taken from K. Mukerji (106).

I.9.4: CROSS-SECTION ANALYSIS OF THE INVESTMENT OF PUBLIC LIMITED COMPANIES IN CERTAIN INDUSTRIES

All the data in this connection were obtained from *Reserve Bank of India Bulletin*, September 1961.

I.10: FOREIGN TRADE EQUATIONS

MT: total merchandise imports at 48–49 prices (in Rs. crores)
p_m: import price index (base 1948–49 = 100)
X: exports at 48–49 prices (in Rs. crores)
p_x: export price index (base 1948–49 = 100)

The figures of imports and exports at current prices were obtained from *Estimates of National Income 1948–49 to 1951–62* (52). The unit value indices of imports and exports were obtained from the *Statistical Abstracts* (66), 1961 and the *Report on Currency and Finance* (130), 1961–62.

M_k: import of capital goods deflated by the general import price index (in Rs. crores)
M_c: import of raw materials and consumer goods (excepting food-grains) deflated by the import price index (in Rs. crores)
M_o: import of food-grains and other miscellaneous imports deflated by the import price index (in Rs. crores)

F: foreign exchange reserves of India at the beginning of the year (in Rs. crores)

The data relating to the above series were obtained from *India's Balance of Payments 1948–49 to 1961–62* (129). The original figures were in current prices. We deflated them by the general import price index in order to maintain the identity (7.21) of Chapter 7, though theoretically a separate price index for each item would have been more appropriate.

FC: foreign capital inflow at current prices (in Rs. crores)

In view of the identity (7.18) of Chapter 7, this was nothing but the annual trade balance. Thus in our definition it included movements of foreign reserves, movement of non-monetary gold, official donation, 'other invisibles', private capital and 'errors and omissions'. All these items should not, strictly speaking be designated as 'foreign capital'. But the name 'foreign capital' is only a convenient expression in this context and the variable as defined by us does possess the desirable characteristic of being exogenous.

Y_w: index of gross domestic product of world at constant factor cost (base 1958 = 100)

The figures for the years 1950 to 1960 were obtained from the *U.N. Statistical Yearbook* (164), 1964. The calendar year figures were taken as approximations for the financial years as well. The figures for 1948 and 1949 were not available in *U.N. Yearbooks*. So we computed them from the regression equation: $Y_w = Ae^{\lambda t}$ fitted to the data for the years 1950–61. The fitted equation was:

(I.10.1) $$\log Y_w = \underset{(0{\cdot}007)}{4.3237} + \underset{(0{\cdot}001)}{0{\cdot}0385}\, t$$

$$\bar{R}^2 = 0{\cdot}9917;\ \delta^2/S^2 = 2{\cdot}021$$

The fit was quite good by every statistical criterion. Therefore, we used this approximation as a tolerable one.

X_w: world export volume index (base 1958 = 100)

X_u: export volume index of underdeveloped countries (base 1958 = 100)

p_{xw}: unit value index of world exports in U.S. dollars (base 1958 = 100)

p_{xu}: unit value index of exports of underdeveloped countries in U.S. dollars (base 1958 = 100)

These data were obtained from U.N. *Statistical Yearbooks* (164) for the years 1964, 1963, 1962 and 1956. The original data were transferred to a common base with 1958 = 100 for our purposes. Two figures that had to be computed were p_{xu} and X_u for 1949. They were not available in *U.N. Yearbooks* under the heading 'underdeveloped countries'. So we constructed them by taking the weighted average of indices of exports volume and export price of the following countries: Latin America (weight: 10·3), Morocco, Tunisia (weight: 3·8), Far East Independent Countries (weight: 3·8), 'Rest of the Sterling Area' (weight: 9·1), 'Middle East Non-Sterling' (weight: 2·0), 'Other Far East' (weight: 4·2). The figures of exports volume and export price index of these countries, as well as their weights, were obtained from the U.N. *Statistical Yearbooks.*

In the above discussion, we have explained the methods of compilation of the variables which we finally accepted in our model as well as those with which we experimented but which we did not select ultimately. However, in view of the volume of the data, it seems desirable to confine ourselves to presenting only the data on the variables that enter into our final model. The data for the common period 1948–49 to 1961–62 for all the variables are given in Table I.1. The data for series extending over longer periods are given in Tables I.2, I.3, and I.4.

TABLE I.1

THE DATA, 1948–49 TO 1960–61

Year	Y_a	K_a	R_2	F_a	L_i	$(M-X)_a$	Y_i	K_i
1948–49	4250	5031	14·80	4952	3829	284	4400	10780
49–50	4360	5126	9·06	4822	3891	376	4460	11152
50–51	4340	5259	12·60	5083	3958	481	4510	11481
51–52	4440	5405	19·26	5200	3922	392	4660	11913
52–53	4600	5560	12·83	5920	4044	203	4860	12309
53–54	4980	5723	13·69	6982	4044	83	5050	12706
54–55	5030	5907	11·96	6804	4126	60	5250	13243
55–56	5020	6124	18·12	6685	4244	140	5460	13844
56–57	5250	6368	35·57	6985	4530	365	5750	14800
57–58	5010	6621	12·76	6351	4961	322	5880	15806
58–59	5560	6872	16·05	7671	4812	387	6090	16765
59–60	5510	7135	21·22	7590	4852	514	6350	17882
1960–61	5910	7399	20·83	8098	5012	350	6840	19046

TABLE I.1 (*continued*)

Year	Y	M	C	pY	p	p_a	p_i	p_c
1948–49	8650	1877	1211	8650	100·00	100·00	100·00	100·0
49–50	8820	1837	1200	9010	102·15	102·98	101·35	103·0
50–51	8850	1844	1205	9530	107·68	112·67	102·88	103·0
51–52	9100	1850	1217	9970	109·56	113·06	106·22	107·5
52–53	9460	1725	1140	9820	103·80	104·57	103·09	105·5
53–54	10030	1757	1173	10480	104·48	106·63	102·38	108·6
54–55	10280	1814	1220	9610	93·48	86·48	100·19	103·4
55–56	10480	2017	1367	9980	95·22	90·04	100·00	98·3
56–57	11000	2191	1494	11310	102·81	105·14	100·70	107·5
57–58	10890	2308	1542	11390	104·59	105·39	103·91	113·6
58–59	11650	2373	1606	12600	108·15	112·23	104·43	118·3
59–60	11860	2531	1747	12950	109·19	113·43	105·51	123·8
1960–61	12750	2730	1956	14160	111·05	116·51	106·14	127·0

TABLE I.1 (*continued*)

Year	p_{im}	W_i	$p_{inv.}$	I_a	T_a	I_i	GC	T_i	p_x
1948–49	100·00	100·0	100·00	52	42	276	(87·0	197	100·00
49–50	102·73	111·9	103·48	93	47	248	86·7	172	103·40
50–51	103·37	109·9	104·08	86	52	218	87·9	179	114·60
51–52	110·52	117·4	111·30	109	50	400	87·2	193	168·90
52–53	107·59	125·7	110·12	113	60	153	26·1	188	118·90
53–54	107·27	126·4	110·24	107	70	434	90·6	170	111·20
54–55	105·88	126·4	109·53	124	70	294	94·5	167	116·80
55–56	105·11	132·8	111·02	133	75	435	82·8	180	107·66
56–57	108·69	135·5	114·90	166	79	844	90·4	214	112·44
57–58	113·97	141·8	119·21	159	83	327	74·1	240	112·44
58–59	115·42	143·6	122·82	160	85	720	92·3	251	111·25
59–60	117·76	148·4	124·69	163	87	534	98·0	284	108·85
1960–61	123·22	157·8	130·55	171	87	727	98·8	224	118·84

TABLE I.1 (*continued*)

Year	p_{xu}	X	Y_w	p_m	MT	FC	M_k	G_i	M_c	G_a
1948–49	102	482	70	100·0	766	284	150·4	127	256·1	28
49–50	95	497	73	97·3	621	90	185·6	94	208·2	43
50–51	97	565	74	109·0	596	3	148·9	97	231·5	77
51–52	122	432	79	130·2	740	233	136·8	150	286·8	101
52–53	111	506	82	128·7	492	31	140·2	89	189·9	116
53–54	103	486	86	114·4	517	52	139·8	118	204·5	143
54–55	105	511	87	115·6	592	87	190·9	228	200·4	189
55–56	105	594	93	111·05	685	121	283·1	244	228·5	241
56–57	104	565	96	116·15	946	464	431·4	390	236·0	202
57–58	104	595	99	125·09	986	565	443·8	450	190·1	207
58–59	100	518	100	117·43	876	435	394·7	421	154·1	223
59–60	97	578	106	114·87	808	299	298·1	559	210·0	242
1960–61	98	531	111	116·95	942	471	359·9	509	217·2	261

TABLE I.2

AGRICULTURAL PRODUCTION, CAPITAL AND RAINFALL, 1920–21 TO 1947–48

Year	Y_a	K_a	R_2	*Year*	Y_a	K_a	R_2
1920–21	3807	4633	18·01	1940–41	4534	4966	9·57
21–22	4537	4647	5·90	41–42	4331	4982	15·34
22–23	4698	4643	11·03	42–43	4539	4956	14·38
23–24	3970	4649	8·40	43–44	4712	4947	8·80
24–25	4236	4646	11·53	44–45	4500	4971	14·17
25–26	4288	4694	9·24	45–46	4132	5028	10·16
26–27	4302	4756	7·84	46–47	4219	5114	15·10
27–28	4339	4694	9·06	47–48	4399	5146	7·20
28–29	4450	4721	9·03				
29–30	4534	4846	7·91				
1930–31	4598	4859	5·71				
31–32	4540	4844	7·29				
32–33	4523	4854	11·32				
33–34	4564	4868	21·84				
34–35	4448	4877	9·25				
35–36	4367	4884	9·45				
36–37	4387	4869	18·24				
37–38	4673	4884	8·32				
38–39	4264	4924	11·57				
39–40	4493	4946	10·51				

TABLE I.3

MONEY WAGES AND COST OF LIVING INDICES, 1939–40 TO 1947–48

Year	W_i	p_c
1939–40	32·9	27·8
40–41	34·6	26·9
41–42	36·5	29·7
42–43	42·5	40·3
43–44	59·1	74·4
44–45	66·5	74·7
45–46	66·3	74·7
46–47	68·6	79·2
47–48	83·3	89·7

TABLE I.4

MONEY, CURRENCY AND INCOME, 1901–02 TO 1947–48

Year	M	C	pY	*Year*	M	C	pY
1901–02	118	102	1085	1924–25	434	341	3154
02–03	123	105	1177	25–26	437	342	3197
03–04	136	116	1116	26–27	412	316	3051
04–05	142	119	1072	27–28	424	330	2969
05–06	159	135	1275	28–29	431	335	3045
06–07	176	150	1529	29–30	400	306	3030
07–08	182	154	1343	1930–31	378	281	2481
08–09	170	141	1504	31–32	377	286	1927
09–10	187	153	1539	32–33	368	268	1900
1910–11	196	158	1559	33–34	377	276	1876
11–12	207	167	1615	34–35	380	276	1923
12–13	222	179	1759	35–36	393	294	2046
13–14	223	181	1740	36–37	410	303	2108
14–15	209	168	1834	37–38	419	308	2294
15–16	227	185	2216	38–39	406	291	2191
16–17	266	216	2663	39–40	448	322	2552
17–18	285	215	2886	1960–41	529	379	2823
18–19	387	315	2835	41–42	633	439	3236
19–20	439	343	3820	42–43	967	674	4137
1920–21	414	311	3522	43–44	1276	839	5247
21–22	427	326	3235	44–45	1499	937	5835
22–23	416	326	3229	45–46	1737	1102	6000
23–24	427	340	2880	46–47	1851	1161	6576
				1947–48	1845	1164	7200

Bibliography

1. Anstey, Vera, *The Economic Development of India*, 4th edition, Longmans, London, 1952.
2. Arora, H. C., and Iyengar, K. R. R., 'Long Term Growth of National Income in India, 1901–1956', in *National Income and Allied Topics*, Vol. I, edited by V. K. R. V. Rao, S. R. Sen, M. V. Divatia and Uma Datta, Asia Publishing House, London, 1960.
3. Arrow, K. J., Chenery, H. B., Minhas, B. S., and Solow, R. M., 'Capital–Labour Substitution and Economic Efficiency', *The Review of Economics and Statistics*, August 1961.
4. Atkinson, F. J., 'A Statistical Review of the Income and Wealth of British India', *Journal of the Royal Statistical Society*, June 1902.
5. Baldwin, R. E., 'Export Technology and Development from a Subsistence Level', *The Economic Journal*, March 1963.
6. Ball, R. J., 'Some Econometric Analysis of the Long Term Rate of Interest in the U.K., 1921–61', *The Manchester School of Economics and Social Studies*, January 1965.
7. Banerji, H., 'An Analysis of Import Demand', *Artha Vijnana*, September 1959.
8. Baring, E., and Barbour, D., Cited in Digby, W., *'Prosperous' British India* (28).
9. Barna, T., 'The Replacement Cost of Fixed Assets in British Manufacturing Industry, in 1955', *Journal of the Royal Statistical Society*, 1957.
10. Bernstein, E. M., 'International Effects of U.S. Economic Policy', prepared in connection with the study of *Employment, Growth and Price Levels* for the Joint Economic Committee, January 1960.
11. Berrill, K., 'Foreign Capital and Take-off', in *The Economics of Take-off into Sustained Growth*, Proceedings of a Conference held by the International Economic Association, edited by W. W. Rostow, Macmillan & Co. Ltd., London, 1963.
12. Bhatia, R. J., 'The Production Function for Indian Manufacturers, 1948', *Journal of the Bombay University*, January 1954.

13. BHATT, V. V., *Aspects of Economic Change and Policy in India, 1800–1960*, Allied Publishers (Private) Limited, Bombay, 1963.
14. BHATTACHARJEE, J. P., 'Trend of Food and Foodgrains in India', in *Studies in Agricultural Economics* edited by J. P. Bhattacharjee, The Indian Society of Agricultural Economics, Bombay, 1958.
15. BHATTACHARJEE, J. P. (Ed.), *Studies in Agricultural Economics*, Tenth International Conference of Agricultural Economists (Mysore, 1958), The Indian Society of Agricultural Economics, Bombay, 1958.
16. BISWAS, D., 'The Indian Money Market: An Analysis of Money Demand', *The Indian Economic Journal*, January 1962.
17. BUCHANAN, D. H., *The Development of Capitalistic Enterprise in India*, Macmillan & Co. Ltd., New York, 1934.
18. BUCHANAN, N. S., *International Investment and Domestic Welfare*, Henry, Holt & Co., New York, 1945.
19. CAGAN, P., 'The Demand for Currency Relative to the Total Money Supply', *The Journal of Political Economy*, August 1958.
20. CHENERY, H. B., 'Overcapacity and the Acceleration Principle', *Econometrics*, January 1952.
21. CLARK, C. G., *The Conditions of Economic Progress*, Macmillan & Co. Ltd., London 1957.
22. CLARK, R., 'The Economic Determinants of Jute Production', *Monthly Bulletin of Agricultural Economics and Statistics*, September, 1957, F.A.O., Rome.
23. COHEN, B. I., 'The Stagnation of Indian Exports, 1951–61', *The Quarterly Journal of Economics*, November 1964.
24. CURZON, LORD, Cited in W. Digby, *'Prosperous' British India* (28).
25. DANDEKAR, V. M., *Second Report on the Poona Schedules of the National Sample Survey (1950–51)*, Gokhale Institute of Politics and Economics, Poona, 1956.
26. DATTA, B., *Essays in Plan Economics: A Commentary on Indian Planning Experience*, World Press, Calcutta, 1963.
27. DATTA, K. L., *Report on the Enquiry into the Rise of Prices in India*, Vols. I–III, Calcutta, 1914.
28. DIGBY, W., *'Prosperous' British India: A Revelation from Official Records*, T. Fisher Unwin, London, 1901.
29. DIVATIA, M. V., and TRIVEDI, H. M., *Industrial Capital in India, 1938–39*, N. M. Tripathy Ltd., Bombay, 1947.
30. DUTT, M. M., 'The Production Function for Indian Manufacturers', *Sankhya: The Indian Journal of Statistics*, Part 4, 1955.

31. DUTT, R., *The Economic History of India Under Early British Rule*, London (7th edition), 1950.
32. DUTTA, M., 'A Prototype Model of India's Foreign Sector', *International Economic Review*, January 1964.
33. DUTTA, M., 'Measuring the Role of Price in International Trade: Some Further Tests', *Econometrics*, July 1965.
34. DUTTA, M., 'Import Structure of India', *The Review of Economics and Statistics*, August 1965.
35. ECKAUS, R. S., 'The Factor Proportions Problem in Underdeveloped Areas', *American Economic Review*, September, 1955.
36. EICHER, C. K., and WITT, L. W. (Ed.), *Agriculture in Economic Development*, McGraw-Hill Book Company, New York, 1964.
37. EZEKIEL, M. J. B., and FOX, K. A., *Methods of Correlation and Regression Analysis: Linear and Curvilinear* (3rd Edition), John, Wiley & Son, Inc., New York, 1959.
38. EZEKIEL, M., 'Impact and Implications of Foreign Surplus Disposal on Developed Economies and Foreign Competitors: the International Perspective', *Journal of Farm Economics*, December 1960.
39. FAIRNBAIRN, C., and DWIGHT, C. J. (compilers), *Tea Shares Manual, 1963*, London, January 1964.
40. FISHER, F. M., 'Dynamic Structure and Estimation in Economy-wide Econometric Models' in *The Brookings Quarterly Econometric Model of the U.S.* edited by J. S. Duesenberry, G. Fromm, L. R. Klein and E. Kuh, Rand McNally and Company, Chicago, 1965.
41. FRIEDMAN, M., 'The Quantity Theory of Money—A Restatement', in *Studies in the Quantity Theory of Money*, edited by M. Friedman, Chicago, 1956.
42. FRIEDMAN, M., 'The Demand for Money: some Theoretical and Empirical Results', *Journal of Political Economy*, August 1959.
43. FRIEDMAN, M., and MEISELMAN, D., 'The Relative Stability of Monetary Velocity and the Investment Multiplier in the U.S., 1897–1958', in *Stabilisation Policies*, a series of research studies prepared for the Commission on Money and Credit, Prentice-Hall, Inc. Englewood Cliffs, N.J., 1963.
44. FRIEDMAN, M., and SCHWARTZ, ANNA J., *A Monetary History of the U.S. 1867–1960*, National Bureau of Economic Research Studies in Business Cycles, 12, Princeton University Press, 1963.
45. GALENSON, W., and LEIBENSTEIN, H., 'Investment Criteria, Productivity and Economic Development', *The Quarterly Journal of Economics*, August 1955.
46. GOLDBERGER, A. S., *Impact Multipliers and Dynamic Properties*

of the Klein–Goldberger Model, North-Holland Publishing Co., Amsterdam, 1959.

47. GOVERNMENT OF INDIA, *Agricultural Situation in India*, Monthly, Ministry of Food and Agriculture, Manager of Publication, Delhi.
48. GOVERNMENT OF INDIA, *Annual Survey of Industries, 1960*, Central Statistical Organisation, Department of Economics, Cabinet Secretariat.
49. GOVERNMENT OF INDIA, *Census of India*, Reports and Papers, Decennial Series, Manager of Publications, Delhi.
50. GOVERNMENT OF INDIA, *Digest of Indian Labour Statistics*, Annual, Labour Bureau, Ministry of Labour and Employment.
51. GOVERNMENT OF INDIA, *Estimates of Gross Capital Formation in India for 1948–49 to 1960–61*, Central Statistical Organisation, Cabinet Secretariat, 1961.
52. GOVERNMENT OF INDIA, *Estimates of National Income, 1948–49 to 1961–62*, Central Statistical Organisation, Cabinet Secretariat, 1963.
53. GOVERNMENT OF INDIA, *Final Report of the National Income Committee*, Department of Economic Affairs, Ministry of Finance, 1954.
54. GOVERNMENT OF INDIA, *India: Pocket Book of Economic Information* (Annual), 1963, Department of Economic Affairs, Ministry of Finance.
55. GOVERNMENT OF INDIA, *Indian Agriculture in Brief* (Annual), 1963, Directorate of Economics and Statistics, Ministry of Food and Agriculture.
56. GOVERNMENT OF INDIA, *Indian Labour Gazette*, 1955, Ministry of Labour.
57. GOVERNMENT OF INDIA, *Monthly and Annual Rainfall*, Vol. XXXI Part III, 1959, The Meteorological Department.
58. GOVERNMENT OF INDIA, *The National Sample Survey*, Reports, Department of Economic Affairs, Ministry of Finance.
59. GOVERNMENT OF INDIA, *The Planning Process*, Planning Commission, 1963.
60. GOVERNMENT OF INDIA, *Progress of Joint Stock Companies in India*, Research and Statistics Division, Department of Company Law Administration, Ministry of Finance, 1955.
61. GOVERNMENT OF INDIA, *Re-appraisal of the Second Plan*, Planning Commission, 1958.
62. GOVERNMENT OF INDIA, *Report on the Census of Indian Manufacturers*, Annual, Manager of Publications, Delhi.
63. GOVERNMENT OF INDIA, *Report on India's Food Crisis and Steps to Meet It* by the Agricultural Production Team sponsored by

the Food Foundation, Ministry of Food and Agriculture, 1959.

64. GOVERNMENT OF INDIA, *Second Five Year Plan*, Planning Commission, Manager of Publications, Delhi, 1956.
65. GOVERNMENT OF INDIA, *Statistical Abstract for British India*, Annual, Department of Commercial Intelligence and Statistics, Manager of Publications, Delhi.
66. GOVERNMENT OF INDIA, *Statistical Abstract of the Indian Union* (Annual), 1961, Central Statistical Organisation, Department of Statistics.
67. GOVERNMENT OF INDIA, *Studies in Economics of Farm Management*, Reports for the years 1954–55, 1955–56 and 1956–57 relating to Bombay, Madras Punjab, Uttar Pradesh and West Bengal issued by The Directorate of Economics and Statistics, Ministry of Food and Agriculture.
68. GOVERNMENT OF INDIA, *Third Five Year Plan: A Draft Outline*, Planning Commission, 1960.
69. GOVERNMENT OF INDIA, *Third Five Year Plan*, Planning Commission, 1961.
70. GOVERNMENT OF INDIA, *The Third Plan Mid-term Appraisal*, Planning Commission, 1963.
71. GRILLICHES, Z., 'Estimates of the Aggregate Agricultural Production Function from Cross-sectional Data', *Journal of Farm Economics*, May 1963.
72. HABERLER, G., *The Theory of International Trade*, London, 1936.
73. HAGEN, E. E., 'An Economic Justification of Protectionism', *The Quarterly Journal of Economics*, November 1958.
74. HARROD, R. F., and HAGUE, D. C. (Ed.), *International Trade Theory in a Developing World*, Proceedings of a Conference held by the International Economic Association, Macmillan & Co., London, 1963.
75. HECKSCHER, E. F., *Mercantilism*, Allen and Unwin, London, 1955.
76. IENGAR, H. V. R., *Monetary Policy and Economic Growth*, Vora & Co. Publishers Ltd., Bombay, 1962.
77. INTERNATIONAL LABOUR OFFICE, *Wage Changes in Various Countries*, Geneva, 1926.
78. JOHNSTON, J., 'An Econometric Model of the U.K.', *The Review of Economic Studies*, October 1961.
79. JOHNSTON, J., *Econometric Methods*, McGraw-Hill Company, Inc., London, 1963.
80. JORGENSON, D. W., 'The Development of a Dual Economy', *The Economic Journal*, June 1961.
81. KAHN, A. E., 'Investment Criteria in Development Programs', *The Quarterly Journal of Economics*, February 1951.

82. KALDOR, N., 'Capitalist Evolution in the Light of Keynesian Economics', *Sankhya: The Indian Journal of Statistics*, May 1957.
83. KALRA, B. R., 'A Note on Working Force Estimates, 1901–61', *Census of India*, 1961, Paper No. 1, Manager of Publications, Government of India, Delhi, 1962.
84. KEYNES, J. M., 'Return of Estimated Value of Foreign Trade of the U.K. at Prices of 1900', Official Papers, *The Economic Journal*, December 1912.
85. KEYNES, J. M., *Indian Currency and Finance*, Macmillan & Co. Ltd., London, 1913.
86. KEYNES, J. M., *The General Theory of Employment, Interest and Money*, Harcourt, Brace & Co., New York, 1936.
87. KHATKHATE, D. R., 'Some Notes on the Real Effects of Foreign Surplus Disposal in Underdeveloped Economies', *The Quarterly Journal of Economics*, May 1962.
88. KHATKHATE, D. R., 'Money Supply Impact of National Currency Counterpart of Foreign Aid: An Indian Case', *The Review of Economics and Statistics*, February 1963.
89. KHUSRO, A. M., 'Liquidity Preference in India', *The Indian Economic Review*, February 1957.
90. KINDLEBERGER, C. P., 'Planning for Foreign Investment', *American Economic Review*, March 1943.
91. KLEIN, L. R., and GOLDBERGER, A. S., *An Econometric Model of the U.S. 1929–1952*, North-Holland Publishing Company, Amsterdam, 1955.
92. KLEIN, L. R., BALL, R. J., HAZLEWOOD, A., and VANDOME, P., *An Econometric Model of the U.K.*, Basil Blackwell, Oxford, 1961.
93. KLEIN, L. R., and SHINKAI, Y., 'An Econometric Model of Japan, 1939–59', *International Economic Review*, January 1963.
94. KNOWLES, L. C. A., *The Economic Development of the British Overseas Empire*, Part II, London, 1928.
95. KOTHARI, V. N., 'Long-term Trends in Employment Pattern in India', *Indian Economic Journal*, April 1960.
96. KOYCK, L. M., *Distributed Lags and Investment Analysis*, North-Holland Publishing Company, Amsterdam, 1954.
97. KUH, E., *Capital Stock Growth: A Micro-econometric Approach*, North-Holland Publishing Company, Amsterdam, 1963.
98. LATANE, H. A., 'Cash Balance and the Interest Rate: A Pragmatic Approach', *The Review of Economics and Statistics*, November 1954.
99. LATANE, H. A., 'Income Velocity and Interest Rates: A Prag-

matic Approach', *The Review of Economics and Statistics*, November 1960.

100. Lewis, W. A., 'Economic Development with Unlimited Supplies of Labour', *The Manchester School of Economic and Social Studies*, May 1954.
101. Little, I. M. D., 'The Real Cost of Labour, and the Choice between Consumption and Investment' in *Pricing and Fiscal Policies* edited by P. N. Rosenstein–Rodan, George, Allen and Unwin Ltd., London, 1964.
102. Mahalanobis, P. C., 'The Approach of Operational Research to Planning in India', *Sankhya: The Indian Journal of Statistics*, December 1955.
103. Meyer, J. R., and Kuh, E., *The Investment Decision: An Empirical Study*, Harvard University Press, Cambridge, Massachusetts, 1959.
104. Morgan, T., 'Trends in Terms of Trade and Their Repercussions on Primary Producers' in *International Trade Theory in a Developing World*, Proceedings of a Conference held by the International Economic Association, edited by R. Harrod and D. C. Hague, Macmillan & Co. Ltd., London, 1963.
105. Mukerji, K., 'A Note on the Long Term Growth of National Income in India, 1900–01 to 1952–53' in *Papers on National Income and Allied Topics*, Vol. II, edited by V. K. R. V. Rao, A. K. Ghosh, M. V. Divatia and Uma Datta, Asia Publishing House, London, 1962.
106. Mukerji, K., *Levels of Economic Activity and Public Expenditure in India*, Asia Publishing House, London, 1965.
107. Mukherjee, M., and Sastry, N. S. R., 'An Estimate of the Tangible Wealth of India', in *The Measurement of National Wealth, Income and Wealth Series VIII*, edited by R. Goldsmith and C. Saunders International Association for Research in Income and Wealth, Bowes & Bowes, London, 1959.
108. Murti, V. N., and Sastry, V. K., 'Foreign Demand for Certain Indian Exports', *Reserve Bank of India Bulletin*, May 1950.
109. Murti, V. N., and Sastry, V. K., 'Elasticities of Demand for Certain In Indian Imports and Exports', *Sankhya: The Indian Journal of Statistics*, December 1951.
110. Murti, V. N., and Sastry, V. K., 'Production Functions for Indian Industry', *Econometrica*, April 1957.
111. Naoroji, Dadabhai, *Poverty and Un-British Rule in India*, Sonnenschein & Co., London, 1901.
112. Narasimham, N. V. A., *A Short Term Planning Model for India*, North-Holland Publishing Company, Amsterdam, 1956.
113. Neisser, H., and Modigliani, F., *National Income and*

International Trade, University of Illinois Press, Urbana, 1953.

114. NURKSE, R., *Problems of Capital Formation in Underdeveloped Countries*, Oxford University Press, Fair Lawn, N.J., 1953.
115. PALVIA, C. M., *An Econometric Model for Development Planning (With Special Reference to India)*, Central Plan Bureau, The Hague, 1953.
116. PATEL, S. J., 'Long-term Changes in Output and Income in India: 1896–1960', *The Indian Economic Journal*, January 1958.
117. PATINKIN, D., *Money, Interest and Prices*, Row, Peterson & Co., Evanston, Illinois, 1956.
118. POLAK, J. J., 'Balance of Payments Problems of Countries Reconstructing with the Help of Foreign Loans', *The Quarterly Journal of Economics*, February 1943.
119. POLAK, J. J., *An International Economic System*, University of Chicago Press, Chicago, 1953.
120. PREBISCH, R., *The Economic Development of Latin America*, United Nations, New York, 1950.
121. RANADE, M. G., *Essays on Indian Economics: A Collection of Essays and Speeches*, Thacker & Co., Bombay, 1899.
122. RANGNEKAR, D. K., *Poverty and Capital Development in India: Contemporary Investment Patterns, Problems and Planning*, Oxford University Press, London, 1959.
123. RANIS, G., and FEI, J. C. H., 'A Theory of Economic Development', *American Economic Review*, September 1961.
124. RAO, V. K. R. V., *The National Income of British India, 1931–32*, Macmillan & Co. Ltd., London, 1940.
125. RAO, V. K. R. V., SEN, S. R., DIVATIA, M. V., and DATTA, UMA (Ed.), *Papers on National Income and Allied Topics*, Vol. I, Asia Publishing House, London, 1960.
126. RAO, V. K. R. V., GHOSH, A. K., DIVATIA, M. V., and DATTA, UMA (Ed.), *Papers on National Income and Allied Topics*, Vol. II, Asia Publishing House, 1962.
127. RESERVE BANK OF INDIA, *All-India Rural Credit Survey, Report of the Committee of Direction*, Vol. I, Bombay, 1954.
128. RESERVE BANK OF INDIA, *Banking and Monetary Statistics of India*, Bombay, 1954.
129. RESERVE BANK OF INDIA, *India's Balance of Payments, 1948–49 to 1961–62*, Bombay, 1963.
130. RESERVE BANK OF INDIA, *Report on Currency and Finance*, Annual, Bombay.
131. RESERVE BANK OF INDIA, *Reserve Bank of India Bulletin*, Monthly, Bombay.

132. ROBERTSON, D. H., *A Study of Industrial Fluctuations*, King, London, 1915.
133. ROBINSON, JOAN, 'The Production Function and the Theory of Capital', *The Review of Economic Studies*, 1953–54.
134. ROSEN, G., *Industrial Change in India: Industrial Growth, Capital Requirements and Technological Change, 1937–1955*, Asia Publishing House, London, 1959.
135. ROSTOW, W. W., 'The Take-off into Self-sustained Growth" *The Economic Journal*, March 1956.
136. ROSTOW, W. W. (ed.), *The Economics of Take-off into Sustained Growth*, Proceedings of a Conference held by the International Economic Association, Macmillan & Co. Ltd., London, 1963.
137. ROYAL COMMISSION, *The Royal Commission on Indian Finance Currency, Report of the Commissioners* (Minutes of Evidence, Appendices, etc.), London, 1913–14.
138. ROYAL COMMISSION, *The Royal Commission on Labour in India, Report of the Commissioners*, London, 1931.
139. SAKSENA, S. P., 'Cost of Living Indices and Wages', in *Economic Problems of Modern India*, Vol. II edited by R. K. Mukherjee and H. L. Dey, Macmillan & Co. Ltd., 1941.
140. SASTRY, V. K., 'Demand for and Supply of Money in India', *Indian Economic Journal*, July 1962.
141. SCHULTZ, T. W., 'Value of U.S. Farm Surpluses to Underdeveloped Countries', *Journal of Farm Economics*, December 1960.
142. SCHULTZ, T. W., *Transforming Traditional Agriculture*, Yale University Press, London, 1964.
143. SELDEN, R. T., 'Monetary Velocity in the United States' in *Studies in the Quantity Theory of Money*, edited by M. Friedman, Chicago University Press, Chicago, 1956.
144. SEN, A. K., *Choice of Techniques*, Basil Blackwell, Oxford, 1960.
145. SEN, A. K., 'Working Capital in the Indian Economy: A Conceptual Framework and Some Estimates' in *Pricing and Fiscal Policies* edited by P. N. Rosenstein-Rodan, George Allen and Unwin Ltd., London, 1964.
146. SEN, S. R., 'Impact and Implications of Foreign Surplus Disposal on Underdeveloped Economies: The Indian Perspective', *Journal of Farm Economics*, December 1960.
147. SETHI, J. D., *Problems of Monetary Policy in an Underdeveloped Country, With Special Reference to India*, Asia Publishing House, Bombay, 1961.
148. SHAH, K. T., and KHAMBATTA, K. J., *Wealth and Taxable Capacity of India*, Bombay, 1924.

149. Shah, V. C., 'Demand for Money in India, 1948–59', *Indian Economic Journal*, August 1961.
150. Shah, V. C., 'Monetary Analysis in India, 1948–49 to 1958–59', *The Indian Economic Journal*, January 1962.
151. Solow, R. M., 'Investment and Technical Progress', in *Mathematical Methods in the Social Sciences*, edited by K. J. Arrow, S. Karlin, and P. Suppes, Stanford, 1960.
152. Solow, R. M., and Kareken, J., 'Lags in Monetary Policy', in *Stabilisation Policies*, a series of research studies prepared for the Commission on Money and Credit, Prentice-Hall, Inc., Englewood Cliffs, N.J., 1963.
153. Tewari, J., 'Productivity of Capital Investment in U.P.', *Bulletin of International Statistical Institute*, 1954.
154. Theil, H., 'Report of the Uppsala Meeting, August 2–4, 1954', *Econometrica*, April 1955.
155. Theil, H., *Economic Forecasts and Policy*, North-Holland Publishing Co., Amsterdam, 1961.
156. Thorner, Alice, 'The Secular Trend in the Indian Economy, 1881–1951', *The Economic Weekly*, July 1962.
157. Thorner, D., 'De-industrialisation in India, 1881–1931' in *First International Conference of Economic History*, Stockholm, 1960.
158. Thorner, D., and Thorner, Alice, *Land and Labour in India*, Asia Publishing House, London, 1962.
159. Tobin, J., 'The Monetary Interpretation of History', A Review Article on M. Friedman and Anna J. Schwartz (44), *American Economic Review*, June 1965.
160. Tsiang, S. C., 'Acceleration, Theory of the Firm, and the Business Cycle', *The Quarterly Journal of Economics*, August 1951.
161. United Nations, *Demographic Yearbook*, Annual, New York.
162. United Nations, *Economic Survey of Asia and the Far East, 1948*, Department of Economic Affairs, Lake Success, New York, 1948.
163. United Nations, *Economic Survey of Asia and the Far East, 1961*, Bangkok, 1962.
164. United Nations, *Statistical Yearbook*, Annual, Statistical Office of the United Nations, Department of Economic and Social Affairs, New York.
165. Uzawa, H., 'On a Two-Sector Model of Economic Growth', *The Review of Economic Studies*, October 1961.
166. Warburton, C., 'The Secular Trend in Monetary Velocity', *The Quarterly Journal of Economics*, February 1949.
167. Wold, H., and Jureen, L., *Demand Analysis, A Study in Econometrics*, John Wiley & Sons, New York, 1953.

Name Index

Subject Index